Learning Microsoft Access 2010

LEARNING Microsoft Access 2010

Ramesh Bangia
B.Sc., Dip. Comp. Sc.
Formerly Managing Editor, Software Today
Formerly Incharge Computer Centre, Hindustan Copper Ltd., New Delhi

KHANNA BOOK PUBLISHING CO. (P) LTD.
DELHI

Learning Microsoft Access 2010 — Ramesh Bangia

First Edition 2011

Published by:
Khanna Book Publishing Co. (P) Ltd.
4C/4344, Ansari Road, Darya Ganj, New Delhi-110 002
Phone: 011-23244447, 23244448
E-mail: contact@khannabooks.com
Website: www.khannabooks.com

Regd. Off: 1694-95, 1st Floor, Nai Sarak, Delhi-110006 (India)
Phone: 011-23283211, 23256658
Fax: 011-23256658

Cover Design & Layout by
Chauhan Offset, Delhi

Printed in India by ZN Printers

PREFACE

Learning of a software is both easy and difficult. It depends upto what level you are planning to learn. If you are learning only for the working use, then it is very easy. But, when you try to go deep into it, then you realise how difficult it is to master it.

Microsoft Access 2010 is such a vast subject that it will take a lot of time to understand it fully. This book has been written in mind to make you aware of the options available in the software and how they can be used. It is like telling the child about the steps and stairs. You are the one who is to climb the stair. This book will just guide you how to use the stairs.

I am indeed debited to my publishers Khanna Book Publishing Co. Pvt. Ltd. for their suggestions and encouragement given in producing this book.

I would like to thank my family specially my wife Sadhna, kids Mayank and Samarth, for without their criticism this book would not have seen the day.

Suggestions for improvement of the book are indeed welcome.

Ramesh Bangia

CONTENTS

Contents

CHAPTER 1

Introduction to Microsoft Office 2010

Introduction

Office 2010 also includes new applications and server-side tools. Chief among these is Groove, a collaboration and communication suite for smaller businesses, which was originally developed by Groove Networks before being acquired by Microsoft in 2005. Also included is Office SharePoint Server 2010, a major revision to the server platform for Office applications, which supports "Excel Services", a client-server architecture for supporting Excel workbooks that are shared in real time between multiple machines, and are also viewable and editable through a web page.

What is Microsoft Office?

There are software and software. But, when you come to using the computer and a single software which can do everything for you, the choice mostly is Microsoft Office. This is not a software but a combination of software which can perform various aspects of your office routines. It can be writing letters, maintaining accounts, keeping databases, making a presentation, etc. This Microsoft Office has a solution for everything.

Office 2010 contains a number of new features, the most notable of which is the entirely new graphical user interface called the Fluent User Interface, replacing the menus and toolbars that have been the cornerstone of Office since its inception with a tabbed toolbar, known as the Ribbon. Office 2010 requires Windows XP with Service Pack 2 or 3, Windows Server 2003 with Service Pack 1 or higher, or Windows Vista.

The 'Ribbon User Interface' is a task-orientated Graphical User Interface (GUI). It features a central menu button, widely known as the 'Office Button'. The Ribbon Interface has been rumoured to be introduced into Microsoft Office 14.

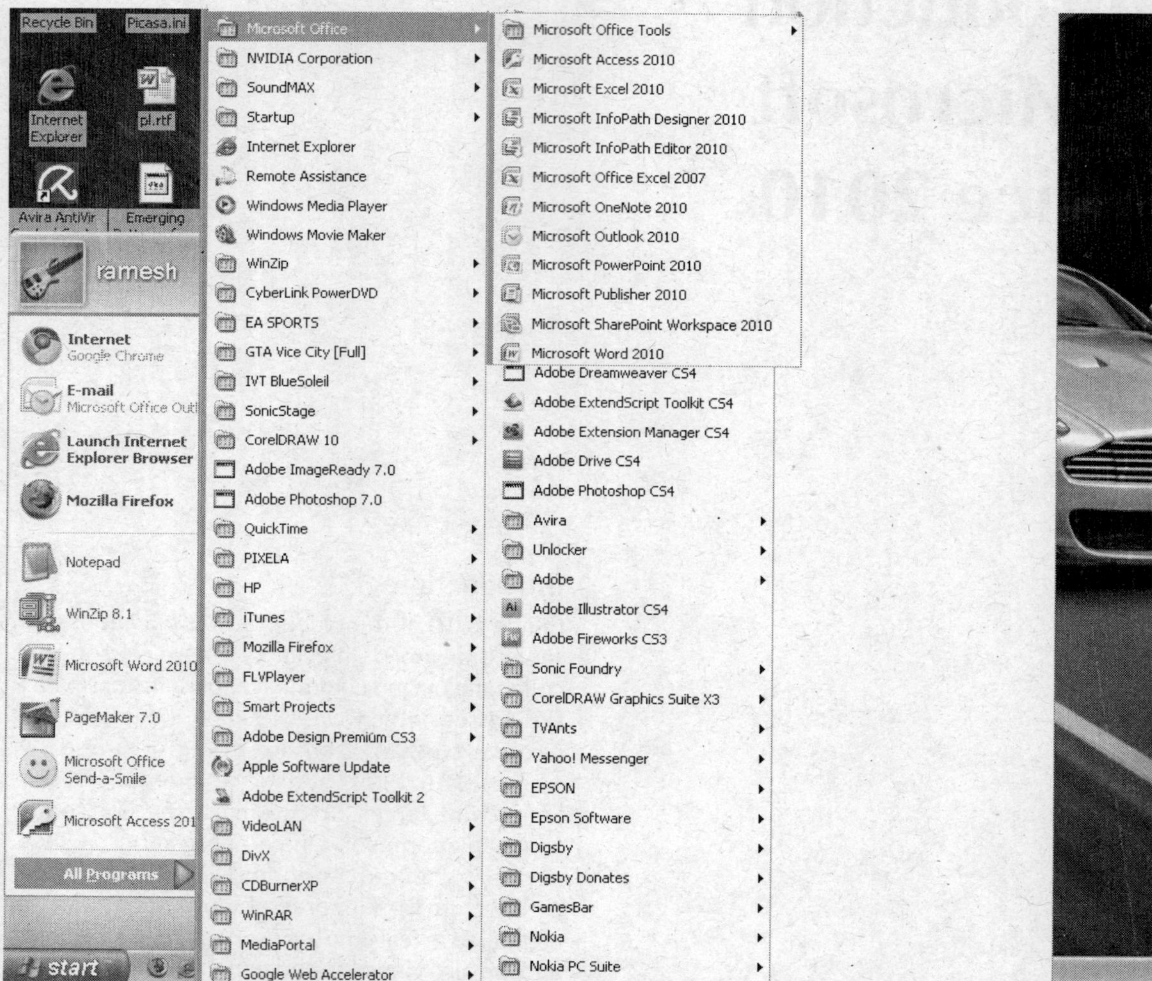

Constituents of Microsoft Office 2010

Microsoft FrontPage has been removed from the Office suite entirely. It has been replaced by Microsoft Office SharePoint Designer, which is aimed towards development of SharePoint portals. Its designer-oriented counterpart Microsoft Expression Web is targeted for general web development. However, neither application is included in any of the Office suites.

Speech recognition and handwriting recognition are now part of Windows Vista. Speech and ink components have been removed from Office 2010. Handwriting and speech recognition work with Office 2010 only on Windows Vista or Windows XP Tablet PC Edition. However, XP users can use an earlier version of Office to use speech recognition.

Let us take a look at the various constituents which are there in Microsoft Office 2010.

Microsoft Office Word 2010

A word processing software which allows you to write letters, edit them and print them after formatting it according to your needs. It has all the possible options of a word processor in the form of font style and size; indents; line spacing; margins; spell checking and grammar checkers to name a few.

Microsoft Office Excel 2010

This spreadsheet program allows you to manipulate and present your data in almost any way you choose. It allows you to work on a tabular pad consisting of columns and rows where you can perform all your mathematical, financial and statistical calculations. These calculations can be as simple as totalling a row or column of values or as complex as figuring the rate of return on an investment under varying circumstances. It also allows you to make a graphical representation of all your data in the form of 2-dimensional or 3-dimensional graph or pie chart.

Microsoft Office Access 2010

A software to take care of most of your database requirements. It allows you to store and organize information in sets of tables, which can be displayed in the form of columns and rows to look like a table or an index card. What's more it allows you to perform calculations and find for you simple statistics like totals and averages. It allows you to sort the data in any form and extract the required information based on the key given by you.

Microsoft Office PowerPoint 2010

Want to make a presentation in a hurry! This is an ideal program of the same. Make sophisticated slide shows and professional looking electronic presentations. It also allows you to add charts, tables and pictures for make the presentation look alive.

Microsoft Office Outlook 2010

It is an electronic tool for managing appointments, addresses, e-mail, and notes. With lots of stress being given to the e-mail these days, it is an ideal software for sending and receiving e-mail.

Microsoft Office Publisher 2010

It is Microsoft's answer to the various other publishing software available in the market like PageMaker. It allows you to create invitations, design business-cards, and letter-heads, make your own calenders, produce newsletter, etc.

Microsoft Office OneNote 2010

It is used to gather information during meetings, brainstorming sessions, interviews, and more. The notes you create can include text, drawings, images, and audio recordings. OneNote uses a freeform page layout, so you can place and move information wherever you want.

Microsoft Office InfoPath 2010

It is helps you collect and work with data by using dynamic, online forms that have a familiar Office interface. Based on the Extensible Markup Language (XML), InfoPath makes it easy to create and use robust forms to more effectively gather and share information throughout your organization.

Microsoft Office Groove 2010

Microsoft Office Groove 2010 is Internet software for making direct connections with the people who are important to you. With Office Groove 2010, you can bring together team members from both inside and outside your company, with no IT assistance required and no need to waste time thinking about firewalls, servers, security, or network access. Additionally, you can enjoy the efficiency of always knowing each other's virtual location, or online presence, thus allowing for organic and quick conversation and collaboration.

Starting Above Software

You can start any of the above mentioned software by one of the following methods:

From Start Button

Click at Start button to access the various commands. Click on Programs to get the various programs. From here click at the program called Microsoft Office 2010 group and then the required program, as shown here.

From Icon of Word

You can choose to have an icon of the software on your desktop. This icon can be created by using the feature of Creating Shortcut.

Working with Various Constituents of Microsoft Office 2010

Let me give you here the tips for working under various constituents of Office 2010.

Microsoft Word 2010

As you know that Word is used for creating a document. So in simple terms, follow the following procedure to create a document.

1. Open Word 2010.
2. Click at New from the Office button.
3. A new blank slate for writing would be opened for you.
4. Type the text as you would otherwise too.
5. Do not bother about any formatting or spelling.
6. Save the document at this stage to avoid loosing the text, if the lights go out.
7. Now format the text of the document according to your needs, i.e., Bold, Italics, etc.
8. If required, change the alignment of the text or part of it.
9. Save again.
10. Close the document from Office button.
11. Now open the same document again.
12. Spell check the whole document, correcting the wrong words.
13. Your document is ready.
14. Print it on the attached printer.
15. See the result of your effort.

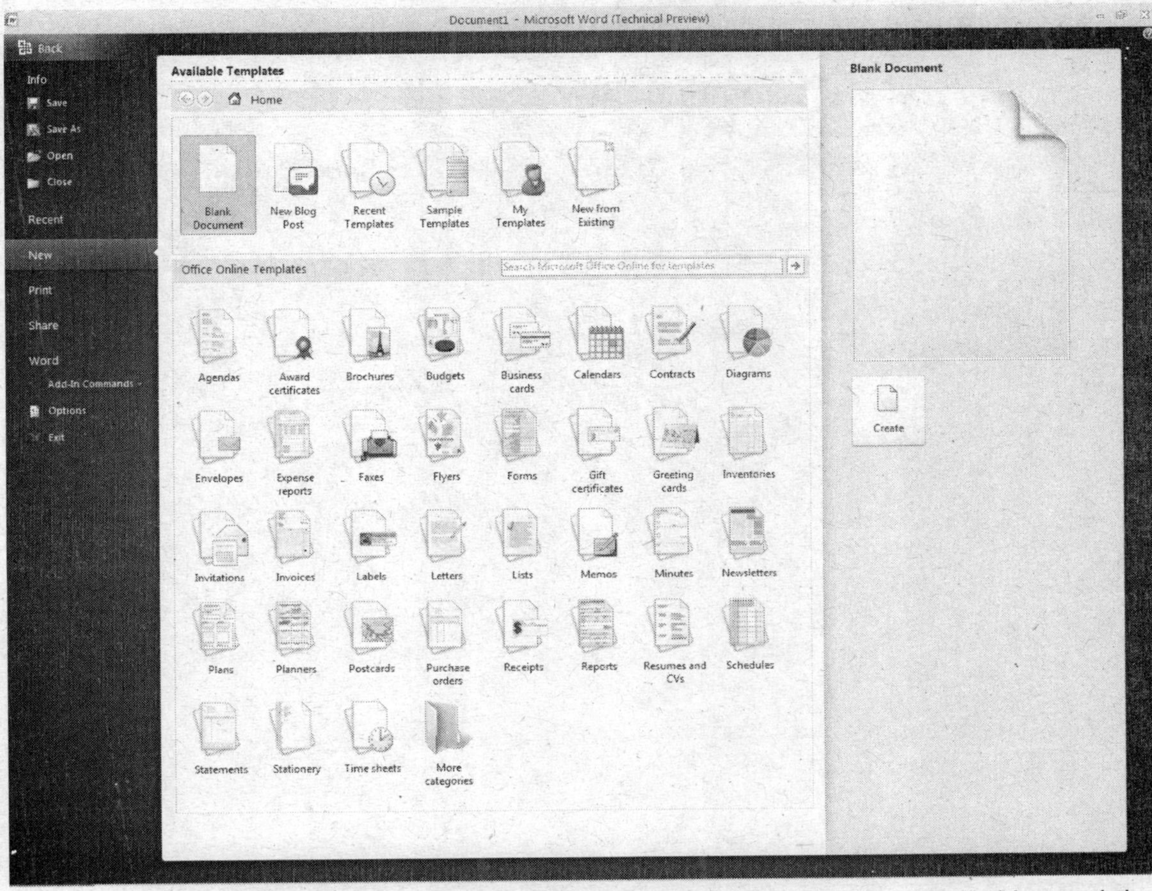

If you follow these steps for creating a document in Word 2010, I am sure that you would never fail.

Microsoft Excel 2010

As you know that Excel is used for creating a spreadsheet. So in simple terms, follow the following procedure to create a spreadsheet.

1. Open Excel 2010.
2. Click at New from the Office button.
3. A new blank spreadsheet would be opened for you.
4. Type the number, text, formula, as the case may be.
5. Do not bother about any formatting at this stage.
6. Save the document at this stage to avoid loosing the typing, if the lights go out.
7. Now format the spreadsheet according to your needs, i.e., Bold, Italics, etc.
8. If required, change the alignment of the cells.
9. Save again.
10. Close the spreadsheet from Office button.
11. Now open the same spreadsheet again.
12. Spell check the whole spreadsheet, correcting the wrong words.
13. Your spreadsheet is ready.

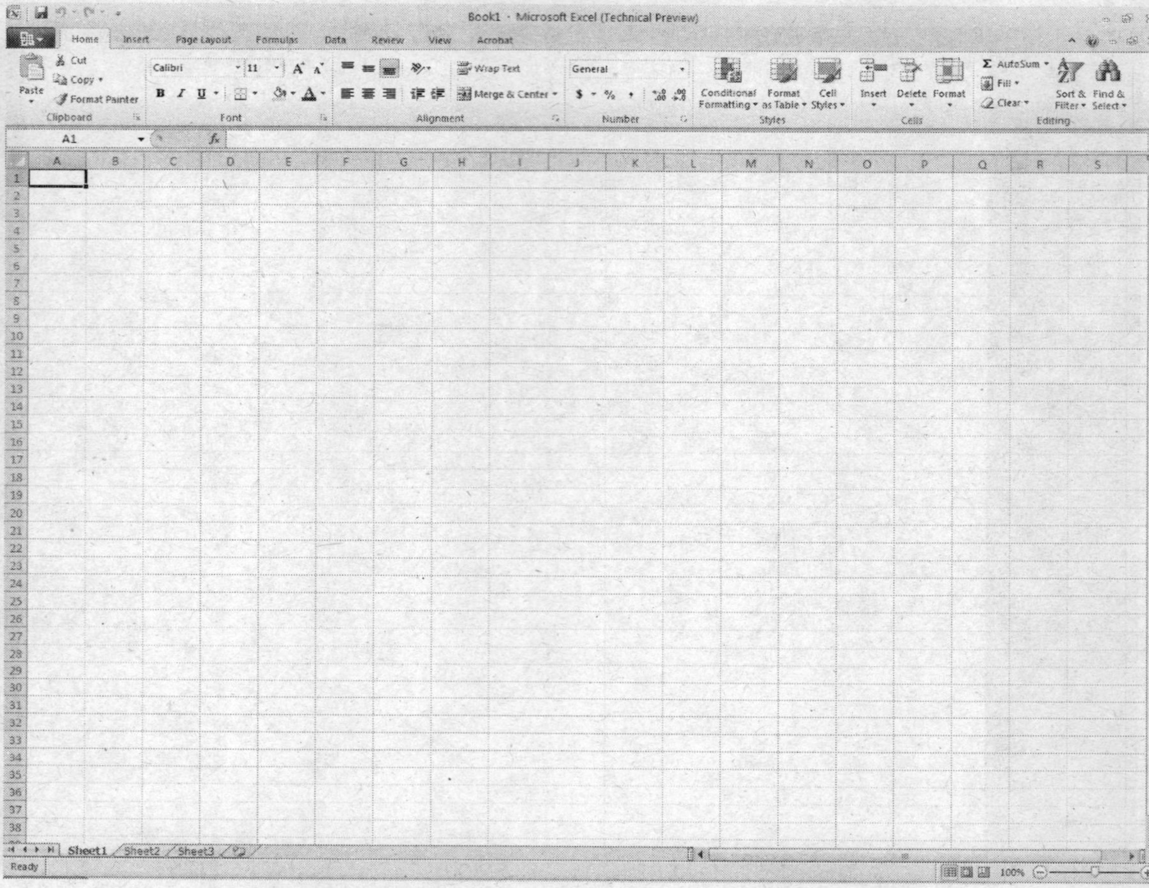

14. Print it on the attached printer.
15. See the result of your effort.

Microsoft PowerPoint 2010

As you know that PowerPoint is used for creating a presentation. So in simple terms, follow the following procedure to create a presentation.

1. Open PowerPoint 2010.
2. Click at New from the Office button.
3. A new blank presentation would be opened for you.
4. Select the type of slide you want to create.
5. Type the text and other details, as the case may be.
6. Save the slide/presentation.
7. Now format the slide according to your needs, i.e., Bold, Italics, etc.
8. If required, change the alignment of the text within presentation.
9. Save again.
10. Add a new slide, if the need be.
11. Close the slide from Office button.

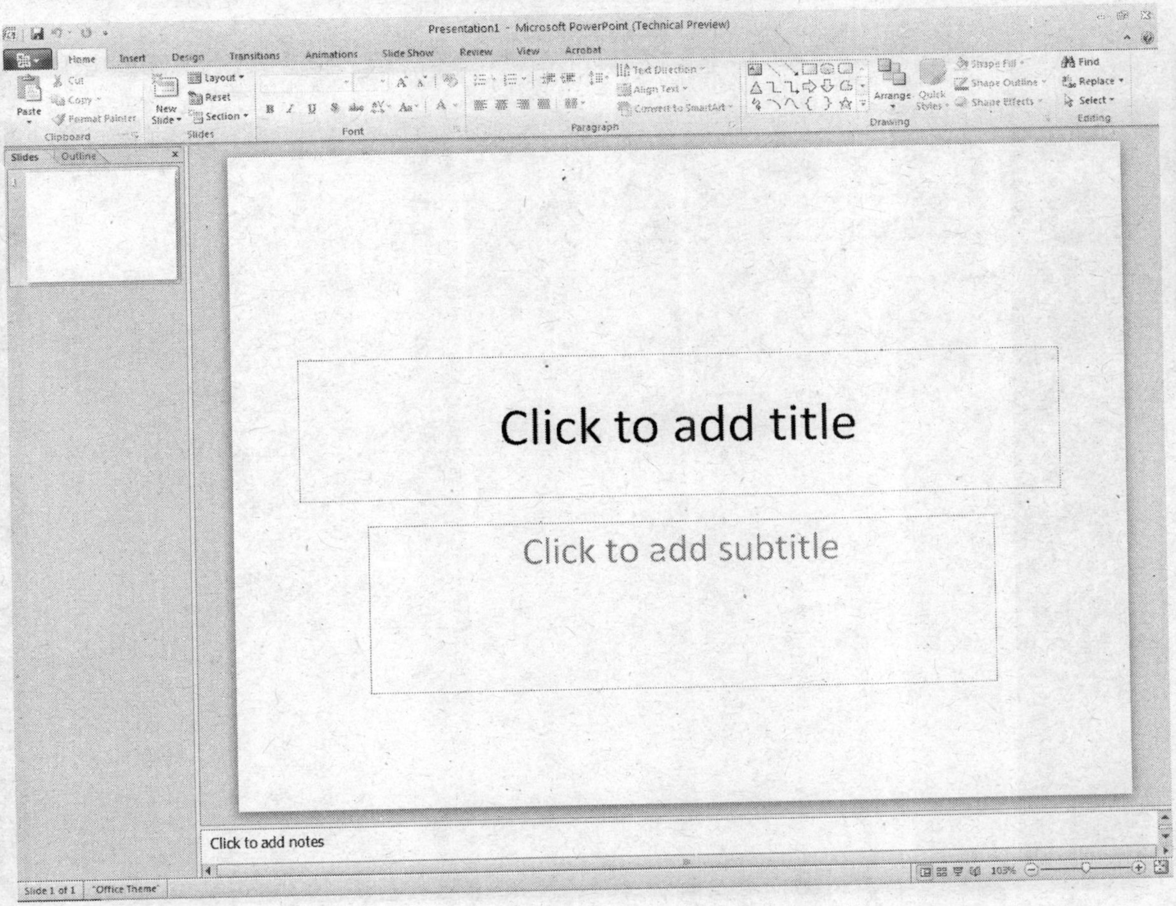

12. Now open the same presentation again.
13. Create a slide show of the slides.
14. Run the slide show to see the effect.

In similar way, you can run the other software of Microsoft Office 2010.

Using the Mouse

Since most of the activities in Microsoft Office are done using the mouse, it is very important to have the complete knowledge of working of mouse while using the constituents of Microsoft Office.

To click

Position the pointer on a menu, a button, or an icon and click the left mouse once.

To double-click

Position the pointer on an item and click the left mouse button twice in quick succession.

To select

1. Position the pointer on the first item to select.
2. Click and hold down the mouse button.

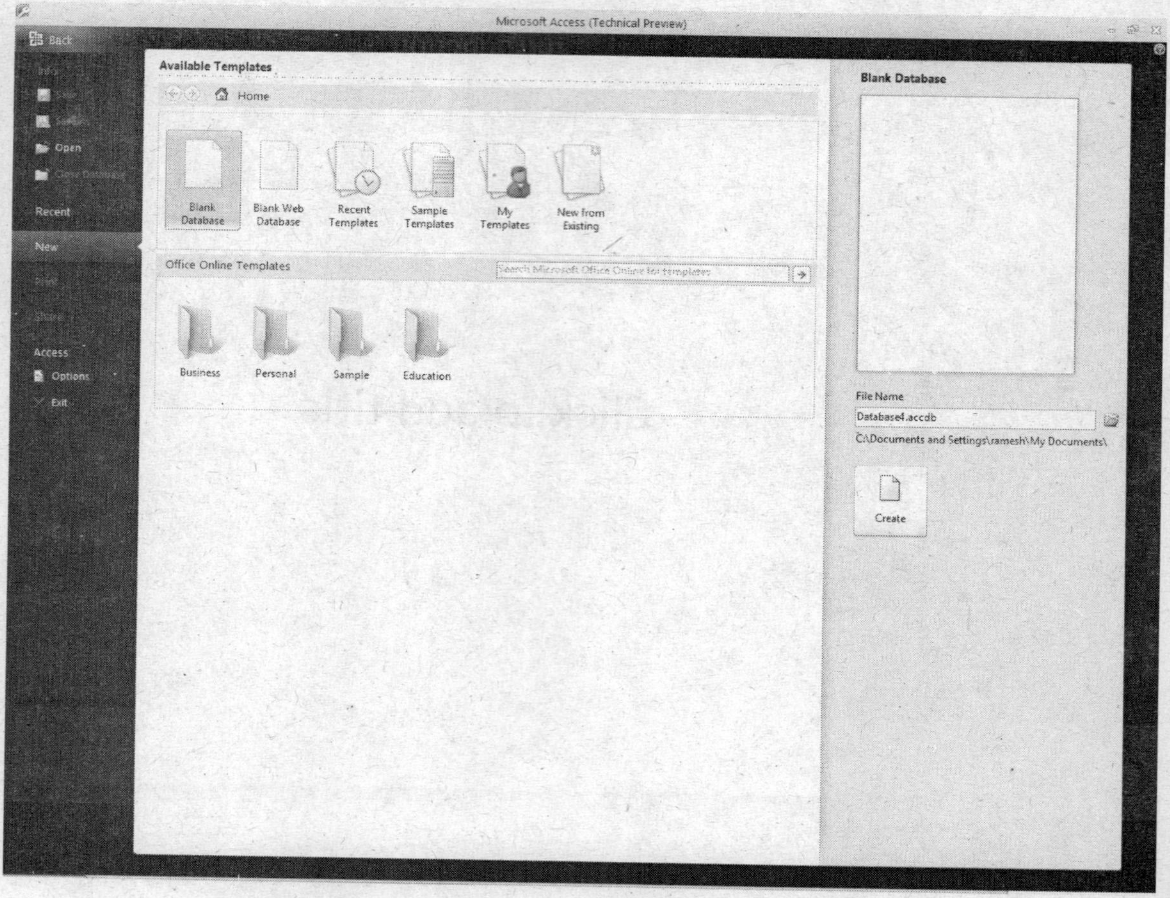

3. Move the mouse pointer across the items to select.
4. Release the mouse button.

To drag

1. Position the pointer on an item.
2. Click and hold down the left mouse button.
3. Move the mouse.
4. Release the mouse button.

To scroll

Drag the scroll button in the scroll bar up or down.

Or

Click a scroll arrow at either end of the scroll bar.

To choose from a menu

1. Click a menu name.
2. Click an item on a menu.

   Or

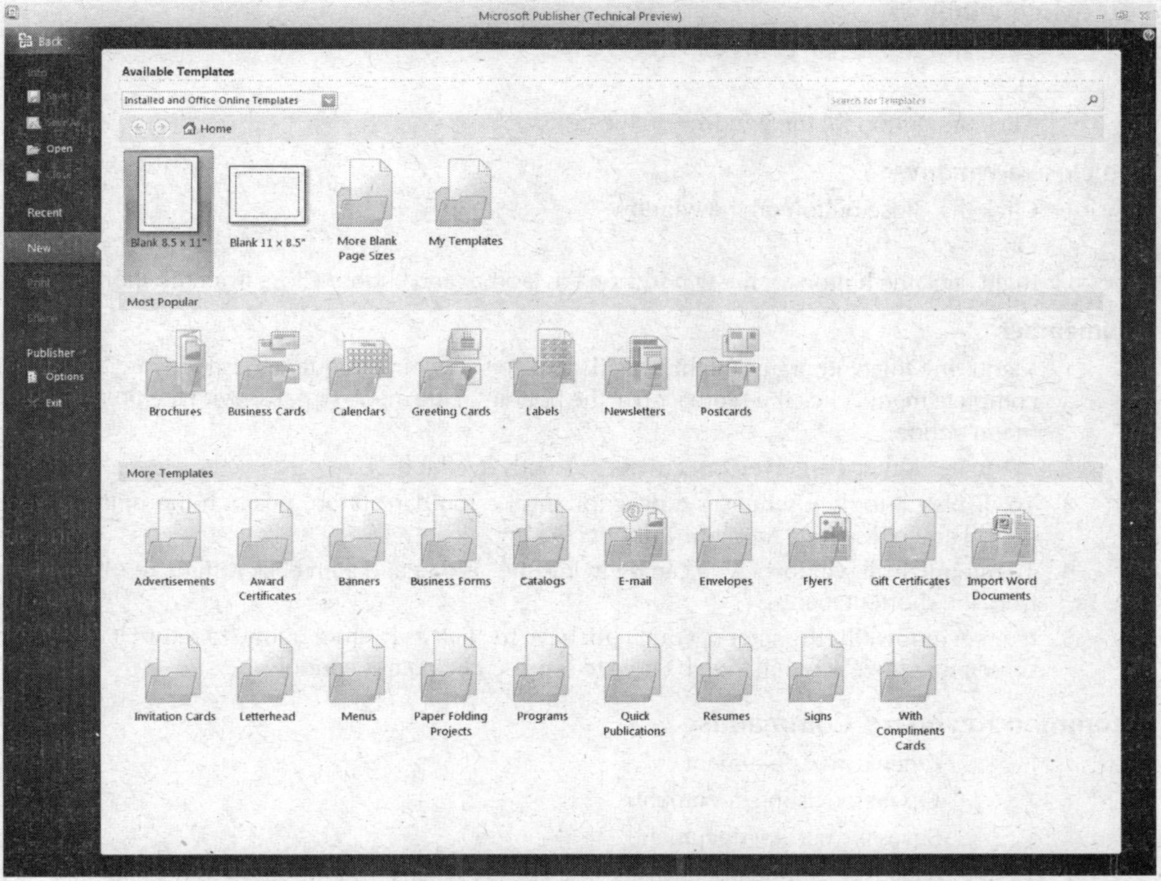

If the item is followed by an arrow, position the mouse pointer on the item to open the submenu and then click an item on the submenu.

To move a window

Position the pointer on the window's title bar and press and hold the mouse button as your drag the window.

To resize a window

Position the pointer on the window's corner and, when you see the diagonal pointer, drag to resize the window.

To minimize a window

Click the Minimize button.

To restore a minimized window

Click the button for the window on the taskbar.

To maximize a window

Click the Maximize button.

To switch windows

Click any visible part of the window

Or

Click the button for the window on the taskbar.

To close a window

1. Click the Close button on the window

   Or

   Right click the button for the window on the taskbar and choose Close from the shortcut menu.

Remember

1. Menus in Office programs might be collapsed to show only frequently used items. To view the complete menu, click the More icon at the bottom of the menu or pause with the pointer on any menu option.
2. Menu items that are grayed out are not currently available.
3. To display a tooltip, which is a description of a toolbar button, position the pointer on the button and pause for a moment without clicking.
4. To minimize all windows, you can rightclick the taskbar and then click Minimize All Windows from the shortcut menu.
5. If one window fills the screen, you might have to click its Restore button to return it to a partial-screen window. You will then be able to see and click other windows.

Common Keyboard Commands

Ctrl + N	Open a new document
Ctrl + O	Opens a existing document
Ctrl + S	Saves the current document
Ctrl + W	Close the current document
Ctrl + P	Prints the current document
Ctrl + C	Copies the highlighted matter to store it in clipboard
Ctrl + X	Cuts the highlighted matter to store it in clipboard
Ctrl + V	Pastes the matter available on the clipboard
F1	Call for help
Shift + F1	Use the What's This? Button
Ctrl + F6	Switch between open documents
Ctrl + Z	Undo an action
Ctrl + Y	Redo an action

CHAPTER 2

What's New in Microsoft Access 2010

Introduction

This chapter gives you a glimpse of the new commands or changes in the existing commands of Microsoft Access 2010.

What's New in Microsoft Office Access 2010

Microsoft Office Access 2010 provides a powerful set of tools that allow you to quickly start tracking, reporting, and sharing information in a manageable environment. With its new, interactive design capabilities, prebuilt library of tracking application templates, and ability to work with data from many data sources, including Microsoft SQL Server, Office Access 2010 allows you to rapidly create attractive and functional tracking applications without requiring deep database knowledge. You can quickly create and adapt applications and reports to changing business needs, and with its new, enhanced deep integration with Microsoft Windows SharePoint Services 3.0, Office Access 2010 helps you share, manage, audit, and back up information.

Office Access 2010 includes a suite of prebuilt tracking applications in the form of templates that you can use to get started quickly. Use them right out-of-the-box or enhance and refine them to track information your way. You can employ new views and layouts, enhanced sorting and filtering, rich text, multivalued fields, split forms, and a host of new features to create richer, better tracking applications and effectively share tracked information with others.

New, improved user interface

Office Access 2010 employs a new user interface designed from the ground up to help make you more productive. You can work faster, learn faster, and find faster. The new interface uses a standard area called the ribbon that replaces the layers of menus and toolbars found in earlier releases of Access.

The ribbon enables you to locate groups of related commands faster. For example, if you need to create a new form or report, you will find it on the Create tab. The new design makes it easier to find the commands that you need, and you will discover features that you otherwise might not have noticed. This is because, with the tabs used in Office Access 2010, commands are placed closer to the surface, instead of nested deep in menus. You will do less digging and more remembering.

You will also get up and running faster, thanks to the new Getting Started with Microsoft Office Access window. This feature offers quick access to the new getting started experience, including access to a library of professionally designed database templates.

Major new interface elements in Office Access 2010 include:

- Getting Started with Microsoft Office Access page — The new startup experience that is displayed when you start Access from the Start menu or a desktop shortcut.
- The ribbon — The area at the top of the program window where you can choose commands.
- Command tab — Commands are displayed and combined so that you can find commands you need when you need them.
- Contextual command tab — A command tab that appears depending on your context — the object that you are working on or the task that you are performing. This tab contains the commands most likely to apply to what you are doing.
- Gallery — A new control that displays a choice visually, so that you can see the results that you will get. Galleries are employed throughout the 2010 Microsoft Office system interface. They let you choose a result without having to worry about how you get it.
- Quick Access Toolbar — A single standard toolbar that appears in the ribbon offering instant, single-click access to the most needed commands, such as Save and Undo.
- Navigation Pane — The area on the left side ot the window that displays database objects. The Navigation Pane replaces the Database window from earlier versions of Access.
- Tabbed documents — Your tables, queries, forms, reports, and macros are displayed as tabbed documents.

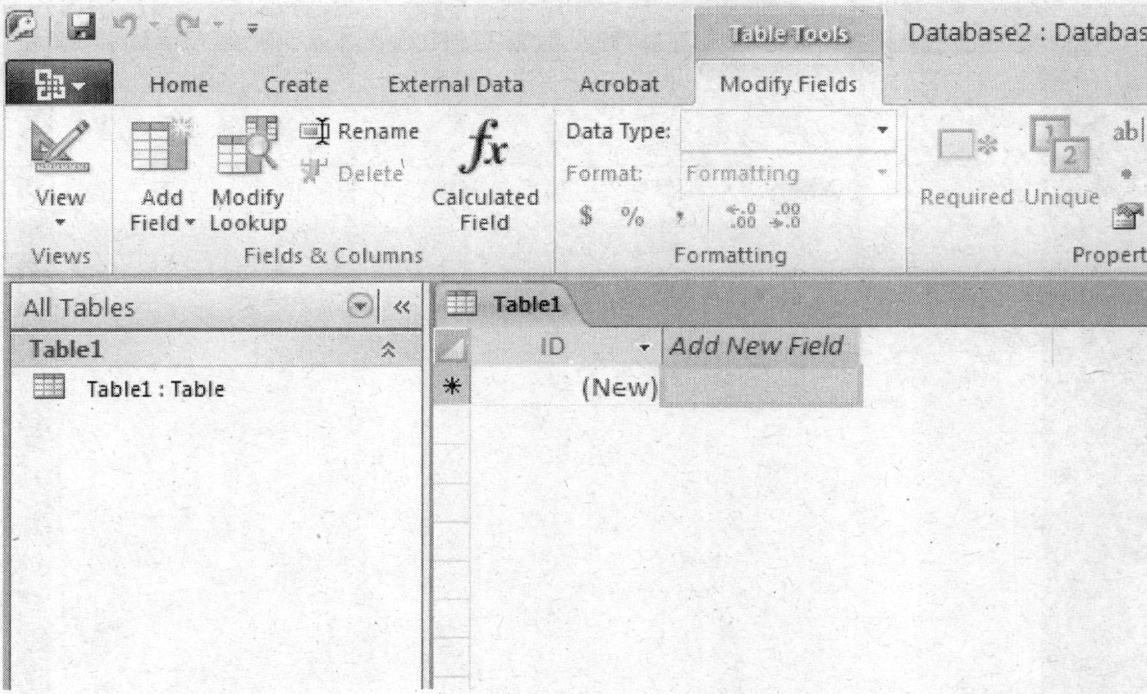

- Status bar — The bar at the bottom of the window that displays status information and includes buttons that let you switch views.
- Mini toolbar — A toolbar-like element that transparently appears above text that you have selected, so that you can easily apply formatting, such as bold or italic, or change the font.

Great templates to get you started

Use the Getting Started with Microsoft Office Access window to quickly get started creating your database. You can create your own database or start with one of our professionally designed database templates.

Each template is a complete tracking application, with predefined tables, forms, reports, queries, macros, and relationships. The templates are designed to be immediately useful out-of-the-box so that you can get up and running quickly. If the template design meets your needs, you are ready to go! If not, you can use the template to get a head start in creating the database that meets your specific need.

Office Access 2010 includes a collection of database templates in the box. You can also use the Getting Started with Microsoft Office Access window to connect to Microsoft Office Online and download the latest new or revised templates.

The templates provided include:

- Assets
- Contacts
- Events
- Faculty
- Issues
- Marketing projects
- Projects

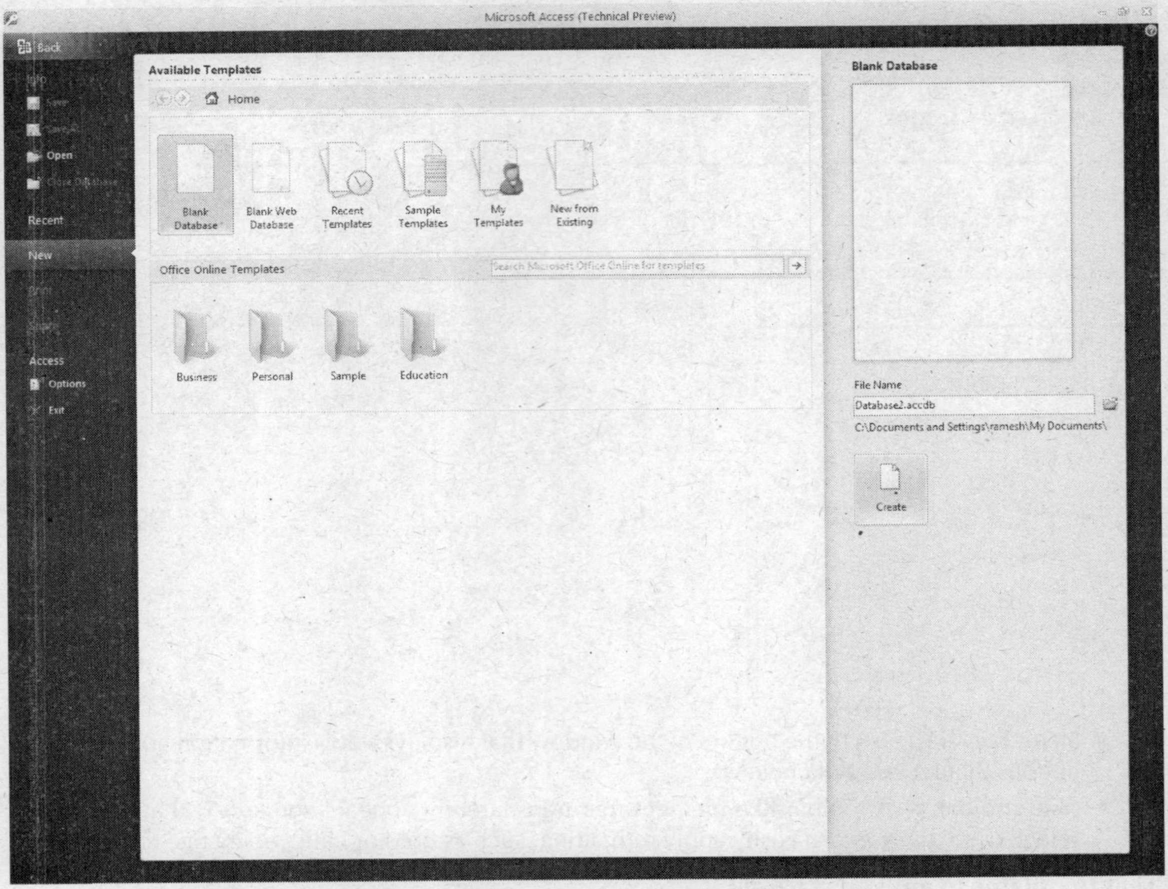

- Sales pipeline
- Students
- Tasks

Enhanced sorting and filtering

Need to quickly find a matching value or sort a column of data? The new Office Access 2010 AutoFilter feature augments already powerful filtering abilities to let you quickly focus on the data that you need. You can easily select among the unique values in a column, useful for when you can't recall the name that you need, or sort the values by using plain language context menu options, such as Sort Oldest to Newest or Sort Smallest to Largest.

You will find the most common filter options surfaced in menu commands, or you can use quick filters to limit information based on the data that you enter. Quick filter options automatically change based on the data type, so you will see sensible choices for text, date, and numeric information.

These new filtering and sorting features are designed to provide you with a consistent experience whether you are using Office Access 2010 or Microsoft Office Excel 2010.

Layout view

The new Layout view lets you make design changes while you browse. This capability lets you make many of the most common design changes while you view a live form or report. For example, you can add a field by dragging from the new Field List pane, or change properties by using the property sheet. Layout view supports the new stacked and tabular layouts — groups of controls that you can manipulate as one, so that you can easily rearrange fields, columns, rows, or whole layouts. You can also remove a field or add formatting easily in Layout view. Design view still remains available for more detailed work, and has also been enhanced to support layouts.

Stacked and tabular layouts

Forms and reports often contain tabular information, such as a column that contains customer names or a row that contains all of the fields for a customer. You can use Office Access 2010 to group these controls into a layout that can easily be manipulated as one unit, including the label. Because you can select controls from different sections, such as the label in the section header or footer, you have considerable flexibility. You can easily:

- Move or resize a layout. For example, move a column to the left or right.
- Format a layout. For example, set a customer name column in bold so that it stands out.
- Add a column (field) to a layout.
- Delete a column (field) from a layout.

Layouts are saved with your design, so they remain available.

Automatic calendar for date picking

Fields and controls that employ the Date/Time data type automatically gain a new feature: support for a built-in interactive calendar for choosing a date. The calendar button automatically appears to the right of the date. Want to know the date for this coming Friday? Click the button and the calendar automatically appears to let you find and choose the date. You can optionally turn off the calendar for a field or a control by using a property.

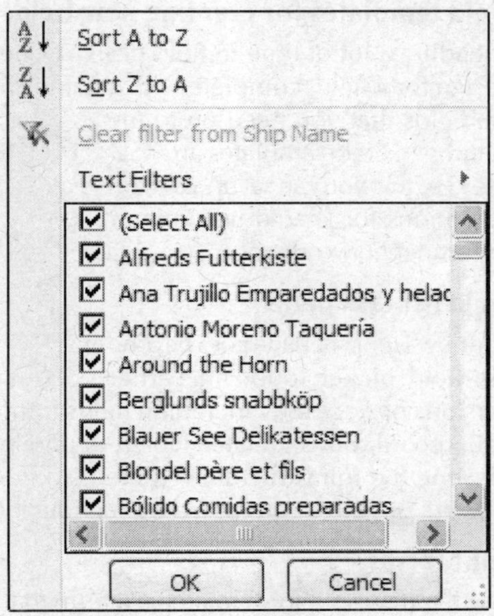

Rich text in memo fields

With the new rich text support in Office Access 2010, you are no longer limited to plain text. You can format text with options, such as bold, italic, different fonts and colors, and other common formatting options, and store the text in your database. Rich formatted text is stored in a Memo field in an HTML-based format that is compatible with the rich text data type in Windows SharePoint Services. You set the new TextFormat property to either RichText or PlainText, and the information is then properly formatted in text box controls and in Datasheet view.

Enhanced quick create by using the Create tab

The Create tab on the ribbon is the new main starting point for adding new objects. Quickly create new forms, reports, tables, SharePoint lists, queries, macros, modules, and more. The creation process takes into account the active object, so if you have a table open, you can create a new form based on that table in just two mouse clicks. The new forms and reports are more visually appealing and immediately useful, because their design has been upgraded. For example, automatically generated forms and reports get professional looking designs with headers that include a logo, a title, and for reports, a date and time; not to mention informative footers and totals.

You will find that objects created by using the new quick create experience take you farther with less effort.

Create tables quickly by using the improved Datasheet view

Creating tables is now easier — just click Table on the Create tab and start entering data in the improved Datasheet view. Office Access 2010 automatically determines the data type, so you are up and running in no time. With the new Add New Field column, it becomes obvious where you can easily add a field — and if you need to change the data type or display format, it is easy to do so by using the ribbon. You can even paste Excel tables into a new datasheet, and Office Access 2010 creates all of the fields and recognizes the data types automatically.

The Add New Field column

Need to add a customer ID field to your orders table? Just drag a field from the new Field List pane onto the datasheet to add a field from another table, and Access automatically creates any needed relationships or prompts you throughout the process.

Total row in datasheets

New to Datasheet view is a Totals row where you can add a sum, count, average, maximum, minimum, standard deviation, or variance. You point and click to choose the one that you want.

Field templates for creating new fields

Spending a lot of time in field design? Check out the new Field Templates pane. A field template is a design for a field, complete with a name, data type, length, and prepopulated properties. You can drag the fields that you need on to the datasheet. Field templates are XSD based so that you can set up standard definitions for shared use in your department or workgroup.

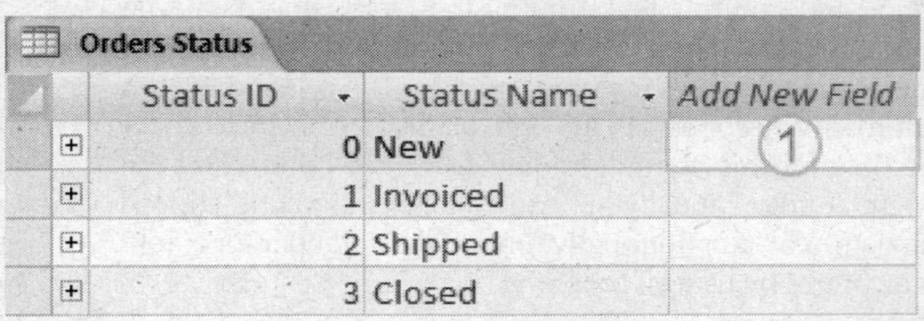

Field list task pane

The new Field List pane goes beyond the field picker found in earlier versions of Access by including fields from other tables. You can drag and drop fields from the table in your record source, related tables, or unrelated tables in the database. Office Access 2010 is smart about creating the infrastructure required, so if a relationship between tables is needed, it is automatically created, or you are prompted throughout the process.

Split forms

Use the new split form to create a form that combines a Datasheet view and a Form view. You can set a property to tell Access whether to place the datasheet on the top, bottom, left, or right.

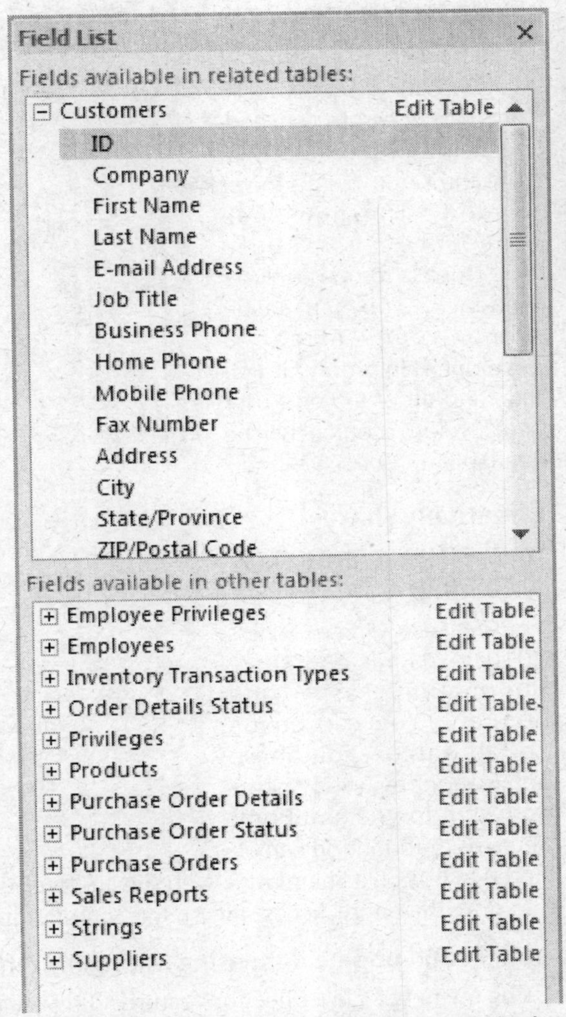

Multivalued fields

You can create a field that holds multiple values. Suppose that you want to store a list of categories to which you have assigned an item. In most database management systems and in earlier versions of Access, you have to model a many-to-many relationship in order to do this correctly.

In Office Access 2010, the hard part is done for you when you choose a multivalued field. Multivalued fields are especially appropriate when you use Office Access 2010 to work with a SharePoint list that contains one of the multivalued field types used in Windows SharePoint Services. Office Access 2010 is compatible with these data types.

Attachment data type for storing pictures, graphics, Office files, or any type of file

The new Attachment data type lets you easily store all types of documents and binary files in your database without unnecessary database bloat. Attachments are automatically compressed when appropriate to maximize space usage. Do you need to attach a Microsoft Office Word 2010 document to a record? Want to save a series of digital pictures in your database? Attachments make these tasks much easier. You can even have multiple attachments attached to a single record.

Use an alternate background color

Datasheets, reports, and continuous forms support a new alternate background color that you can set independently of the regular background color. Shading every other line is easy and you can choose any color.

Navigation Pane

The new Navigation Pane provides easy access to all of your objects and replaces the Database window. Organize your objects by object type, date created, date modified, related table (based on object dependencies), or in custom groups that you create. Need more space to work on your form design? The Navigation Pane docks on the left and you can easily collapse it so that it takes up little space, but still remains available.

Embedded macros

Use the new trusted, embedded macros to avoid having to write code. An embedded macro is stored in a property and is part of the object to which it belongs. You can modify the design of an embedded macro without having to worry about other controls that might use the macro — each embedded macro is independent. Embedded macros are trusted because they are automatically prevented from performing certain potentially unsafe operations.

CHAPTER 2

Improved Help viewer

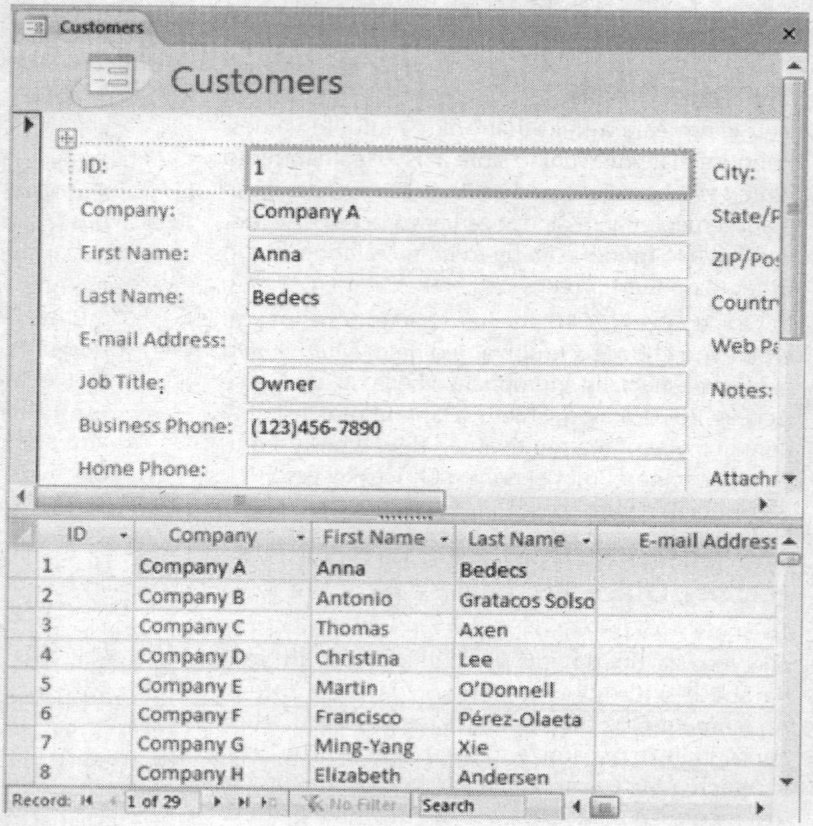

Unlike previous versions of Access, Office Access 2010 offers easy access to both end-user help and developer help from the same Help viewer window. The new help experience has been redesigned in response to user feedback. You can easily scope your search to developer Help only, if you like, and all of the end user and developer content will be available on Office Online.

Effectively share tracked information with others

You can use Office Access 2010 to gather and share information easily and securely. You can create collaborative database applications by using Access and Windows SharePoint Services. Information can be stored in lists on a SharePoint Web site and accessed through linked tables in an Access database, or you can store the entire Access file on the SharePoint site.

Collect and update data using Microsoft Office Outlook 2010

Using the new Data Collection feature, Office Access 2010 can automatically create a Microsoft Office InfoPath 2010 or HTML form and embed it in the body of an e-mail message. You can then send it to recipients selected from your Outlook contacts, or from your Access database.

You choose whether you want to collect new information or update existing information. Recipients then complete the form and return it. Office Outlook 2010 recognizes the incoming forms and lets you automatically save the data in your Office Access 2010 database — no retyping required.

Move your database to a SharePoint site

You can easily change your standalone database to a Windows SharePoint Services shared solution that uses Access tables linked to SharePoint lists. The Move to SharePoint Site Wizard is smart, automatically migrating primary keys and relationships in ways that make sense.

The immediate benefits of a Windows SharePoint Services shared solution include shared browser-based access, centralized backup, SharePoint site based database deployment, and all of the benefits of using a rich, Access based client in a server based solution. IT departments gain a measure of predictability and control by sourcing database access on the SharePoint site. Users can subscribe to e-mail alerts when records are added, deleted, or changed in a SharePoint list.

Integration with Windows SharePoint Services workflow

Office Access 2010 supports workflow by using the Windows Workflow Services found in Windows SharePoint Services. You can create solutions that employ workflow routing and approval, automatically assign tasks to other users, report on project status, and ensure that tasks are completed on time, for example.

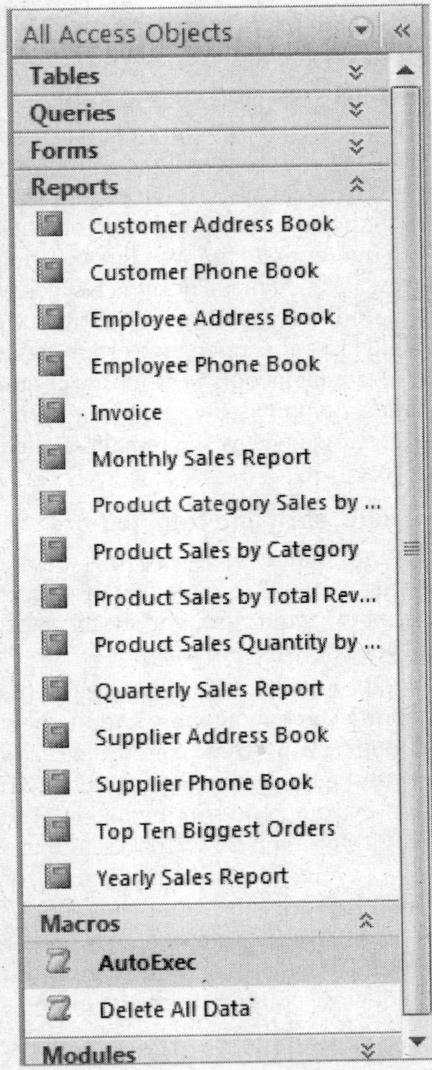

Improved performance for tables linked to SharePoint lists

Optimizations made to the internal processing of tables linked to SharePoint lists enable a faster, smoother experience.

One-to-one mapping with Windows SharePoint Services data types

With new support for multivalued fields and attachments, Office Access 2010 now supports all of the data types found in Windows SharePoint Services, making the design and building of Windows SharePoint Services shared applications much simpler.

Take SharePoint lists offline with Access

Need to take some work home with you? You can take your SharePoint lists offline with one click by using Office Access 2010. Work on your data in Access and then synchronize your changes, or reconnect with the SharePoint site at a later time.

Export to PDF and XPS

Now you can export data to a PDF (Portable Document Format) or XPS (XML Paper Specification) format for printing, posting, and e-mail distribution, provided that you first install the Publish as PDF or XPS add-in. Exporting a form, report, or datasheet to a PDF or XPS file lets you capture information in an easily distributed form that retains all of your formatting characteristics, but doesn't require others to have Access installed on their computers to print or review your output. You can export to a PDF or XPS format file from Office Access 2010 only after you install the add-in. Here's some information about the file formats:

- Portable Document Format (PDF) PDF is a fixed-layout electronic file format that preserves document formatting and enables file sharing. The PDF format ensures that when the file is viewed online or printed, it retains exactly the format that you intended, and that data in the file cannot be easily copied or changed. The PDF format is also useful for documents that will be reproduced by using commercial printing methods.
- XML Paper Specification (XPS) XPS is an electronic file format that preserves document formatting and enables file sharing. The XPS format ensures that when the file is viewed online or printed, it retains exactly the format that you intended, and that data in the file cannot be easily copied or changed.

Improved import and export experience

New features in Office Access 2010 make it easier to import and export data. You can save an import or export operation and then reuse the saved operation the next time that you have to perform the same task. The Import Spreadsheet Wizard lets you override the data type chosen by Access, and you can import, export, and link to the new Office Excel 2010 file formats.

Create and adapt reports to suit your business needs

Report view and Layout view

Two new views let you work with reports interactively. By using the new Report view, you can browse a rich, accurate rendering of your report without having to print or preview it. To focus on certain records, use the filter feature, or use a find operation to search for matching text. You can use the copy command to grab text for copy and paste operations by using the Clipboard, or click the active hyperlinks displayed in your report to follow a link by using your browser. Report view adds the ability to browse, but Layout view lets you make design changes while you browse. This capability lets you make many of the most common design changes while you view a live report. For example, add a field by dragging from the new Field List pane, or change properties by using the property sheet. Layout view supports the new stacked and tabular layouts — groups of controls that you can manipulate as one, so that you can easily rearrange fields, columns, rows, or whole layouts. You can also remove a field or add formatting easily in Layout view. Design view still remains available for more detailed work, and has also been enhanced to support layouts.

Group, sort, and total feature

New to Office Access 2010 is a better and more accessible way to group and sort in reports and add totals. You will find the new user interface easier to navigate and understand, and when it is used with the new Layout view, you see the effect of your changes instantly.

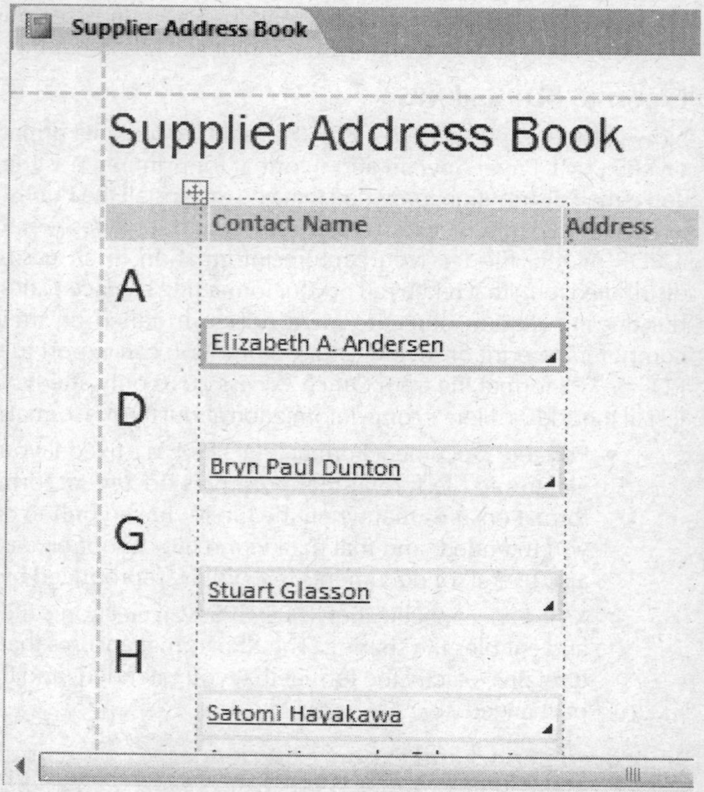

Need to see total sales by region in a report? Use Layout view and the new Grouping pane to add a group level and request a total — and see the changes live in your report immediately! The new Totals drop-down makes adding a sum, average, count, maximum, or minimum to your report headers or footers easy. Simple totals no longer require manually creating a calculated field. Now you just point and click.

Improved look of automatically created reports

The new Quick Create feature automatically generates reports with professional looking designs, with headers that include a logo, a title, a date and time, and informative footers and totals.

Manage and audit information

Enhanced Office Access 2010 security features and strong integration with

Windows SharePoint Services enable you to more effectively manage and help secure your information tracking applications. By storing your tracking application data in lists on Windows SharePoint Services, you can audit revision history, recover deleted information, and set data access permissions.

Enhanced security

In order to help make Office Access 2010 more secure and to maintain consistency with other 2010 Office release products, Office Access 2010 includes new and improved security features. Unified trust decisions are integrated with the Microsoft Office Trust Center. Trusted locations make it easy to trust all databases in secure folders. You can load an Office Access 2010 application with code or macros disabled to provide a more secure, "sandboxed" experience. Trusted macros are run in Sandbox mode.

Revision tracking by using Windows SharePoint Services

You can view revision history at the record level with the help of Windows SharePoint Services. Need to know who changed a row or when it was changed? You can find out by viewing the revision history.

Permission setting by using Windows SharePoint Services

Set access permissions to SharePoint lists with the help of Windows SharePoint Services. You can selectively allow or deny certain users access. You can assign limited reading permissions or full editing rights.

Retrieve from the Recycle Bin by using Windows SharePoint Services

You can use the new Recycle Bin in Windows SharePoint Services 3.0 to easily view deleted records and recover information that was erroneously deleted.

Open Access forms and reports from Windows SharePoint Services

Windows SharePoint Services users can open lists in rich Access views directly from a SharePoint site. Office Access 2010 forms, reports, and datasheets can appear listed alongside other views on a SharePoint site. When you choose an Access view, Office Access 2010 starts and opens the requested form, report, or datasheet. This makes it easy for you to run a rich Office Access 2010 report on a SharePoint site without having to first start Office Access 2010. You can also choose to open a list in Access, and if a database doesn't exist, it is created automatically and prepopulated with a set of forms and reports based on your list.

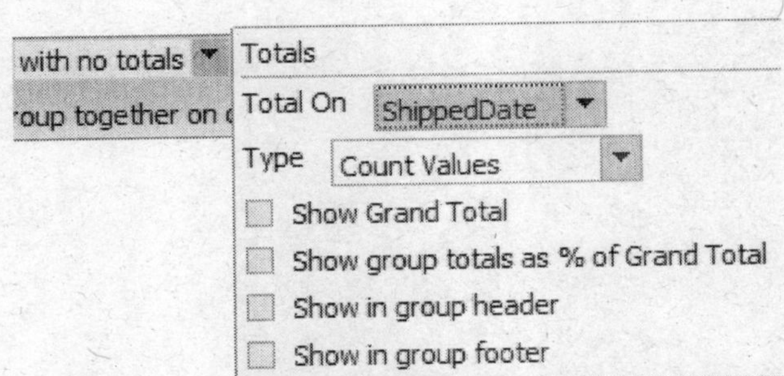

Memo field history tracking

Memo fields are useful for storing large amounts of information. Starting with Office Access 2010, you can set a property that tells Access to retain a history of all changes to a Memo field. You can then view a history of those changes. This feature also supports the tracking feature in Windows SharePoint Services so that you can also use Access to view your SharePoint list content history.

Office Diagnostics

Microsoft Office Diagnostics is a series of diagnostic tests that can help you to discover why your computer is crashing. The diagnostic tests can solve some problems directly and may identify ways that you can solve other problems. Microsoft Office Diagnostics replaces the following Microsoft Office 2003 features: Detect and Repair and Microsoft Office Application Recovery.

Proofing Tools

The following are some new features of the spelling checker:

- The spelling checker has been made more consistent across the 2010 Microsoft Office system programs. Examples of this change include:
- Several spelling checker options are now global. If you change one of these options in one Office program, that option is also changed for all the other Office programs.
- In addition to sharing the same custom dictionaries, all programs can manage them using the same dialog box.
- The 2010 Microsoft Office system spelling checker includes the post-reform French dictionary. In Microsoft Office 2003, this was an add-in that had to be separately installed.
- An exclusion dictionary is automatically created for a language the first time that language is used. Exclusion dictionaries let you force the spelling checker flag words you want to avoid using. They are handy for avoiding words that are obscene or that don't match your style guide.

CHAPTER 3

Introduction to Relational Database

Introduction

A database is an integrated collection of well defined data and information, centrally controlled in all its aspects, created and stored in a typical structure for an organisation. In an organisation, the database could be, one or more, depending upon the needs and the operations of the organisation. The data structure and its storage should be such that it facilitates shareability, availability, evolvability and integrity of the data. The database separates a design of the information system from the data design and its management.

Information

Information is the result of processing, manipulating and organizing data in a way that adds to the knowledge of the receiver. In other words, it is the context in which data is taken.

Information as a concept bears a diversity of meanings, from everyday usage to technical settings. Generally speaking, the concept of information is closely related to notions of constraint, communication, control, data, form, instruction, knowledge, meaning, mental stimulus, pattern, perception, and representation. Many people speak about the Information Age as the advent of the Knowledge Age or knowledge society, the information society, and information technologies, and even though informatics, information science and computer science are often in the spotlight, the word "information" is often used without careful consideration of the various meanings it has acquired.

Data vs Information

Data in everyday language is a synonym for information. In the exact sciences there is a clear distinction between data and information, where data is a measurement that can be disorganized and when the data becomes organized it becomes information. Data can be about reality, or fiction such as a fictional movie. Data about reality consists of propositions. A large class of practically important propositions are measurements or observations of a variable. Such propositions may comprise numbers, words, or images.

Data are raw facts whereas Information is the processed data.

If the raw data is processed as per certain rules or policy, the result obtained is called information. It means that when we process data to achieve meaningful results, it becomes information. For example:

- Results summary of an examination
- Purchase and sales of any goods items.
- The number of employees works in HR department, etc.

This can be physically represented as:

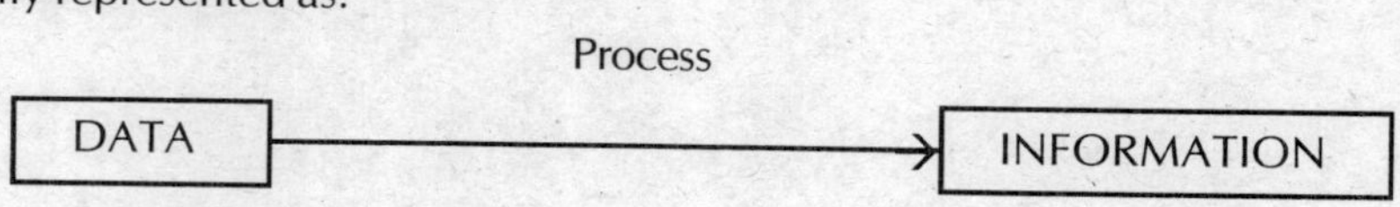

Thus, information is the processed data.

Quality of Information

Information helps you take decision for current action which you are performing. So much emphasis should be given to the quality of the information. If you given the wrong information, naturally, the net result would be wrong too. For example, if the meter reading of electric supply is wrongly noted, then the billing would be wrong too. There are some factors which contribute towards value of information are: timeliness, availability, accuracy, presentation and its completeness.

Characteristics of the levels of information, these levels of management which use this kind of information.

Top Level Management

- Top levels are heavily focus on planning.
- It deals with complex and some uncertain activities.
- Deals with fewer people.
- Concentrate with strategic decisions.

Middle Level Management

- Middle levels lesser focus on planning but more than low level management.

- It deals with less complying but better defined variable.
- Number of people involved are more than top level but less than lower level.
- Concerned with tectical decisions.

Low or Supervisory Level Management

- Minimum focus on planning.
- Very large number of people involved in it.
- It deals with straight forward activities.
- Concerned with operation decisions.

Information Processing

Information System (IS) is the system of persons, data records and activities that process the data and information in a given organization, including manual processes or automated processes. Usually the term is used erroneously as a synonymous for computer-based information systems, which is only the Information technologies component of an Information System. The computer-based information systems are the field of study for Information technologies (IT); however these should hardly be treated apart from the bigger Information System that is always envolved in.

The IT Department partly governs the information technology development, use, application and influence on a business or corporation . A computer based information system, following a definition of Langefors, is a technologically implemented medium for recording, storing, and disseminating linguistic expressions, as well as for drawing conclusions from such expressions. Information systems are also social systems whose behaviour is heavily influenced by the goals, values and beliefs of individuals and groups, as well as the performance of the technology.

In information systems, an information system consists of three components: human, technology, organisation. In this view, information is defined in terms of the three levels of semiotics. Data which can be automatically processed by the application system corresponds to the syntax-level. In the context of an individual who interprets the data they become information, which correspond to the semantic-level. Information becomes knowledge when an individual knows (understands) and evaluates the information (e.g., for a specific task). This corresponds to the pragmatic-level.

In general systems theory, an information system is a system, automated or manual, that comprises people, machines, and/or methods organized to collect, process, transmit, and disseminate data that represent user information.

In rough set theory, an information system is an attribute-value system.

In telecommunications, an information system is any telecommunications and/or computer related equipment or interconnected system or subsystems of equipment that is used in the acquisition, storage, manipulation, management, movement, control, display, switching, interchange, transmission, or reception of voice and/or data, and includes software, firmware, and hardware.

In computer security, an information system is described by five objects:

Structure:

- Repositories, which hold data permanent or temporarily, such as buffers, RAM, hard disks, cache, etc.
- Interfaces, which exchange information with the non-digital world, such as keyboards, speakers, scanners, printers, etc.
- Channels, which connect repositories, such as buses, cables, wireless links, etc. A Network is a set of logical or physical channels.

Behaviour:

- Services, which provide value to users or to other services via messages interchange.
- Messages, which carries a meaning to users or services.

In the mathematical area of domain theory, a Scott information system (after its inventor Dana Scott) is a mathematical structure that provides an alternative representation of Scott domains and, as a special case, algebraic lattices.

Fields of Information Systems

Information systems deal with the development, use and management of an organization's IT infrastructure. In the post-industrial, information age, the focus of companies has shifted from being product oriented, to knowledge oriented, in a sense that market operators today, compete on process and innovation, rather than product : the emphasis has shifted from the quality and quantity of production, to the production process itself, and the services that accompany the production process. The biggest asset of companies today, is their information, represented in people, experience, know-how, innovations (patents, copyrights, trade secrets), and for a market operator to be able to compete, he/she must have a strong information infrastructure, at the heart of which, lies the information technology infrastructure.

Thus, the study of information systems, focuses on why and how technology can be put into best use to serve the information flow within an organization.

Information Systems has a number of different areas of work:

- Information Systems Strategy
- Information Systems Management
- Information Systems Development

Each of which branches out into a number of sub disciplines, that overlap with other science and managerial disciplines such as computer science, pure and engineering sciences, social and behavioral sciences, and business management.

What is a Database?

Conventionally, in an information system, the information is obtained by developing the systems and integrating them. The calls for breaking the system into various subsystems and developing the information systems independently. In this approach, each system will have its master files and transaction files. They have to be processed separately at different times, depending upon the needs and schedules. The file layouts and the access methods could be different in different systems.

Therefore, the files will be updated at different times. This approach does affect the quality of the information across all the systems due to various reasons. The data in many systems are common and there is repetition of data storage in various systems. This is called data redundancy. The redundancy of data gives rise to problems of keeping the data current and same in all the files. The data management is complex in such a situation. The reports generated out of such files show discrepancies in the information. Since the data files are different for different systems, data sharing is not possible. These files need to be created at different times.

Transaction updating is also carried out at different times. It requires the increase of a magnetic media for storage because the systems are developed independently. The redundancy causes lack of integrity and inconsistency of the data in the various files.

Why a Database?

To better understand what drives the design of databases, you must understand the difference between data and information. Data are raw facts. The word "raw" is used to indicate that the facts have not yet been processed to reveal their meaning.

Let's summarize some key points:

- Data constitute the building blocks of information.
- Information is produced by processing data.
- Information is used to reveal the meaning of data.
- Good, relevant and timely information is the key to good decision making.
- Good decision making is the key to organizational survival in a global environment

Such data must be generated properly and it must be stored properly in a format that is easy to access and process. And, like any basic resource, the data environment must be managed carefully. Data management is discipline that focuses on the proper generation, storage and retrieval of data. Given the crucial role played by data, it should not surprise you that data management is a core activity for any business, government agency, service organization or charity.

Typically, efficient data management requires the use of a computer database. A database is a shared, integrated computer structure that houses a collection of:

- End user data, that is raw facts of interest to the end user.
- Metadata or data about data, through which the data are integrated.

The metadata provide a description of the data characteristics and the set of relationship that link the data found within the database. In a sense, a database resembles a very well-organized electronic filling cabinet in which powerful software, known as a database management system (DBMS) helps manage the cabinet's contents.

Because data are the crucial raw material from which information is derived, there are many good reasons why DBMSs are important in our information-based society. The following points are worth stressing.

- Since data are so important, we must have a good way of managing such data. As you will discover the DBMS helps make data management much more efficient and effective than it was before the DBMS became a reality.
- The DBMS contains a query language that makes it possible to produce quick answers to adhoc queries. (A query is a question and an adhoc query is a spur-of-the-moment question.) For example, end users, when dealing with large amounts of sales data, might want quick answers to questions (adhoc queries) such as:

  What was the dollar volume of sales by product during the past six months?

  What is the sales bonus figure for each of our salespeople during the past three months?

  How many of our customers have credit balances of Rs. 30,000 or more?
- The DBMS helps create an environment in which end users have better access to more and better-managed data than they did before the DBMS became the data management standard. Such access makes it possible for end users to respond quickly to changes in their environment. The availability of data, combined with the tools that transform data into usable information, empowers the end users to make quick and informed decisions that can make the difference between success and failure in the global economy.
- Wider access to well-managed data prompts an integrated view of the organization's operations. Thus it becomes much easier to see how actions in one segment of the company affect other segments. The DBMS environment promotes a clearer view of the big picture.
- You will discover that the probability of data consistency is greatly reduced in a properly designed database that is managed through a DBMS. Better data make it possible to generate better information on which better decisions are based.

The advantages of using a DBMS are not limited to the few we have just listed. In fact, you will discover many more advantages as you learn more about the technical details of the database and its proper design.

A DBMS is a collection of program that manages the database structure and controls access to the data stored in the database. The DBMS makes it possible to share the data in the database among multiple applications or users.

In effect, the DBMS serves as the intermediary between the user and the database by translating user requests into the complex code required to fulfill those requests. The DBMS hides much of the database's internal complexity from the application programs that use the database. The application program might be written by a programmer, using a programming language such as COBOL or it might be created through a DBMS utility program.

Keep in mind that the DBMS is the database software you buy commercially; you do not have the option of making design changes to it. Therefore, when we speak of database design, we mean the design of the database structure that will be used to store and manage data, rather than the design of the DBMS software. Once the database design is completed, the DBMS handles all the complicated activities required to translate the designer's view of the structures into structures that are usable to the computer.

Characteristics of Data in a Database

Database design has two important terms as Data and Fields. Data is the information that goes into your database. An individual's last name—Tendulkar, for example—is data. Fields are the types of data that make up the database. A field is another name for an attribute or category, so an entire category of data, such as a group of names, is considered to be a field. Names, phone numbers, customer numbers, descriptions, locations, and stock numbers are common fields that your database might contain.

You should not only know the type of information which is being fed into the database, but you must also know the format in which it is going to be printed. Information comes from a database in the form of reports. When you ask the computer for a list of all homes in the area priced between Rs. 1,00,000 and Rs. 1,50,000, or for a list of employees earning less than Rs. 15.00 per hour, you are also asking for a report. When you request Sachin Tendulkar's address, you are also asking for a report. A report is a summary of information.

Whether the computer displays a few lines on the screen or hundreds of lines on a stack of paper, it is providing a report based on the data contained within the database file.

Office Database Data

Each office has to maintain details of its several employees. It may, for example, maintain the files of the following:

Personal File
Accounts File
Leave Record File

Details of these files can be worked out (it may be different from office to office) as follows:

Personal File

Name
Address
Telephone number
Joining Date
Designation
Qualifications

Accounts File

- Name
- Basic Salary
- HRA
- DA
- I Tax
- PF

Leave Records File

- Name
- Casual Leave
- Priviledge Leave
- Sick Leave
- Accumulated Leaves

If you notice all these files have one field in common which is Name and this is called the *Primary Key* and is the link between all the 3 files.

A look at the fields of the Personal file will give us an idea about the database to be created for it.

Personal File

Name	Alphanumeric
Address	Alphanumeric
Telephone number	Numeric
Joining Date	Date
Designation	Alphanumeric
Qualifications	Alphanumeric

Once we create all these tables the office database will be created. A database, therefore, comprises of tables. Tables in turn contain records. If we are to decide what tables should be part of the office database, we have to ask ourselves what is the information which needs to be stored in the database. Once we have this information we can decide about the tables.

A Database is a collection of all the required information pertaining to a particular subject. Thus, all the data pertaining to a office is put together in a database. Two things should be borne in mind while storing data.

- The data is to be stored in a single database since it pertains to a single subject.
- The distinction between the various groups should be maintained since different types of details are stored for each group.

To satisfy these conditions, the data for each category is stored in a separate table. All the tables are part of a single database.

Thus, in the Office Database we have 3 tables as follows:

Office Database

- Personal Table
- Accounts Table
- Leave Record Table

The point to be noted here is that data in this database is stored in the form of tables, is also known as relations.

What is a Database Management System (DBMS)?

Let us see the general architecture of a database. The architecture of a DBMS is divided into three levels: the external level, the conceptual level and the internal level. The view at each of these levels is described by a scheme.

A scheme is an outline or a plan that describes the records and relationships existing in the view. The word scheme, which means a systematic plan for attaining some goal, is used interchangeably in the database literature with the word schema. The word schemas is used in the database literature for the plural instead of schemata, the grammatically corrrect word. The scheme also describes the way in which entities at one level of abstraction can be mapped to the next level.

External or User View

The external or user view is at the highest level of database abastraction where only those portions of the database of concern to a user or application program are included. Any number of user views (some of which may be identical) may exist for a given global or conceptual view.

Each external view is described by means of a scheme called an external schema. The external schema consists of the definition of the logical records and the relationships in the external view. The external schema also contains the method of deriving the objects in the external view from the objects in the conceptual view. The objects include entities, attributes, and relationships. (The term view, scheme, and schema are sometimes used interchangeably when there is no confusion as to what is implied.

Conceptual of Global View

At this level of database abstraction all the database entities and the relationships among them are included. One conceptual view represents the entire database, This conceptual view is defined by the conceptual schema. It describes all the records and relationships included in the conceptual view and, therefore, in the database. There is only one conceptual schema per database. This schema also contains the method of deriving the objects in the conceptual view from the objects in the internal view.

The description of data at this level is in a format independent of its physical representation. It also includes features that specify the checks to retain data consistency and integrity.

Internal View

We find this view at the lowest level of abstraction, closest to the physical storage method used. It indicates how the data will be stored and describes the data structures and access methods, to be used by the database. The internal view is expressed by the internal schema, which contains the definition of the stored record, the mehod of representing the data fields, and the access aids used.

Mapping between Views

The conceptual database is the model or abstraction of the objects of concern to the database. The view is the subset of the objects modeled in the conceptual database that is used by an application. There could be any number of views of a conceptual database. A view can be used to limit the portion of the database that is known and accessible to a given application.

Two mappings are required in a database system with three different views. A mapping between the external and conceptual views gives the correspondence among the records and the relationships of the external and conceptual views. The external view is an abstraction of the conceptual view, which in its turn is an abstraction of the internal view. It describes the contents of the database as perceived by the user or application program of that view. The user of the external view sees and manipulates a record corresponding to the external view. There is a mapping from a particular logical record in the external view to one (or more) conceptual record(s) in the conceptual view.

Need for DBMS

A good database does not just happen; the structure of its contents must be designed carefully. In fact, database design is such a crucial aspect of working with databases that most of this book is dedicated to the development of good database design techniques. Even a good DBMS will perform poorly with a badly designed database. A well-designed database facilitates data management and becomes a valuable information generator. A poorly designed database is likely to become a breeding ground for redundant data, that is, unnecessarily duplicated data. Redundant data are often the source of difficult-to-trace information errors.

A database contains redundant data when the same data about the same entity are kept in different locations. (An entity is a person, place or thing about which data are to be collected and stored.) for example, data redundancy exists when a customer's telephone number is stored in a customer file, a sales agent file and an invoice file.

If the customer's phone number changes, the correction might not be made in all the locations where it occurs. Therefore, the existence of redundant data can produce uncorrected data entries and you probably won't know which value is the correct one. Reports might yield different results, depending on which version of the data was used. In short, uncontrolled data redundancies are typical of a poorly designed database.

A poorly designed database tends to generate errors that are likely to lead to bad decisions. A bad database design eventually can be self-correcting: organizations using poorly designed databases often fail because their managers do not have access to timely (or even correct) information, thereby eliminating the bad database design.

Because the database is the source from which information is generated, its design is the subject of detailed study in the modern data environment. Database design is simply too important to be left to luck. That's why college students study database design, why organizations of all types and sizes send personnel to database design seminars and why database design consultants often make an excellent living.

A Practical Approach to Database Design

Because information is clearly important in our so-called information age, the ability to produce useful databases has tremendous practical value. For this reason, we will focus our attention on the principles and concepts that have a direct bearing on the practical aspects of database design. If you want to learn how to design a useful database, this book will point you in the right direction. If you want to develop a thorough understanding of the outer limits of database theory, this is not the book for you.

In addition to including the material necessary to build an appropriate database vocabulary and to understand basic database concepts, we have also developed two complete applications through the logical design stage. (the logical design is the structural blueprint of the database). We believe that exposure to the practical aspects of the design process will properly set the stage for your own successful designs.

Type of DBMS

The DBMS, on which the database system is based can be classified according to the number of users, the database site locations(s) and the expected type and extent of use.

The number of users determines whether the DBMS is classified as single – user or multiuser. A single-user DBMS supports only one user at a time. In other words, if user A is using the database users B and C must wait until user A has completed his/her database work. If a single-user database runs on a personal computer, it is also called a desktop database. In contrast, a multiuser DBMS supports multiple users at the same time.

If the multiuser database supports a relatively small number of users (usually fewer than fifty) or a specific department within an organization, it is called a work group database. If the database is used by the entire organization, it is called a workgroup database. If the database is used by the entire organization and supports many users (more than fifty, usually hundreds) across many departments, the database is known as an enterprise database.

The database site location might also be used to classify the DBMS. For example, a DVMS that supports a database located at a single site is called a centralized DBMS. A DBMS that supports a database distributed across several different sites is called a distributed DBMS.

Perhaps the types of use and the extent of such use yield the most relevant and currently favored DBMS classification. For example, transactions such as product or service sales, payments and supply purchases reflect critical day-to-day operations. Such transactions are time-critical and must be recorded accurately and immediately – the sale of a product must be recorded and reflected in the inventory immediately.

A DBMS that powers a database primarily designed to support such "immediate response" transactions is classified as a transactional DBMS or a production DBMS. In contrast a decision support database focuses primarily on the production of information required to make tactical or strategic decisions at middle and high management levels. Decision support, provided by a decision support system (DSS), typically requires extensive "Data messaging" (data manipulation) to extract information from historical data to formulate pricing decisions, sales forecasts, market positioning and so on.

Because most DSS information is based on historical data, the data retrieval time factor is not likely to be as critical as it is for the transactional database. Additionally, the DSS information tends to be based on complex data derived from many sources.

To make such complex data more easily retrievable, the DSS database structure is quite different from that of a transaction – oriented database. In fact, the term data warehouse is used to describe the database design favored by DSSs.

Quite clearly, properly database design requires the database designer to precisely identify the database's expected use. Designing a transactional database emphasizes data integrity, data consistency and operational speed. The design of a decision support database recognizes the use of historical and aggregated data. Designing a database to be used in centralized, single-user environment requires a different approach from that used in the design of a distributed, multiuser database.

Relational Database Management System (RDBMS)

A relational database management system (RDBMS), such as Access, stores data in related tables. For instance, a table containing employee data (names and addresses) may be related to a table containing payroll data (pay date, pay amount, and cheque number). Queries allow the user to ask complex questions (such as "What is the sum of all paychecks issued to Amitabh Bachchan in 2007") from these related tables, with the answers displayed as on-screen forms and printed reports.

RDBMS Terminology

The architecture of DBMS packages has evolved from the early monolithic systems, where the whole DBMS software package was one tightly integrated system, to the modern DBMS packages that are modular in design, with a client/server system architecture. The evolution mirrors and trends in computing, where large centralized mainframe computers are being replaced by hundreds of distributed workstations and personal computers connected via communications networks to various types of server machines – Web servers, database servers, file servers, application servers and so on.

In a basic client/server DBMS architecture, the system functionality is distributed between two types of modules. A client module is typically designed so that it will run on a user workstation or personal computer. Typically, application programs and user interfaces that access the database run in the client module. Hence, the client module handles user interaction and provides the user-friendly interfaces such as forms- or menu based GUIs (Graphical User Interfaces). The other kind of module, called a server module, typically handles data storage, access, search and other functions.

Data Models, Schemas and Instances

One fundamental characteristic of the database approach is that it provides some level of data abstraction by hiding details of data storage that are not needed by most database users. A data model – a collection of concepts that can be used to describe the structure of a database – provides the necessary means to achieve this abstraction. By structure of a database, we mean the data types, relationships and constraints that should for the data. Most data models also include a set of basic operations for specifying retrievals and updates on the database.

In addition to the basic operations provided by the data model, it is becoming more common to include concepts in the data model to specify the dynamic aspect or behavior of a database application. This allows the database designer to specify a set of valid user defined operations that are allowed on the database objects.

An example of a user-defined operation could be COMPUTE_GPA which can be applied to a STUDENT object. On the other hand generic operations to insert, delete, modify or retrieve any kind of object are often included in the basic data model operations. Concepts to specify behavior are fundamental to object oriented data models but are also being incorporated in more traditional data models. For example, object-relational models extend the traditional relational model to include such concepts, among others.

Categories of Data Models

Many data models have been proposed, which can we categorize according to the types of concepts they use to describe the database structure. High-level of conceptual data models provide concepts that are close to the way many users perceive data, whereas low-level or physical data models provide concepts that describe the details of how data is stored in the computer.

Concepts provided by low-level data models are generally meant for computer specialists, not for typical and users. Between these two extremes is a class of representation (or implementation) data models, which provide concepts that may be understood by end users but that are not too far removed from the way data is organized within the computer. Representational data models hide some details of data storage but can be implemented on a computer system in direct way.

Conceptual data models use concepts such as entities, attributes and relationships. An entity represents a real-world object or concept, such as an employee or a project, that is described in the database. An attribute represents some property of interest that further describes an entity, such as the employee's name or salary. A relationship among two or more entities for example a works-on relationship between an employee and a project.

Representational or implementation data models used most frequently in traditional commercial DBMSs. These include the widely used relational data model, as well as he so-called legacy data models – the network and hierarchical models – that have been widely used in the past.

Schemas, Instances and Database State

In any data model, it is important to distinguish between the description of the database and database itself. The description of a database is called the database schemas, which is specified during database design and is not expected to change frequently. Most data models have certain conventions for displaying schemas as diagrams. A displaying schema is called a schema diagram.

A schema diagram displays only some aspects of a schema, such as the names of record types and data items and some types of constraints. The actual data in a database may change quite frequently. For example, the database changes every time we add a student or enter a new grade for a student. It is also called the current set of occurrences or instances in the database.

In a given database state, each schema construct has its own current set of instances; for example, the STUDENT construct will contain the set of individual student entities (records) as its instances. Many database states can be constructed to correspond to a particular database schema. Every time we insert or delete a record or change the value of a data item in record, we change one state of the database into another state.

The distinction between database schema and database state is very important. When as define a new database, we specify its database schema only to the DBMS. At the point, the corresponding database state is the empty state with no data. We get the initial state of the database when the database is first populated or loaded with the initial data. From then on, every time an update operation is applied to the database, we get another database state. At any point in time, the database has a current state.

The DBMS is partly responsible for ensuring that every state of the database is a valid state – that is, a state that satisfies the structure and constraints specified in the schema. Hence, specifying a correct schema to the DBMS is extremely important and the schema must be designed with the utmost care. The DBMS stores the descriptions of the schema constructs and constraints – also called the meta-data – in the DBMS catalog so that DBMS software can refer to the schema whenever it needs to. The schema is sometimes called the intension and a database state an extension of the schema.

Relational Data Structure

There are several implicit relationships among the various entity types. In fact, whenever an attribute of an entity type refers to another entity type, some relationship exists. For example, the attribute Manager of DEPARTMENT refers to an employee who manages the department; the attribute ControllingDepartment of PROJECT refer to the department that controls the project; the attribute Supervisor of EMPLOYEE refers to another employee (the one who supervises this employee); the attribute Department of EMPLOYEE refers to the department for which the employee works; and so on.

In the ER model, these references should not be represented as attributes but as relationship, which are discussed in this section. The COMPANY database schema will be refined in section to represent relationships explicitly. In the initial design of entity types, relationships are typically captured in the form of attributes. As the design is refined, these attributes get converted into relationships between entity types.

Relational Data Integrity

Microsoft Access is a relational database development system. Access data is stored in related tables, where data in one table (such as customers) is related to data in another data (such as orders). Access maintains the relationship between related tables, making it easy to extract a customer and all of the customer's orders, without losing any data or pulling order records not owned by the customer.

After you have created the tables, they need to be related to each other. For example, if you have a Contents table and a Sales table, you must relate the Contents table to the Sales table in order to see all the sales records for a Contact. If you had only one table, you would have to repeat the Contact name and address for each sale record.

Two tables let you look up information in the Contact table for each sale by using the related fields Contant ID (in Contacts) and Buyer ID (in Sales). This way, when a customer changes address, for example, the address changes only in one record in the Contact table; when the Sales information is on-screen, the correct contact address is always visible.

History of Databasetes

We now give a brief historical overview of the applications that use DBMSs and how those applications provided the impetus for new types of database systems.

Early database applications Using Hierarchical and Network Systems

Many early database applications maintained records in large organizations, such as corporations, universities, hospitals and banks. In many of these applications, there were large numbers of records of similar structure. For example, in a university application, similar information would be kept for each student, each course, each grade record and so on. There were also many types of records and many interrelationships among them.

One of the main problems with early database systems have the intermixing of conceptional relationships with the physical storage and placement of records on disk. For example, the grade records of a particular student could be physically stored next to the student record. Although this provided very efficient access for the original queries and transactions that the database was designed to handle, it did not provide enough flexibility to access records efficiently when new queries and transactions were identified. In particular, new queries that required a different storage organization for efficient processing were quite difficult to implement efficiently. It was also quite difficult to reorganize the database when changes were made to the requirements of the application.

Another shortcoming of early systems was that they provided only programming language interfaces. This made it time-consuming and expensive to implement new queries and transactions, since new programs had to be written, tested and debugged. Most of these database systems were implemented on large and expensive mainframe computers starting in the mid-1960s and through the 1970s and 1980s. the main types of early systems were based on three main paradigms: hierarchical systems, network model based systems and inverted file systems.

Providing Application Flexibility with Relational Database

Relational databases were originally proposed to separate the physical storage of data form its conceptual representation and to provide a mathematical foundation for databases. The relational data model also introduced high-level query languages that provided and alternative to programming language interfaces; hence, it was a lot quicker to write new queries.

Relational representation of data somewhat resembles the example we presented in figure. Relational systems were initially targeted to the same applications as earlier systems, but were meant to provide flexibility to quickly develop new queries and to reorganize the database as requirements changed. Early experimental relation systems developed in the late 1970s and the commercial RDBMSs (relational database management systems) introduced in the early 1980s were quite slow, since they did not use physical storage pointers or record placement to access related data records.

With the development of new storage and indexing techniques and better query processing and optimization, their performance improved. Eventually, relational database became the dominant type of database systems for traditional database applications. Relational database now exist on almost all types of computers, from small personal computers to large servers.

Object-Oriented Applications and the Need for More Complex Databases

The emergence of object-oriented programming languages in the 1980s and the need to store and share complex-structured objects led to the development of object-oriented databases. Initially, they were considered a competition to relational databases, since they provided more general data structures. They also incorporated many of the useful object oriented paradigms, such as abstract data types, encapsulation of operations, inheritance and object identity.

However the complexity of the model and the lack of an early standard contributed to their limited use. They are now mainly used in specialized applications, such as engineering design, multimedia publishing and manufacturing systems.

Interchanging Data on the Web for e-Commerce

The World Wide Web provided a large network of interconnected computers. Users can create documents using a Web publishing language, such as HTML (HyperText Markup Language) and store these documents on Web servers where others users (clients) can access them. Documents can be linked together through hyperlinks which are pointers to other documents.

In the 1990s electronic commerce (e-commerce) emerged as a major application on the Web. It quickly became apparent that parts of the information on e-commerce Web pages were often dynamically extracted data from DBMSs. A variety of techniques were developed to allow the interchange of data on the Web. Currently, XML (extended Markup Language) is considered to be the primary standard for interchanging data among various types of databases and web pages. XML combines concepts from the models used in document systems with database modeling concepts.

Extending Database Capabilities for New Applications

The success of database systems in traditional applications encouraged developers of other types of applications to attempt to use them. Such applications traditionally used their own specialized file and data structures. The following are examples of these applications:

- Scientific applications that store large amounts of data resulting from scientific experiments in areas such as high-energy physics or the mapping of the human genome.
- Storage and retrieval of images, from scanned news or personal photographs to satellite photograph images and images from medical procedures such as X-rays or MRI (magnetic resonance imaging).
- Storage and retrieval of videos, such as movies or video clips from news or personal digital cameras.
- Data mining applications that analyze large amounts of data searching for the occurrences of specific patterns or relationships.
- Spatial applications that store spatial locations of data such as whether information or maps used in geographical information systems.
- Time series applications that store information such as economic data at regular points in time, for example, daily sales or monthly gross national product figures.

It was quickly apparent that basic relational systems were not very suitable for many of these applications, usually for one or more of the following reasons:

- More complex data structures were need for modeling the application than the simple relational representation.
- New data types were needed in addition to the basic numeric and character structures types.
- New operations and query language constructs were necessary to manipulate the new data types.
- New storage and indexing structures were needed.

This led DBMS developers to add functionality to their systems. Some functionality was general purpose, such as incorporating concepts from object-oriented databases into relational systems. Other functionality was special purpose, in the form of optional modules that could be used for specific applications. For example, users could buy a time series module to use with their relational DBMS for their time series application.

CHAPTER 4

Creating a Database in Microsoft Access 2010

Introduction

Creating database with a Wizard is probably the easiest and fastest method of creating a database where you have to fill up some information and the database is ready for you. It not only creates Tables for you but all the Forms, Reports, etc., connected with it are done too.

Creating Database using the Wizard

Access can create a blank database or a database using one of many templates available from the Microsoft Web site. No matter how you create a database, you will likely need to modify it to customize it for the type of data you want.

To create a blank database, follow these steps:

1. Click the Office button and choose New.

   The Getting Started with Microsoft Access screen appears.

2. Click the Blank Database icon.

   The file name text box appears in the right corner of the screen.

3. Type a descriptive filename for your database.

   You may want to click the Browse icon to specify a different folder or drive to store your database.

4. Click Create.

   Access displays a blank table and an Add New Field text box. Displaying your database in rows and columns in Datasheet view.

Creating Database using the Template

Just like it's easier to copy someone else's work, it's easier to use an existing database templates and

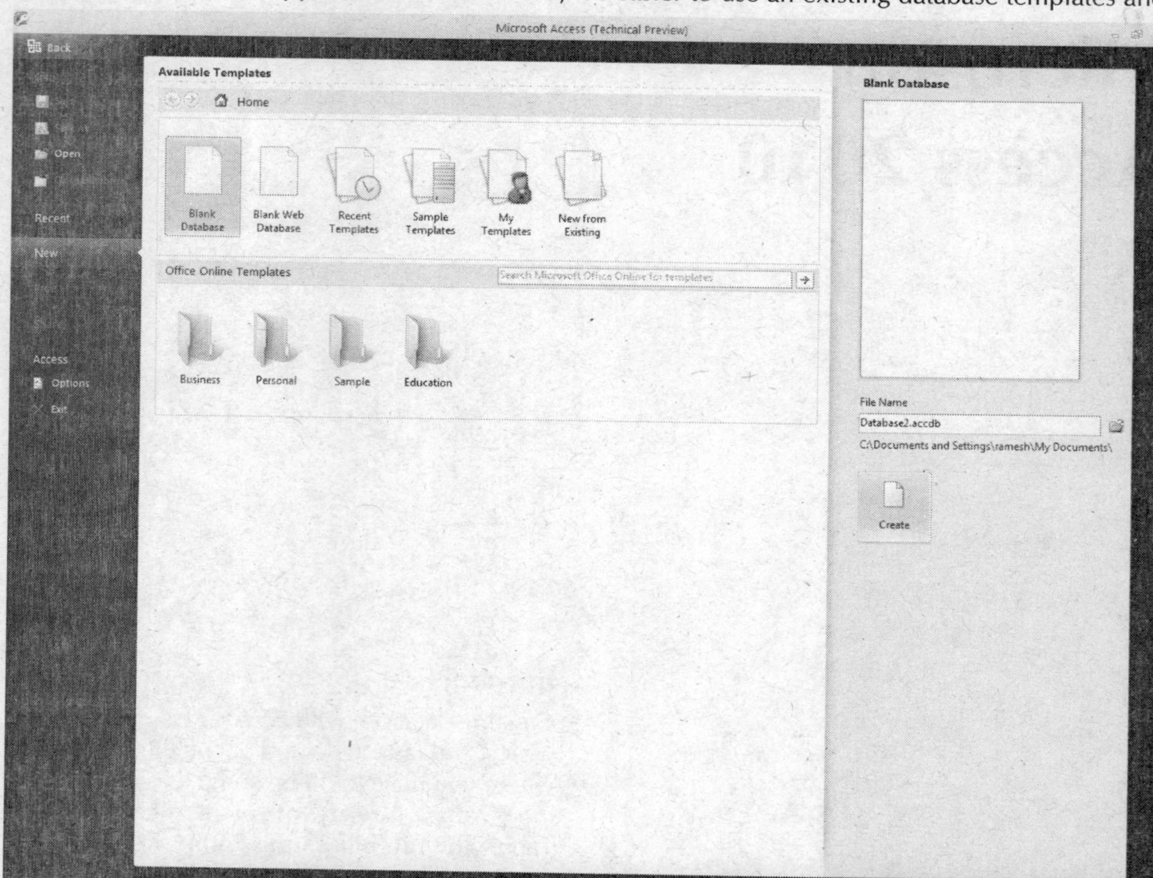

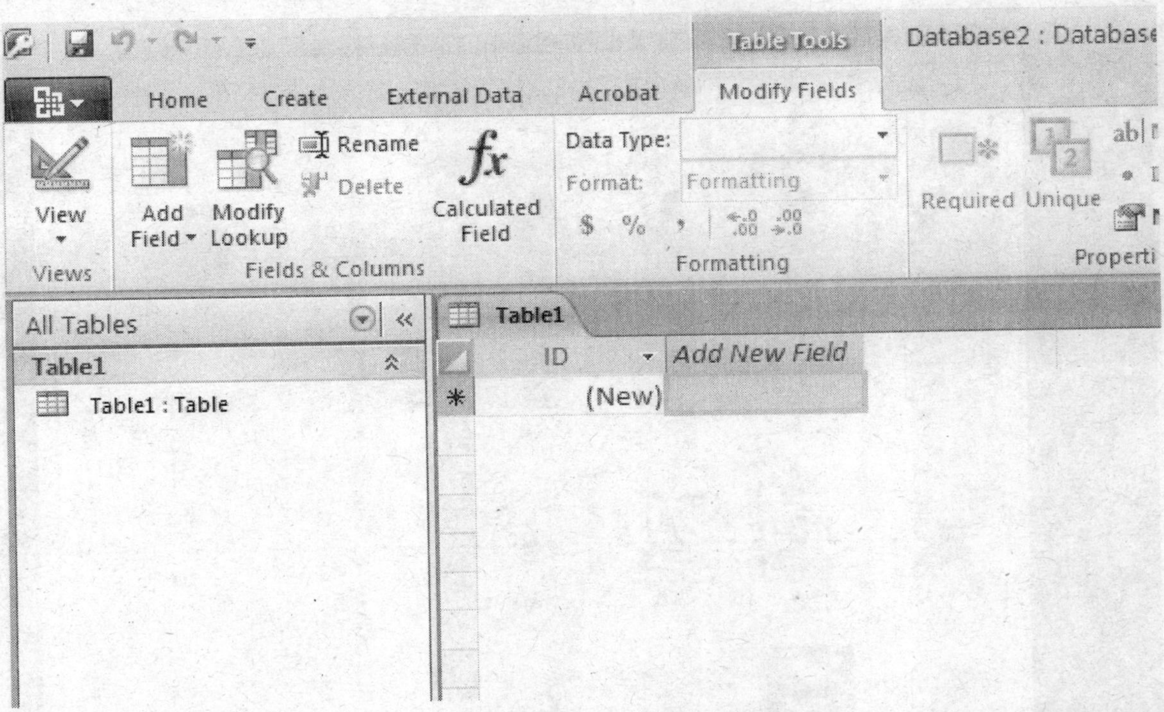

modify it for your own needs. You need an Internet connection to retrieve any database templates from the Microsoft Web site.

To create a database file from a template, follow these steps:

1. Click the Office button and choose New.
   The Getting Started with Microsoft Access screen appears.
2. Click a category under the From Microsoft Office Online categroy such as Business or Education or choose Local Templates.
   A list of available templates appear.
3. Click a template. Access displays a default name in the File Name text box in the bottom right corner of the screen.
4. Type a descriptive name for your database in the File Name text box and then click Create.
   Access displays your database in rows and columns (Datasheet View).
   On the next page, see the database of Marketing Project Home.

Working with Fields of Database

After you have created a database and it has given you a database in the Datasheet View. It becomes apparent that you add fields, name them and then fill up the data in them (or import it).

Naming a Field

If you create a database from scratch, Access displays generic field names such as Field1. If you create a database from a template, you will see the descriptive field names, but you may still want to rename the fields to something else.

To rename a field, follow these steps:

1. Click the Office Button and then choose Open.

Microsoft Access (Technical Preview)
Back
Open
Recent
New
Access
Options
Exit
Available Templates
Home
Sample Templates
105
107
1100
Assets
Bugs
CharitableContributions
Contacts
Details_Part
Events
Faculty
Issues
MarketingProjects
Multiple_Part
Northwind
Notes_Part
Projects
File Name
105.accdb
C:\Documents and Settings\ramesh\My Documents\
Create

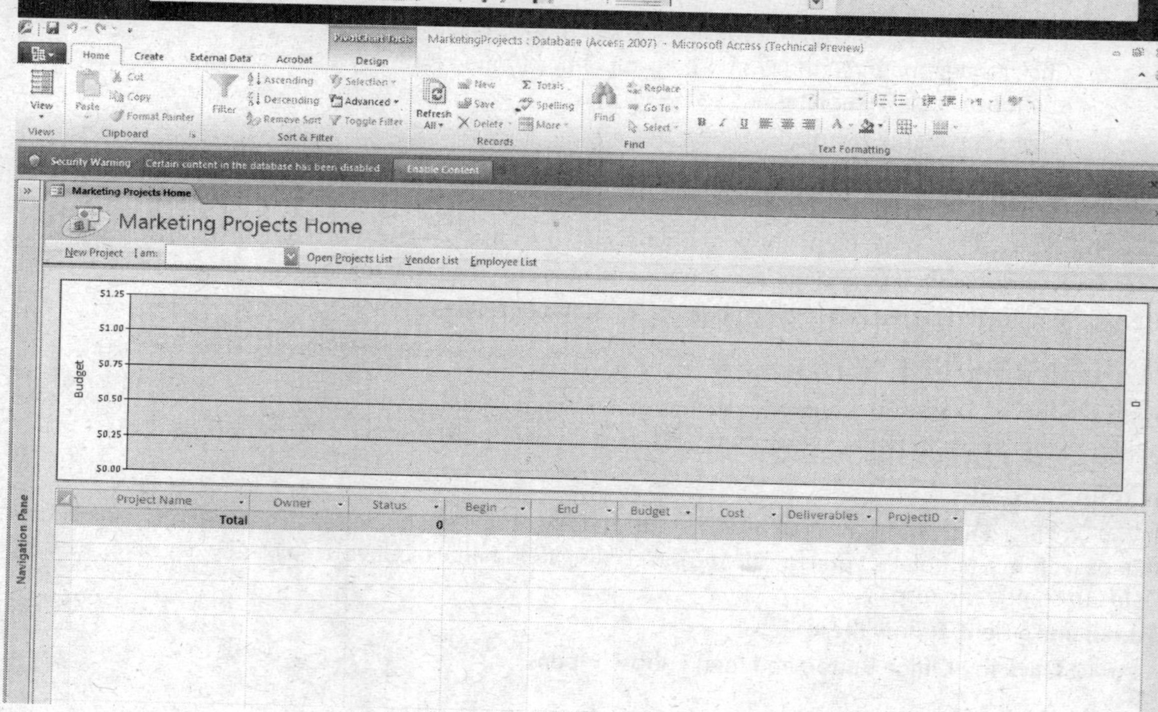
MarketingProjects : Database (Access 2007) - Microsoft Access (Technical Preview)
Home
Create
External Data
Acrobat
Design
View
Paste
Cut
Copy
Format Painter
Filter
Ascending
Descending
Remove Sort
Selection
Advanced
Toggle Filter
Refresh All
New
Save
Delete
Totals
Spelling
More
Find
Replace
Go To
Select
Views
Clipboard
Sort & Filter
Records
Find
Text Formatting
Security Warning
Certain content in the database has been disabled
Enable Content
Marketing Projects Home
Marketing Projects Home
New Project
I am:
Open Projects List
Vendor List
Employee List
$1.25
$1.00
$0.75
$0.50
$0.25
$0.00
Budget
Project Name
Owner
Status
Begin
End
Budget
Cost
Deliverables
ProjectID
Total
0
Navigation Pane

The Open dialog box appears.

2. Click the Access database file you want to modify and then click Open.
   Access displays your chosen database.
3. In the All Tables pane on the left of the screen, double-click the table that contains the fields you want to rename.
   Access displays the Datasheet view of your database.
4. Click the Datasheet tab.
5. Click the field (column head) that you want to rename.
6. Click the Rename icon in the Fields & Columns group.
   Access highlights the field name.
7. Type a new name for your field and then click outside the field name when you are done.

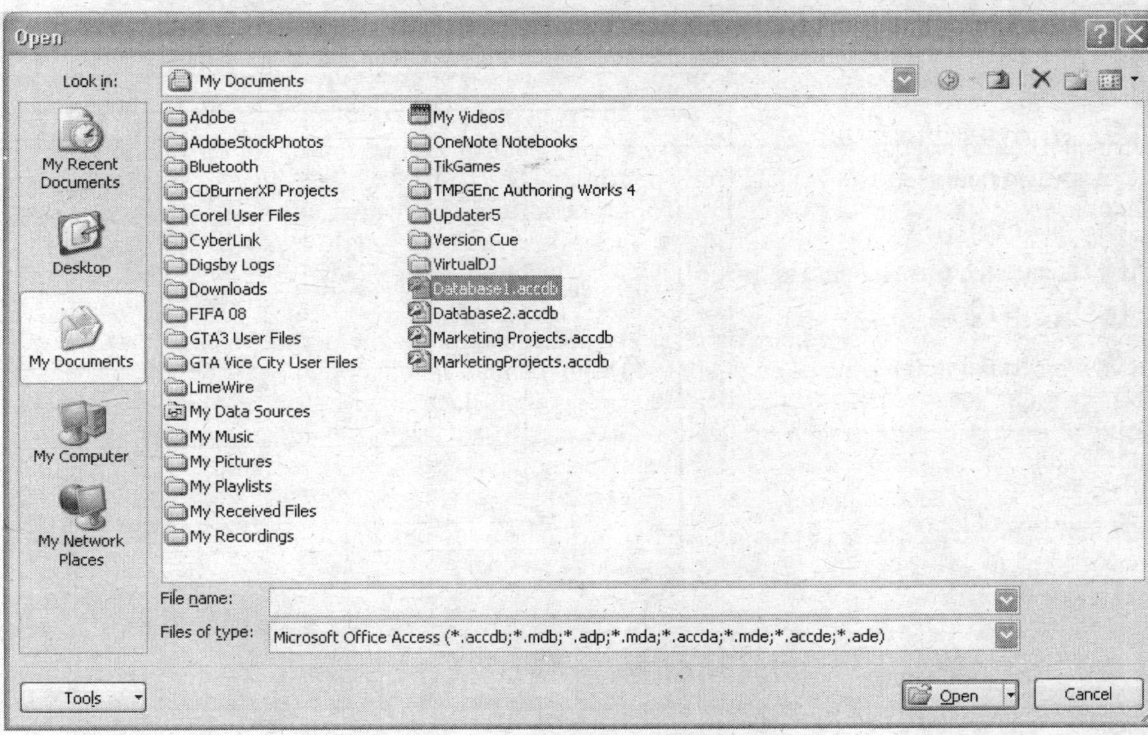

Adding/Deleting a Field

Sometimes you may need to add a field to make room to store new information. Other times, you may want to delete a field that you don't really want after all.

To add a field to a database table, follow these steps:

1. Click an existing field in your database table.
2. Click the Datasheet tab.
3. Click the Insert button in the Fields & Columns group.
   Access inserts a new field (column) in your database table.

To delete a field from a database table, follow these steps:

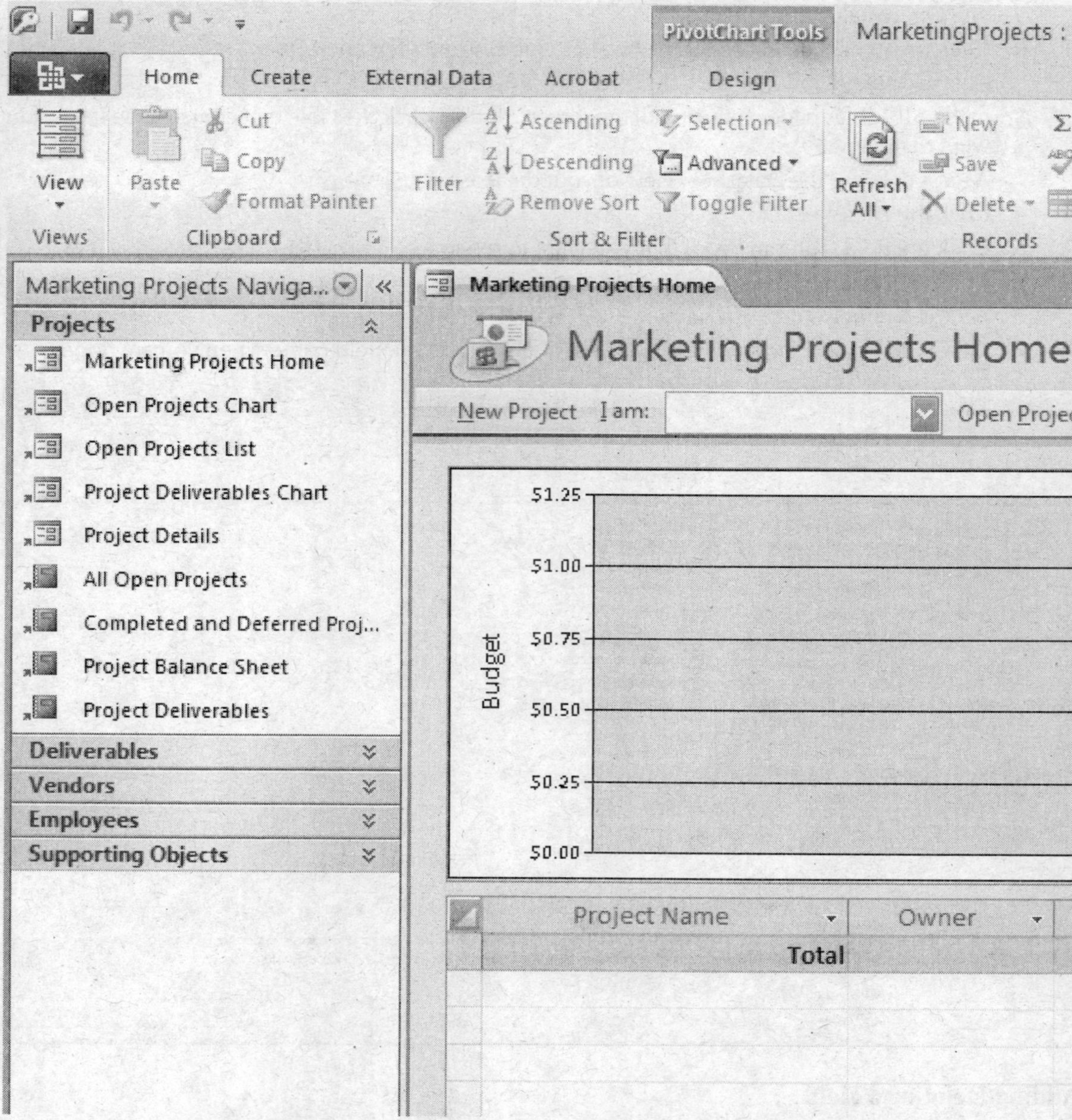

1. Click the field you want to delete.
   Access highlights the entire column in your database table.
2. Click the Datasheet tab.
3. Click the Delete button in the Fields & Columns group.
   A dialog box appears, asking whether you want to permanently delete all the data in the field.
   If you delete a field, you also delete any data that may be stored in the field. Depending on how much data you have stored, you could wipe out a lot of information by deleting a signle field, so be careful.

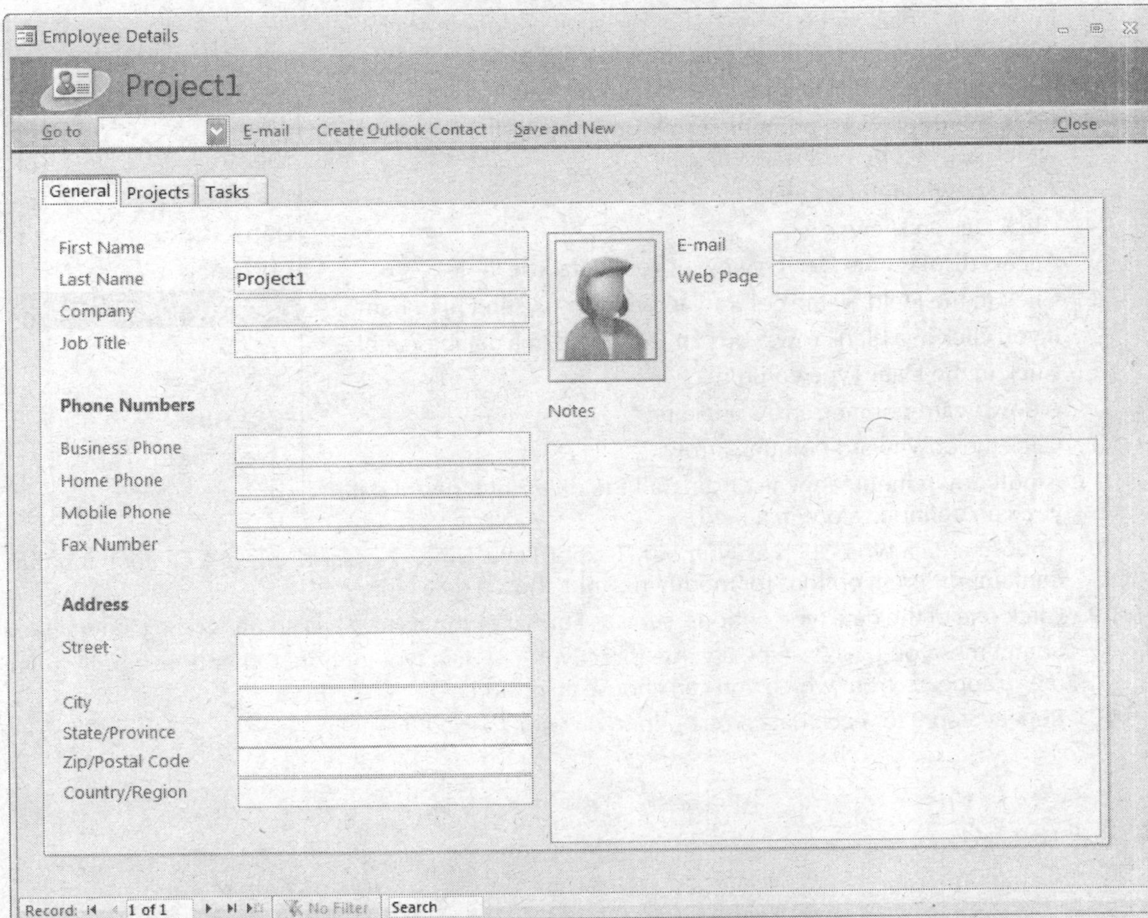

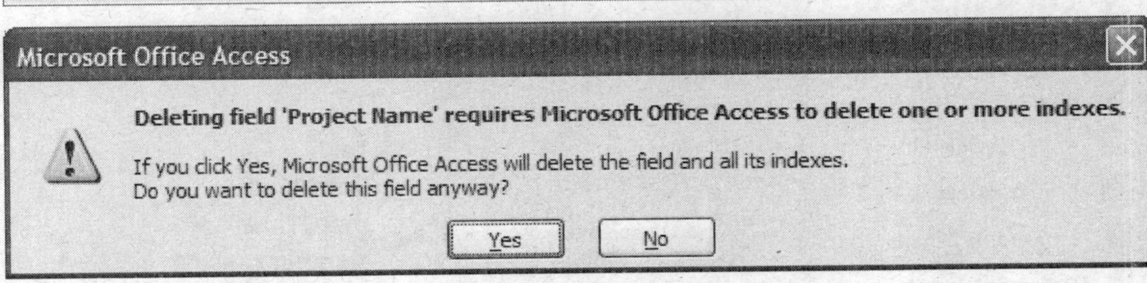

4. Click Yest (or No).

   If you click Yes, Access deletes your chosen field.

Setting the Type and Size of a Field

The type of a field defines the type of data the field can hold (numbers, text, dataes, and so on), and the size of a field defines the amount of data the field can hold (no numbers larger than 250 digits, any text string fewer than 120 characters, and so on).

To define the type and amount of a data a field can store, follow these steps:

1. Click the Home or Datasheet tab.

2. In the All Tables pane on the left of the screen, double-click the table that contains the fields you want to define.
   Access displays the Datasheet view of your table.
3. Click the downward-pointing arrow underneath the View icon, which appears in the Views group.
   A pull down menu appears.
4. Click Design View.
   Access displays the Design view of your database table.
5. Click in the Field Name column and edit an existing filed name.
   If you click in a blank row, you can add a field to a database table.
6. Click in the Data Type column.
   A downward-pointing arrow appears.
7. Click the downward-pointing arrow.
   A pull-down menu appears, listing all the different types of data you can define to store in a field.

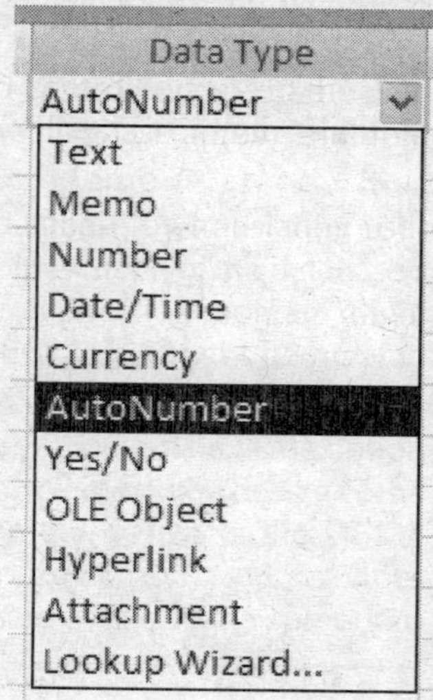

8. Choose a data type, such as Number, Text or Data/Time. Access displays a General tab that contains different options for modifying your chosen data type.
9. Click one of the data type options, such as Format or Input Mask, listed under the General tab.
   Sometimes you have to type a value directly into a data type option. Other time a pull-down menu appears, from which you can choose an option.
10. Repeat Step 9 for each data type option you want to modify.

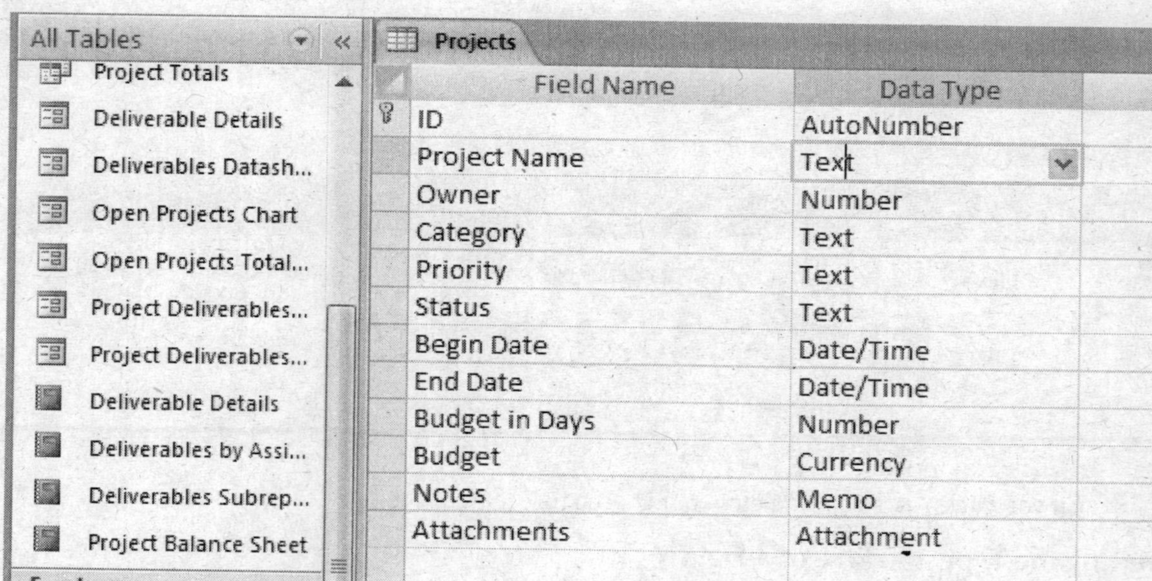

A Five-Step Design Method

Following is a version of the design method that is modified especially for use with Access. This is a top-down approach, starting with the overall system design and ending with the forms design, and it consists of five steps.

The five-step design design methodology is particularly well-suited for Access databases.

Overall System Design

Report Design (Output)

Basic Data Design

Table Design

User Interface Design

These five design steps, along with the database system illustrated by the examples in this book, teach a great deal about Access and provide a great foundation for creating database applications — including tables, queries, forms, data pages, reports, macros, and simple VBA (Visual Basic for Applications) modules.

General | Lookup

Display Control	Combo Box
Row Source Type	Table/Query
Row Source	SELECT [Employees Extended].ID, [Employees Extended].[Employee Name]
Bound Column	1
Column Count	2
Column Heads	No
Column Widths	0";2"
List Rows	16
List Width	2"
Limit To List	Yes
Allow Multiple Values	No
Allow Value List Edits	Yes
List Items Edit Form	Employee Details
Show Only Row Source V	No

The time you spend on each step depends entirely on the circumstances of the database you're building. For example, sometimes the users give you an example of a report they want printed from their Access database, and the sources of data on the report are so obvious that designing the report takes a few minutes. Other times, particularly when the users' requirements are complex, or the business processes supported by the application require a great deal of research, you may spend many days on Step 1.

As you read through each step of the design process, always look at the design in terms of outputs and inputs. Although you see actual components of the system (cars, buyers, sellers, and transactions), remember that the focus of this chapter is how to design each step. As you watch the Access Auto Auctions system being designed, pay attention to the design process, not the actual system.

Step 1: The overall design — from concept to reality

All software developers face similar problems, the first of which is determining how to meet the needs of the end user. It's important to understand the overall requirements before zeroing in on the details.

The five-step design method shown earlier helps you to create the system that you need, at an affordable price (measured in time or dollars)- The Access Auto Auctions database, for example, allows the client to sell items (vehicles and parts) to customers. The Access Auto Auctions database automates the following tasks:

- Entering and maintaining contact information for customers and sellers (name, address, and financial history)
- Entering and maintaining sales information (sales date; payment method; total amount, including tax; buyer ID; and other fields)
- Entering and maintaining sales line item information (details of items actually purchased)
- Viewing information from all the tables (sales, contacts, sales line items purchased, and payment information)
- Asking all types of questions about the information in the database
- Producing a current contacts directory
- Producing a monthly invoice report
- Producing a customer sales history
- Producing mailing labels and mail-merge reports

These nine tasks that the Access Auto Auctions automates have been expressed by the client. You may need to consider other tasks as you start the design process.

Most of the information that is necessary to build the system comes from the eventual users. This means that you need to sit down with them and learn how the existing process works. To accomplish this you need to do a thorough needs analysis of the existing system and how you might automate it.

One way to accomplish this is to prepare a series of questions that give insight to the client's business and how the client uses his data. For example, when considering automating an auto auction business, you may consider asking these questions:

- What reports and forms are currently used?
- How are sales, customer, contacts, and other records currently stored?
- How are billings processed?

As you ask these questions and others, the client will probably remember other things about his business that you should know.

A walkthrough of the existing process is also necessary to get a "feel" for the business. Most likely, you'll have to go back several times to observe the existing process and how the employees work.

When you prepare to follow the remaining steps, keep the client involved — let him know what you're doing and ask lor his input as to what you want to accomplish, making sure it is within the scope of his needs.

Step 2: Report design

Although it may seem odd to start with reports, in many cases users are more interested in the printed output from a database than they are in any other aspect of the application. Reports often include virtually every bit of data managed by an application. Because reports tend 10 be comprehensive, reports are often the best way to gather important information about a database's requirements. In the case of the Access Auto Auctions database, the printed reports contain detailed and summarized versions of most all the data in the database.

After you've defined the Access Auto Auctions' overall systems in terms of what must be accomplished, you can begin report design-When you see the reports that you will create in this section, you may wonder, "Which comes first — the chicken or the egg?" Does the report layout come first, or do you first determine the data items and text that make up the report? Actually, these items are considered at the same time.

It isn't important how you lay out the fields in a report. The more time you take now, however, the easier it will be to construct the report. Some people go so far as to place gridlines on the report so that they will know the exact location they want each bit of data to occupy. In this example, you, can just do it visually.

Step 3: Data design: What fields are required?

The next step in the design phase is to take an inventory of all the information or data fields that are needed by the reports. One of the best methods is to list the data items in each report. As you do so, take careful note of items that are included in more than one report. Make sure that you keep the same name for a data item that is in more than one report because the data item is really the same item.

Another method is to see whether you can separate the data items into some logical arrangement. Later, these data items are grouped into table structures and then mapped onto data-entry screens (forms). You should enter customer data (buyers and sellers), for example, as part of a contact table process, not as part of a sales entry.

Determining contact information

First, look at each report you have reviewed or attempted to make for the Access Auto Auctions system. For this system, start with the customer data and list the data items, as shown in Table 1-1.

TABLE 1-1 Customer-Related Data Items Found in the Reports

Contacts Report	*Invoice Report*
Customer Name	Customer Name
Street	Street
City	City
State	State
ZIP CodePhone Numbers	ZIP CodePhone Number
Type of Customer	
E-Mail Address	
Web Site Information	
Contact Log Information (four fields)	
Discount Rate	
Customer Since	
Last Sales Date	
Sales Tax Rate	
Credit Information (four fields)	

As you can see by comparing the type of contact (customer) information needed for each report, there are many common fields. Most of the data fields pertaining to the customer are found in both reports.

Table 1-1 shows only some of the fields that are used in each report — those related to customer information. Fields appearing on both reports appear on the same rows in the table, which allows you to see more easily which items are in which reports. You can look across a row instead oflooking for the same names in both reports.

Because the related row and the field names are the same, you can easily make sure that you have all the data items. Although locating items easily is not critical for this small database, it becomes very important when you have to deal with large tables containing many fields.

Determining sales information

After extracting the customer data, you can move on to the sales data. In this case, you need to analyze only the Invoice report for data items that are specific to the sales. Table 1-2 lists the fields in the report that contain information about the sales.

TABLE 1-2 Sales Data Items Found in the Reports

Individual Invoice Report	*Line Item Data*
Invoice Number	
Sales Date Invoice Date	
Payment Method	
Payment Salesperson Discount (overall for sale)	
Tax Location Tax Rate	
Product Purchased (multiple lines)	Product Purchased
Quantity Purchased (multiple lines)	Quantity Purchased
Description of Item Purchased (multiple lines)	Description of Item Purchased
Price of Item (multiple lines)	Price of Item
Discount for each item (multiple lines)	Discount for Each Item
Taxable? (multiple lines)	Taxable?
Payment Type (multiple lines)	
Payment Date (multiple lines)	
Payment Amount (multiple lines)	
Credit Card Number (multiple lines)	
Expiration Date (multiple lines)	

As you can see when you examine the type of sales information needed for the report, a couple of items (fields) are repeating (for example, the Product Purchased, Number of items Purchased, and Price of Item fields). Each invoice can have multiple items, and each of these items needs the same type of information — number ordered and price per item.

Each sales invoice will probably have more than one item that is sold and being invoiced. Also, each invoice may include partial payments, and it is possible that this payment information will have multiple lines of payment information, so these repeating items can be put into their own grouping.

Determining line item information

You can take all the individual items that you found in the sales information group in the preced-ing section and extract them to their own group for the invoice report. Table 1-2 shows the information related to each line item.

Unless a numeric field needs to be specifically stored in a table, simply recalculate it when you run the report (or form). You should avoid creating fields in your tables that can be created based on other fields — these calculation fields can be easily created and displayed in a form or report.

Step 4: Table design

Now for the difficult part: You must determine what fields are needed for the tables that make up the reports. When you examine the multitude of fields and calculations that make up the many documents you have, you begin to see which fields belong to the various tables in the database. (You already did much of the preliminary work by arranging the fields into logical groups.) For now, include every field you extracted. You will need to add others later (for various reasons), although certain fields won't appear in any table.

It is important to understand that it isn't necessary to add every little bit of data into the database's tables. For instance, users may express a desire to add vacation and other out-of-office days to the database to make it easy to know which employees are available on a particular day

However, it is very easy to burden an application's initial design by incorporating too many ideas during the initial development phases. Because Access tables are so easy to modify later on, it is probably best to put aside noncritical items until the initial design is complete. Generally speaking, it's not difficult to accommodate user requests after the database development project is under way.

After you've used each report to display all the data, it's time to consolidate the data by purpose (for example, grouped into logical groups) and then compare the data across those functions. To do this step, first you look at the contact information and combine all of its different fields to create one set of data items. Then you do the same thing for the sales information and the line item infor-mation. Table 1-3 compares data items from these three groups of information.

TABLE 1-3 Comparing the Data Items from the Contact Information, Sales Information, and Line Item Information

Contacts Data	***Invoice Data*** -	***Line Items***
Customer Name	Invoice Number	Product Purchased
Street	Sales Date	Quantity Purchased
City	Invoice Date	Description of Item Purchased
State	Payment Method	Price of Item
ZIP Code	Payment Salesperson	Discount for Each Item
Phone Numbers (two fields)	Discount (overall for this sale)	Taxable?
Type of Customer	Tax Location	
E-Mail Address	Tax Rate	
Web Site Information	Payment Type (multiple lines)	
Contact Log Information (four fields)	Payment Date (multiple lines)	
Discount Rate	Payment Amount (multiple lines)	
Customer Since	Credit Card Number (multiple lines)	
Last Sales Date	Expiration Date (multiple lines)	
Sales Tax Rate		
Credit Information (four fields)		

Consolidating and comparing data is a good way to start creating the individual table definitions for Access Auto Auctions, but you have much more to do.

As you learn more about how to perform a data design, you also learn that the contacts data must be split into two groups. Some of these items are used only once for a contact while other Herns may have multiple entries. An example is the Contact Log information. Each contact may have multiple log items recorded in the database. This is also true for the Sales column — the payment information can have multiple lines of information.

It is necessary to further break these types of information into their own columns, thus separating all related types of items into their own columns — an example of the normalization part of the design process. For example, one customer can have multiple contacts with the company. One customer may make multiple payments toward a single sale. Of course, we've already broken the data into three categories above: contacts, invoices, and sales line items.

Keep in mind that one customer may have multiple invoices, and each invoice may have multiple line items on it. The contact category represents customer (buyer or seller) information, the invoice category contains information about individual sales, and the line items category contains informa-tion about each invoice. Notice that these three columns are all related; for example, one customer can have multiple invoices and each invoice may require multiple detail lines (line items).

The relationships between tables can be different. For example, each sales invoice has one and only one customer, while each customer may have multiple sales. A similar relationship exists between the sales invoice and the line items of the invoice.

Assuming that the three groupings represent the main three tables of your system, less additional fields, you need to link tables together. This step, of course, means adding table relationships to the database design.

Database table relationships require a unique field in both tables involved in a relationship. Without a unique identifier in each table, the database engine is unable to properly join and extract related data.

None of the tables in our design has a unique identifier, which means that you need to add at least one more field to each table to serve as the anchor for a relationship to other tables. For example, you could add a ContactID field to the Contacts table, then add the same field to the Invoice table, and establish a relationship between the tables through the ContactID field in each table.The database engine uses the relationship between the Contacts and Invoices table to link customers with their invoices. Linking tables is done through special fields, known as key fields.

With an understanding of the need for linking one group of fields to another group, you can add the required key fields to each group. Table 1-4 shows two new groups and link fields created for each group of fields. These linking fields, known as primary keys and foreign keys, are used to link these tables together.

The field that uniquely identifies each row in a table is called the primary key. The corresponding field in a related table is called the foreign key. In our example, the ContactID field in the Contacts table is a primary key, while the ContactID field in the Invoices table is a foreign key.

Let's assume a certain record in the Contacts table has 12 in its ContactID field. Any records in the Invoices table with 12 in its ContactID field is "owned" by contact number 12. Special rules apply to choosing and managing primary and foreign keys. The notion of primary and foreign keys is the single most important concept behind relational databases.

With the key fields added to each table, you can now find a field in each table that links it to other tables in the database. For example, Table 1-4 shows a ContactID field in both the Contacts table (where it is the table's primary key) and the Invoice table (where it is a foreign key).

You have identified the core of the three primary tables for your system, as reflected by the first three columns in Table 1-4. This is the general, or first, cut toward the final table designs. You have also created two additiona! tables (columns) from fields shown in Table 1-3.

Taking time to properly design your database and the tables contained within it is arguably the most important step in developing a database-oriented application. By designing your database efficiently, you maintain control of the data — eliminating costly data-entry mistakes and limiting your data entry to essential fields.

Although this book is not geared toward teaching database theory and all of its nuances, this is a good point to briefly describe the art of database normalization. You should know that normalization is the process of breaking data down into constituent tables.

Earlier in this chapter you read about how many Access developers add dissimilar information, such as contacts, invoice data, and invoice line items, into one large table.

A large table containing dissimilar data quickly becomes unwieldy and hard to keep updated. Because a contact's phone number appears in every row containing that customer's data, multiple updates must be made when the contact's phone number changes.

TABLE 1-4 Main Tables with Keys

Contacts Data	*Invoice Data*	*Line Items Data*	*Contact tog Data*	*Sales Payment Data*
ContactID	InvoiceID	InvoiceID	ContactLogID	InvoiceID
Customer Name	ContactID	Line Number	ContactID	Payment Type
Street	Invoice Number	Product Purchased	Contact Date	Rayment Date
City	Sales Date	Quantity Purchased	Contact Notes	Payment Amount
State	Invoice Date	Description of Item Purchased	Follow Up?	Credit Card Number
ZIP Code	PaymentMethod	Price of Item	Follow-Up Date	Expiration Date
Phone Numbers (two fields)	Payment Salesperson	Discount for Each Item		
Type of Customer	Discount (overall for this sale)	Taxable?		
E-Mail Address	Tax Location			
Web Site Information	Tax Rate			
Discount Rate				
Customer Since				
Last Sales Date				
Sales Tax Rate				

Normalization is the process of breaking data into smaller, more manageable tables. Each table defines one and only one entity, such as a contact or an invoice, but not both.

The contact and invoice tables are related through a primary key (ContactiD in the customers table) and a foreign key (also named ContactiD) in the invoices table.

Step 5: Form design: Input

After you've created the data and established table relationships, it's time to design your forms. Forms are made up of the fields that can be entered or viewed in Edit mode. If at all possible, your screens should look much like the forms that you use in a manual system. This setup makes for the most user-friendly system.

When you're designing forms, you need to place three types of objects on-screen:

- Labels and text box data-entry fields (the fields on Access forms and reports are usually called controls)
- Special controls (multiple-line text boxes, option buttons, list boxes, check boxes, business graphs, and pictures)
- Graphical objects to visually enhance them (colors, lines, rectangles, and three-dimensional effects)

When designing a form, place your fields (text boxes, check boxes, list boxes, and radio buttons) just where you want them on the form. Ideally, if the form is being developed from an existing printed form, the Access data-entry form should resemble the printed form. The fields should be in the same relative place on the screen as they are in the printed counterpart.

Labels display messages, titles, or captions. Text boxes provide an area where you can type or dis-play text or numbers that are contained in your database. Check boxes indicate a condition and are either unchecked or checked (selected). Other types of controls available with Access include list boxes, combo boxes, option buttons, toggle buttons, and option groups.

CHAPTER 5

Creating a Table in Microsoft Access 2010

Introduction

Creating database tables is as much art as it is science. A good working knowledge of the user's requirements is a primary requirement for any new database project. In this chapter, let's take a look at the steps required lo create basic Access tables.

Creating a New Table

In the following sections, you'll study the process of adding tables to an Access database, including the relatively complex subject of choosing the proper data type to assign to each field in a table.

It is always a good idea lo plan tables on paper first, before sitting down at Access and using the Access tools to add tables to the database. Many tables, especially small ones, really don't require a lot of forethought before adding them to the database. After all, not much planning is required to design a table holding lookup information such as the names of cities and states. However, more complex entities such as customers and products usually require considerable thought and effort to properly implement.

Although you can create the table interactively without any forethought, carefully planning a data-base system is a good idea. You can make any changes later, but doing so wastes time; generally, the result is a system that is harder to maintain than one that is well planned from the beginning. Before you get started, you should understand the table design process. In the following sections, we'll be exploring the new, blank table added by Access as the new data-base was created. It's important to understand the steps required to add new tables to an Access database. Because the steps required to add tables have changed so dramatically from earlier ver-sions of Access, even experienced Access developers will want to read the following sections.

The importance of naming conventions

As your databases grow in size and complexity, the need to establish a naming convention for the objects in your databases increases. As you already know, changes to the name of an object are not propagated throughout the database. Even wiih the Name AutoCorrect option turned on (Office button "^ Access Options ^> Current Database O Name AutoCorrect Options), Access only cor-rects the most obvious name changes. Changing the name of a table breaks virtually every query, form, and report that uses the information from that table. Your best defense is ío adopt reasonable object names and use a naming convention early on as you begin building Access databases and to stick with the naming convention throughout the project.

Access imposes very few restrictions on the names assigned 10 database, objects. Therefore, it is entirely possible to have two distinctly different objects (for instance, a form and a report, or a table and a macro) with the same name. (You can't, however, have a table and a query with the same name, because tables and queries occupy the same namespace in the database.)

Although simple names like Contacts and Orders are adequate, as a database grows in size and complexity you may become confused about which object a particular name refers to. For instance, later in this book, you'll read about manipulating database objects through code and macros. When working with Visual Basic for Applications (VBA), the programming language built into Access 2010, there must be no ambiguity or confusion between referenced objects. Having both a form and a report named Contacts might be confusing to you or your code.

The simplest naming convention is to prefix object names with a three- or four-character string indicating the type of object carrying the name. Using this convention, tables are prefixed with tbl and queries with cjry. The prefix for forms, reports, macros, and modules are f rm, rpt, mcr, and has or mod, respectively In this book, most compound object names appear in mixed case: tblBookOrders, tblBookOrderDetails, and so on. Most people find mixed-case names easier to read and remember than names that appear in all-uppercase or all-lowercase characters (such as TBLBOOKORDERS or tblbookorderdetails).

Also, at times, we'll use informal references for database objects. For instance, the formal name of the table containing contact information in the previous examples is tblContacts. An informal reference to this table might be "the contacts table."

In most instances, your users never see the formal names of database objects. One of your chal-lenges as an application developer is to provide a seamless user interface that hides all data-management and data-storage entities that support the user interface. You can easily control the text that appears in the title bars and surfaces of the forms, reports, and other user interface com-ponents to hide the actual names of the data structures and interface constituents.

Take advantage of the long object names that Access permits to give your tables, queries, forms, and reports descriptive, informative names. There is no reason why you should confine a table name to ConInfo when ContactInf ormation is handled just as easily and is much easier to understand.

Descriptive names can be carried to an extreme, of course. There's no point in naming a form frmUpdateContactInformation if f rmupdateinf o does just as well. Long names are more easily misspelled or misread than shorter names, so use your judgment.

Finally, although Access lets you use spaces in database object names, you should avoid spaces at all costs. Spaces do not add to readability and can cause major headaches, particularly when upsiz-ing to client-server environments or using OLE automation with other applications. Even if you don't anticipate extending your Access applications to client-server or incorporating OLE or DDE automation into your applications, get into the habit of not using spaces in object names.

The table design process

Creating a table design is a muhistep process. By following the steps in order, your table design can be created readily and with minimal effort:

1. Create a new table.
2. Enter field names, data types, and (optionally) descriptions.
3. Enter properties for the fields.
4. Set the tables primary key.
5. Create indexes for necessary fields.
6. Save the table's design.

Generally speaking, some tables are never really finished. As users' needs change, or the business rules governing the application change, you may find it necessary to open an existing table in Design view. This book, like most books on Access, describes the process of creating tables as if every table you ever work on is brand new. The truth is, however, that most of the work that you do on an Access application is performed on existing objects in the database. Some of those objects you have added yourself, while other objects may have been added by another developer at some time in the past. However, the process of maintaining an existing database component is exactly the same as creating the same object from scratch.

Just a quick note about modifying tables once they're built: Adding a new field to a table almost never causes problems. Existing queries, forms, and reports, and even VBA code, will continue using the table as before. After all, these object won't reference the new field because the field was added after their creation. Therefore, you can add a new field and incorporate the field where needed in your application, and everything works as expected.

The trouble comes from removing or renaming a field in a table. Even with AutoCorrect turned on, Access wii! no"t update field name references in VBA code, in control properties, and in expressions throughout the database. Changing an existing field (or any other database object, for that matter) is always a tad idea. You should always strive to provide your tables, fields, and other database objects with good, s'rong, descriptive names at the time you add them to the database, rather than planning to go back later and fix them.

Adding a new table to the database

Begin by selecting the Create tab on the ribbon at the top of the Access screen. The Create tab contains all of the tools necessary ro create not only tables, but also forms, reports, and oiher database objects. There are two main ways to add new tables to an Access database, both of which are invoked from the Tables group on the Create tab;

- Clicking on the Table button: Adds a complete new table to the database.
- Clicking on the Table Design button: Adds a table in Design view to the database.

For our example, we'll be using the Table Design button, but first, let's take a look at the Table button. Begin by clicking on the Table button to add a new table to the Access environment. The new table appears in Datasheet view in the tabbed region of the Access screen. A portion of the new table is shown above. Notice that the new table appears in Datasheet view, with an ID column already inserted, and an Add New Field column to the right of the ID field. The Add New Field column is intended to permit users to quickly add tables to an Access data-base. All that is needed is to simply begin entering data into the Add New Field column. You assign the field a name by right-clicking the field's heading, selecting Rename Column, and entering a name for the field. In other words, building an Access table can be very much like creating a spreadsheet in Microsoft Excel. This approach was usually referred to as "creating a table in Datasheet view" in previous versions of Microsoft Access.

Although it is entirely possible to build an access table without ever switching to Design view, we believe that this is a terrible idea. Building tables by entering data and casually providing names for the table's fields circumvents one of the most critical steps in building in the serious database system. Relational database systems such as Access are constructed by breaking data into constituent enti-ties, and then building a table for each entity. The tables in an Access database should carefully and accurately reflect the entities they describe. Seemingly small issues, such as deciding which data type to assign to a field, has a dramatic impact on the utility, performance, and integrity of the database and its data.

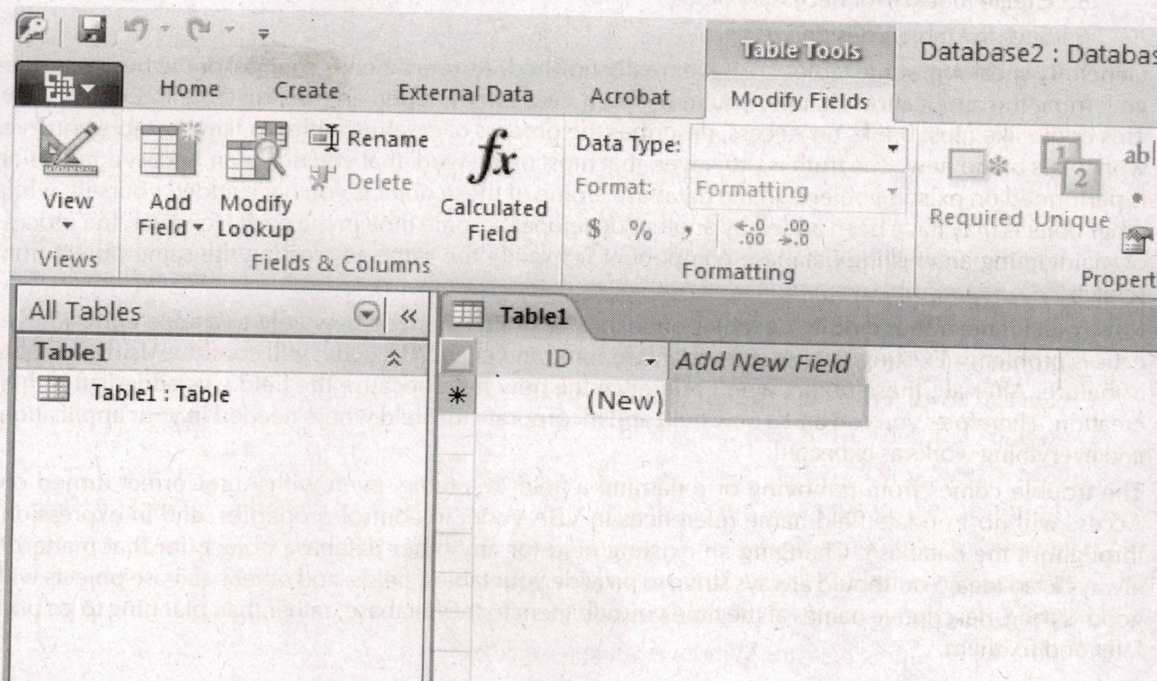

Each table added to an Access database, and each field added lo every table, should have a purpose in the overall database design. Even when adding tables using the Table button, it is far too easy to add tables that do not conform to the rules and which do not fit well into the databases design.

The second approach to add new tables is to use the Table Design button, located on the right side of the Tables grouping on the Create tab. Access opens a new table in Design view, as shown below.

The table designer is quite easy to understand, and each column is clearly labeled. At the far left is the Field Name column, where you input the names of fields you add to the table. You assign a data type to each field in the table, and (optionally) provide a description for the field.

For this exercise, well create the Contacts table for the Access Auto Auctions application. The basic design of this table is outlined in Table 4-1.

TABLE 4-1 The Access Auto Auctions Contacts Table Design

Field Name	***Data Type***	***Description***
ContactID	Auto Number	Primary key
ContactType	Text 50	Type of contact (Wholesaler, dealer, parts store, other)
FirstHame	Text 50	Contact's first name
LastName	Text 50	Contact's last name
Company Address	Text 50	The Contact's employer or other affiliation Contact's address
City	Text 50	Contact's city
State	Text 50	Contact's state
ZipCode	Text 50	Contact's zip code
Phone	Text 50	Contact's phone
Fax	Text 50	Contact's fax
E-Mail	Text 100	Contact's e-mail address
WebSite	Text 100	Contact's Web address
OrigCustDate	DateTime	The date the contact first purchased something from Access Auto Auctions
TaxLocation	Text 50	Used to determine the applicable sales tax
CreditLimit	Currency	Customer's credit limit in dollars
CurrentBalance	Currency	Customer's current balance in dollars
CreditStatus	Text	A description of the customer's credit status
LastSalesDate	DateTime	The most recent date the customer purchased something from Access Auto Auctions
DiscountPercent	Double	The customary -discount provided to the customer
Notes	Memo	Notes and observations regarding this customer
Active	Yes/No	A yes/no value, indicating whether the customer is still buying or selling to Access Auto Auctions

Some of the fields in the preceding table are rather generous in the amount of space allocated for the field's data- For instance, it is unlikely that anyone's name occupies 50 characters, but there is no harm in providing for very long names. Access only stores as many characters as are actually entered into a text field. Therefore, allocating 50 characters does not actually use 50 characters for every name in the database.

The design spelled out in Table 4-1 is a good starting point for the Contacts table. Looking once again at the above figure, you see that the Table Design window consists of two areas:

- The field entry area (top): Use the field entry area to enter each field's name and data type. You can also enter an optional description.
- The field properties area (bottom): The property area at the bottom of the window is for entering more different specifications, called properties, for each field. These properties include field size, format, input mask, and default value, among others. The actual properties displayed in the properties area depend upon the data type of the field.

You can switch between the upper and lower areas of the table designer by clicking the mouse when the pointer is in the desired pane or by pressing F6.

Using the Design ribbon tab

The Design tab on the Arcess ribbon contains many controls that assist in creating a new table definition.

Primary Key

Use this button to designate which of the fields in the table you want to use as the table's primary key. By tradition, the primary key appears at the top of ihe list of fields in the table. Moving a field is easy: Simply left-click on the gray selector to the left of the field's name to highlight the field in the Table Designer, and drag the field to its new position.

Insert Rows

Although it makes very little difference to the database engine, many developers are fussy about the sequence of fields in a table. Also, particularly when assigning an index or composite index to a table, you want the fields to be next to each other in the tables field list. The Insert Row button inserts a blank row just above the position occupied by the mouse cursor. For instance, if the cursor is currently in the second row of the Table Designer, clicking the insert Row button inserts an empty row in the second position, moving the existing second row to the third position.

Delete Rows

Conversely, the Delete Rows button removes a row from the tables design. Be careful, however, because Access does not ask you to confirm the deletion before actually removing the row.

Property Sheet

The Property Sheet button opens the Properties window for the table. These properties enable you to specify important table characteristics such as a validation rule to apply to the entire table, or an alternate sort order for the table's data.

Indexes

Indexes are discussed in much more detail later in this chapter. Clicking the Indexes button opens the Indexes dialog box, enabling you to specify the details of indexes on the fields in your table.

Working with fields

Fields are created by entering a field name and a field data type in each row of the field entry area of the Table Design window. The field description is an option to identify the field's purpose. The description appears in the status bar at the bottom of the screen during data entry. After entering each fields name and data type, you can further specify how each field is used by entering properties in the property area.

Naming a field

A field name should be descriptive enough to identify the field to you as the developer, to the user of the system, and to Access. Field names should be long enough to quickly identify the purpose of the field, but not overly long.

To enter a field name, position the pointer in the first row of the Table Design window under the Field Name column. Then type a valid field name, observing these rules:

- Field names can be from 1 to 64 characters.
- Field names can include letters, numbers, and many special characters.
- Field names cannot include a period (.}, exclamation point (!), brackets ([ ]), or accent grave (').
- You can't use low-order ASCII characters, for example Qrl + J or Ctrl + L (ASCII values 0 to 31).
- You can't start with a blank space.
- You can't use a double quotation mark (") in the name of a Microsoft Access project file.

You can enter field names in upper-, lower-, or mixed case. If you make a mistake while typing the field name, position the cursor where you want to make a correction and type the change. You can change a field name at any time — even if it's in a table and the field contains data — for any reason.

Access is not case sensitive, so the database itself doesn't care whether you name a table tblContacts or TblContacts, The selection of upper-, lower-, or mixed case is entirely your decision and should be aimed at making your table names descriptive and easy to read.

After your table is saved, if you change a field name that is also used in queries, forms, or reports, you have to change it in those objects as well. One of the leading causes of errors in Access applications stems from changing the names of fundamental database objects such as tables and fields, but neglecting to make all of the changes required throughout the database. Overlooking a field name reference in the control source of a control on the form or report, or deeply embedded in VBA code somewhere in the application, is far too easy.

Specifying a data type

The next step is to actually create your tables and define your fields for those tables. You must also decide what type of data each of your fields will hold- In Access, you can choose any of several data types (these data types are detailed later in this chapter):

- **Text**: Alphanumeric characters, up to 255 characters
- **Memo**: Alphanumeric characters, very long strings up to 65,538 (64K) characters
- **Number**: Numeric values of many types and formats
- **Date/Time**: Date and time data
- **Currency**: Monetary data
- **AutoNumber**: Automatically incremented numeric counter
- **Yes/No**: Logical values, Yes/No, True/False
- **OLE Object**: Pictures, graphs, sound, video, word processing, and spreadsheet files
- **Hyperlink**: A field that links to a picture, graph, sound, video, and word processing and spreadsheet files

One of these data types must be assigned to each of your fields. You must also specify the length of the Text fields, or accept the default of 50 characters for Text fields.

Designing data-entry rules

The last major design decision concerns data validation, which becomes important as users enter data. You want to make sure that only good data (data that passes certain defined tests) gets into your system. You have to deal with several types of data validation. You can test for known individual items, stipulating that the Gender field can accept only the values Male, Female, or Unknown, for example. Or you can test for ranges, specifying that the value of Weight must be between 0 and 1,500 pounds.

Designing lookup tables

Sometimes you need to design entire tables to perform data validation or just to make it easier to create your system; these are called lookup tables. For example, because Access Auto Auctions needs a field to determine the customer's tax rate, you may decide to use a lookup table that contains the tax location, and tax rate. Another example is when a customer pays an invoice using some specific method — cash, credit card, money order, and on and on.

Because the tax rate can change, storing tax rates makes much more sense than hard-coding tax rates into the application. Using lookup tables, Access looks up the current tax rate in tblTaxRates whenever an invoice is created. The tax rate applied to an invoice is stored along with the other invoice data in the Invoice/Sales table because it is time-dependent data, and the value stored in tblTaxRates may be different in the future.

Another purpose of a lookup table is to limit data entry in a field to a specific value. For example, you can use a table containing payment types (cash, check, MasterCard, and so on). The payment types table (tblPaymentTypes) can be used as a lookup table to ensure only approved payment methods can be entered in the Invoice table.

When you create a field in a table, you can use the data type Lookup Wizard. It is not an actual data type, but is instead a way of storing a field one way and displaying it another way.

Although you can create a field on a data-entry form that limits the entry of valid contact types to seller, buyer, or both, you create a table with only one field — ContactType — and use the ContactType field in tblContacts to link to this field in the ContactType lookup table.

You create a lookup table in exactly the same way as you create any other table, and it behaves in the same way. The only difference is in the way you use the table's data.

Several lookup tables are included in the Access Auto Auctions application: tblPaymentType, tblTaxRates, and tblCategories.

Assigning field data types

After you name«a field, you must decide what type of data the field holds. Before you begin enter-ing data, you should have a good grasp of the data types that your system will use. Ten basic types of data are shown in Table 4-2; some data types (such as numbers) have several options.

TABLE 4-2 Data Types Available in Microsoft Access

Data Type	Type of Data Stored	Storage Size
Text	Alphanumeric characters	0-255 characters
Memo	Alphanumeric characters	0-65,536 characters
Number	Numeric values	1, 2, 4, or 8 bytes, 1 6 bytes for Replication ID (GUID)
Date/Time	Date and time data	8 bytes
Currency	Monetary data	8 bytes
AutoNumber	Automatic number increments	4 bytes, 1 6 bytes for Replication ID (GUID)
Yes/No	Logical values: Yes/No, True/False	1 bit (0 or –1)
OLE Object	Pictures, graphs, sound, video	Up to 1GB (disk space limitation)
Hyperlink	Link to an Internet resource	0-64,000 characters
Attachment	A special field (new in Access 2010) that enables you to attach external files to an Access database	Varies by attachment
Lookup Wizard	Displays data from another table	Generally 4 bytes

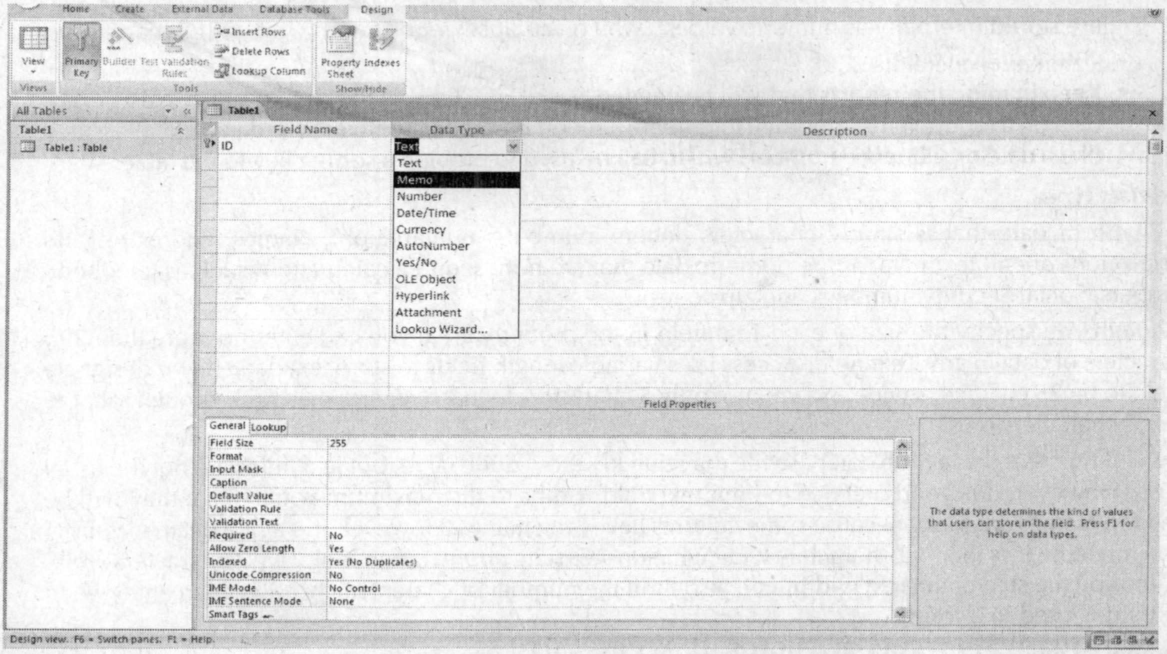

The following figure shows the Data Type drop-down list used to select the data type for the field you just created.

Here are the basic rules to consider when choosing the data type for new fields in your tables:

- **The data type should reflect the data stored in the field**. For instance, you should select one of the numeric data types to store numbers like quantities and prices. Do not store data like phone numbers or Social Security numbers in numeric fields, however. Your application will not be performing numeric operations like addition or multiplication on phone numbers, and this data should not be stored in numeric fields. Instead, use text fields for common data such as Social Security numbers and phone numbers.

  Also, numeric fields never store leading zeros. Putting a zip code such as 02173 into a numeric field means only the last four digits (2173) are actually stored.

- **Consider the storage requirements of the data type you've selected.** Although you can use a long integer data type in place of a simple integer or byte value, the storage requirements of a long integer (4 bytes) is twice that of a simple integer. This means that twice as much memory is required to use and manipulate the number and twice as much disk space is required to store its value. Whenever possible, use byte or integer data types for simple numeric data.
- **Will you want to sort or index the field?** Because of their binary nature, memo and OLE object fields cannot be sorted or indexed. Use memo fields sparingly. The overhead required to store and work with memo fields is considerable.
- **Consider the impact of data type on sorting requirements.** Numeric data sort differ-ently than text data. Using the numeric data type, a sequence of numbers will sort as expected: 1, 2, 3, 4, 5, 10, 100. The same sequence stored as text data will sort like this: 1, 10, 100, 2, 3, 4, 5. If it's important to sort text data in a numeric sequence, you'll have to first apply a conversion function to the data before .sorting.
- **Is the data text or date data?** When working with dates, you're almost always better off storing the data in a Date/Time field than as a Text field. Text values son differently than date data (dates

are stored internally as numeric values), which can upset reports and other output that rely on chronological order..

- **Keep in mind the reports that will be needed.** You won't be able to sort or group memo or OLE data on a report. If it's important to prepare a report based on memo or OLE data, add a Tag field like a date or sequence number, which can be used to provide a sorting key to the table.

Text data type

Any type of data that is simply characters (letters, numbers, punctuation). Names, addresses, and descriptions are all text data, as are numeric data that are not used in a calculation (such as telephone numbers, Social Security numbers, and zip codes).

Although you specify the size of each Text field in the property area, you can enter no more than 255 characters of data in any Text field. Access uses variable length fields to store text data. If you designate a field to be 25 characters wide and you use only 5 characters for each record, then only enough room to store 5 characters is used in your database.

You will find that the **.accdb** database file may quickly grow quite large, but text fields are not the usual cause. However, it is good practice to limit text field widths to the maximum you believe they will be used for. Names are tricky because some cultures have long names. However, it is a safe bet that a postal code might be less than 12 characters wide while a U.S. state abbreviation is always 2 characters wide. By limiting the size of the text width, you also limit the number of characters that users can enter when the field is used in a form.

Memo data type

The Memo data type holds a variable amount of data from 0 to 65,536 characters for each record. Therefore, if one record uses 100 characters, another requires only 10, and yet another needs 3,000, you use only as much space as each record requires.

Notice that you did not specify a field size for the Memo data type. Access allocates as much space is necessary for the memo data.

Number data type

The Number data type enables you to enter numeric data; that is, numbers that will be used in mathematical calculations. (If you have data that will be used in monetary calculations, you should use the Currency data type, which performs calculations without rounding errors.)

The exact type of numeric data stored in a number field is determined by the Field Size prop-erty. Table 4-3 lists the various numeric data types, their maximum and minimum ranges, the deci-mal points supported by each numeric data type, and the storage (bytes) required by each numeric data type.

TABLE 4-3 Numeric Field Settings

Field Size Setting	***Range***	***Decimal Places***	***Storage Size***
Byte	0 to 255	None	1 byte
Integer	-32,768 to 32,767	None	2 bytes
Long Integer	-2,147,483,648 to 2,147,483,647	None	4 bytes
Double	-1.797×10^{308} to 1.797×10^{308}	15	8 bytes
Single	-3.4×10^{18} to 3.4×10^{38}	7	4 bytes
Replication ID	N/A	N/A	1 6 bytes
Decimal	1-28 precision	15	8 bytes

Many errors are caused by choosing the wrong numeric type for number fields. For instance, nolice that the maximum value for the Integer data type is 32,767. We once saw a database that ran perfectly for several years and then started crashing with overflow errors. It turned out that the overflow was caused by a particular field being set to the Integer data type, and when the company occasionally processed very large orders, the 32,767 maximum was exceeded.

It is best to design your tables very conservatively and allow for larger values than you ever expect to see in your database. This is not to say that it is a good idea to use the Double data type for all numeric fields. The Double data type is very targe (8 bytes) and is quite slow when used in calculations for another numeric operation. Instead, the Single data type is probably best for most floating-point calculations, and the Long integer is best for most data where decimal points are irrelevant.

Date/Time data type

The Date/Time data type is a specialized number field for holding dates or times (or dates and times). When dates are stored in a Date/Time field, it is easy to calculate days between dates and other calendar operations. Date data stored in Date/Time fields sort and filter properly as well.

Currency

The Currency data type is another specialized number field. Currency numbers are not rounded during calculations and preserve 15 digits of precision to the left of the decimal point and 4 digits to the right. Because the Currency data type uses a fixed-decimal-point position, they are faster in numeric calculations than doubles.

AutoNumber

The AutoNumber field is another specialized Number data type. When an AutoNumber field is added to a table, Access automatically assigns an integer value to the field (beginning at 1) and increments the value each time a record is added to the table. Alternatively (determined by the New Values property), the value of the AutoNumber field is a random integer that is automatically inserted into new records.

Only one AutoNumber field can appear in a table. Once assigned to a record, the value of an AutoNumber field cannot be changed programmatically or by the user. AutoNumber fields are equivalent to the Long Integer data type and occupy 4 bytes, but display only positive values. The range of possible values for AutoNumber fields, then, range from 1 to 4,294,9Є7,296 — more than adequate to use as the primary key for most tables.

Yes/No

Yes/No fields accept only one of two possible values. Internally stored as a 1 or 0 bit, the Yes /No field is used to indicate yes/no, on/off, or true/false. A Yes /No field occupies a single bit of storage.

OLE Object

The OLE Obj ect field stores OLE data, highly specialized binary objects such as Microsoft Word documents, Excel worksheets, sound or video clips, and images. The OLE object is created by an OLE server application and can be linked to the parent application or embedded in the Access table. OLE objects can only be displayed in bound object frames in Access forms and reports, OLE objects can be as large as 1GB or more in size. OLE fields cannot be indexed.

Attachment

The Attachment data type is new for Access 2010. In fact, the Attachment data type is one of the reasons Microsoft changed the format of the Access data file. The older MDB format is unable to accommodate attachments.

The Attachment data type is relatively complex, compared to the other type of Access fields. Please see the section titled "Understanding the Attachment Data Type" later in this chapter for details on this interesting type of field.

Hyperlink data type

The Hyperlink data type field holds combinations of text and numbers stored as text and used as a hyperlink address. It can have up to three parts:

- The visual text that appears in a field (usually underlined).
- The Internet address — the path to a file (UNC, or Universal Naming Convention, path) or page (URL or Uniform Resource Locator).
- Any sub-address within the file or page. An example of a sub-address is the name of an Access 2000 form or report. Each part is separated by the pound symbol (#).

Lookup Wizard

The Lookup Wi zard data type inserts a field that enables the end user to choose a value from another table or from the results of an SQL statement. The values may also be presented as a combo box or list box. At design time, the Lookup Wizard leads the developer through the process of defining the lookup characteristics when this data is assigned to a field.

Dragging a field created by the Lookup Wizard from the field list as you design a form, a combo box or list box is automatically created on the form. The list box or combo box also appears on a query datasheet that contains the field.

Entering a field description

The field description is completely optional; you use it only to help you remember a field's uses or to let another developer understand the fields purpose. Often you don't use the description col-umn at all, or you use it only for fields whose purpose is not obvious. If you enter a field descrip-tion, it appears in the status bar whenever you use that field in Access — in the datasheet or in a form. The field description can help clarify a field whose purpose is ambiguous or give the user a fuller explanation of the values valid for the field during data entry.

Creating tblContacts

Working with the different data types (plus the Lookup Wizard), you should be ready to create the final working copy of tblContacts. When creating the table, you must add a field that is used to link this table to two other tables (tblSales and tblContactLog) in the Access Auto Auctions application.

AutoNumber fields and Access

Access gives special considerations to AutoNumber fields and assigning values to AutoNumber fields. You cannot change a previously defined field from another type to AutoNumber. If you try to change an existing field in a table to the AutoNumber field type, Access displays a Control can't be edited: It' s bound to AutoNumber field "Contact ID" error in the status bar (the exact error you see will differ, of course, depending on which field is designated as the AutoNumber).

Completing tblContacts

With tblContacts in Design view, you're now ready to create or modify all the fields of tblContacts. Table 4-1, earlier in this chapter, shows the completed field definitions for tblContacts. If you're following the examples, you should be able to complete the table design. Enter the field names and data types exactly as shown. You may also need to rearrange some of the fields. The next few pages explain how to change existing fields (which includes rearranging the field order, changing a field name, and deleting a field).

Here are the steps for adding fields to a table structure:

1. Place the cursor in the Field Name column in the row where you want the field to appear.

2. Enter the field name and press Enter or Tab.
3. In the Data Type column, click the down arrow and select the data type.
4. Place the pointer in the Description column and type a description (optional).

Repeat each of these steps to create each of the data entry fields for tblContacts. You can press the down-arrow (↓) key to move between rows, or simply use the mouse and click on any row. Remember that F6 moves you from the top to the bottom of the Table Design window and back.

Changing a Table Design

As you create your table, you should be following a well-planned design. Yet changes are sometimes necessary, even with a plan. You may find that you want to add another field, remove a field, change a field name or data type, or simply rearrange the order of the field names. You can make these changes to your table at any time. After you enter data into your table, however, things get a bit more complicated. You have to make sure that any changes made don't affect the data entered previously.

In previous versions of Access, changing a field name usually meant that any queries, forms, reports, macros, or modules that referenced that field name would no longer work and had to be manually found and changed. Since Access 2002, the AutoCorrect feature auto-matically seeks out most occurrences of the name and changes it for you.

Inserting a new field

To insert a new field, in the Table Design window, place your cursor on an existing field and choose Insert > Rows or click the Insert Rows button in the toolbar. A new row is added to the table, and existing fields are pushed down. You can then enter a new field definition. Inserting a field does not disturb other fields or existing data. If you have queries, forms, or reports that use the table, you may need to add the field to those objects as well.

Deleting a field

There are three ways to delete a field. While ihe table is in Design View:

- Select the field by clicking the row selector and pressing the Delete key.
- Right-click on the selected field and choose Delete Rows from the shortcut menu.
- Select the field and click the Delete Rows button from the Tools group on the ribbons Design tab.

When you delete a field containing data, you'll see a warning that you will lose data in the table for the selected field. If the table is empty, you won't care. If your table contains data, however, make sure that you want to eliminate the data for that field (column). You will also have to delete the same field from queries, forms, reports, macros, and VBA code that use the field name.

When you delete a field, you can immediately select the Undo button and return the field to the table. But you must do this step before you save the changed table's defini-tion or make any other changes to the table's design. If you attempt to delete a field that is part of a relationship (primary or secondary key field), Access informs you that you cannot delete it until you delete the reference in the Relationships window.

If you delete a field, you must also delete all references to that field throughout Access. Because you can use a field name in forms, queries, reports, and even table-data validation, you must exam-ine your system carefully to find any instances where you may have used the specific field name.

Changing a field location

One of the easiest changes to make is to move a field's location. The order of your fields, as entered in the table's Design View, determines the initial display sequence in the datasheet that displays your data. If you decide that your fields should be rearranged, click on a field selector and use the mouse to drag the field to its new location.

Changing a field name

You change a field's name by selecting an existing field name in the Table Design screen and enter-ing a new name; Access updates the table design automatically. As long as you are creating a new table, this process is easy.

Changing a field size

Making a field size larger is simple in a table design. However, only text and number fields can be increased in size. You simply increase the Field Size property for text fields or specify a differnt field size for number fields. You must pay attention to the decimal-point property in number fields to make sure that you don't select a new size that supports fewer decimal places than you currently have.

Whe you want to make a field size smaller, make sure that none of the data in the table is larger than the new field width. If it is, the existing data will be truncated. Text data types should be make as small as practical to limit the amount of data entered by the user.

Data conversion issues

If in spite of your best efforts, it becomes necessary to change the data type of a field containing data, you may suffer data loss as the data-type conversion occurs. You should be aware of the effects of a data-type conversion on existing data.

- **Any data type to AutoNumber**: Can't be done. The AutoNumber field type must be created fresh in a new field.
- **Text to Number, Currency, Date/Time, or Yest/No**. In most cases, the conversion be made without damaging the data. Inappropriate value are automatically deleted. For instance, a text field containing "January 28, 2010" will be faithfully converted to a Data/Time field. If however, you change a field containing "January 28, 2010" to a Yes/No data type, its value will be deleted.
- **Memo to Text**. A straightforward conversion with no loss or corruption of data. Any text longer than the field size specified for the Text field is truncated and lost.
- **Number to Text**. No losss of information. The number value is converted to text using the General Number format.
- **Number to Currency**. Because the Currency data type uses a fixed decimal point, some precision may be lost as the number is truncated.
- **Date/Time to Text**. No loss of information. Date and time data are converted to text with the General Date format.
- **Currency to Text.** No loss of information. The currency value is converted to text without the currency symbol.
- **Currency to Number.** Simple, straightforward conversion. Some data may be lost as the currency value is converted to fit the new number field. For instance, when converting Currency to Long Integer, the decimal portion is truncated.
- **AutoNumber to Test**. Conversion occurs without loss of data, except in a case where the width of the text field is inadequate to hold the entire AutoNumber value. In this case, the number is truncated.
- **AutoNumber to Number**. Simple, straightforward conversion. Some data may be lost as the AutoNumber value is converted to fit the new number field. For instance, an AutoNumber larger than 32,767 will be truncated if it is convened to an Integer field.

- **Y&s/No to Text**. Simple conversion of Yes/No value to text. No loss of information. OLE Data Type: Cannot be converted to any other type of data.

Assigning field properties

The field properties built into Access tables are powerful allies that can help you manage the data in your tables. In most cases, the field property is enforced by the database engine, which means the property is consistently applied throughout the application. For instance, if you've set the Default Value property in the table design, the default value is available in the table's Datasheet view, on forms, and in queries.

Each field data type has its own set of properties. For instance, numeric fields have a Decimal Places property, and Text fields have a Text Align property. Although many data types share a num-ber of properties (such as Name) in common, there are enough different field properties to make it easy to become confused or to improperly use the properties. The following sections discuss some of the more important and frequently used field properties.

Common properties

Here is a list of all the general properties (note that they may not all be displayed, depending on which data type you chose):

- **Field Size**. When applied to Text Fields, limits size of the field to the specified number of characters (1-255). The default is 50.
- **New Values**. Applies to AutoNumber fields. Allows specification of increment or random type.
- **Format**. Changes the way data appears after you enter it (uppercase, dates, and so on). There are many different types of formats that may be applied to Access data.
- **Input Mask**. Used for data entry into a predefined format (phone numbers, zip codes, Social Security numbers, dates, customer IDs). Applicable to both numeric and text data types.
- **Decimal Places.** Specifies number of decimal places for Numeric and Currency data types.
- **Caption**. Optional label for form and report fields. Access uses the Caption property instead of the field name in these situations.
- **Default Value**. The value automatically provided for new data entry into the field. This value can be any value appropriate for the field's data type. A default is no more than an initial value; you can change it during data entry. To specify a default value, simply enter the desired value into the Default Value property setting. A default value can be an expression, as well as a number or a text string.
- **Validation Rule**. Ensures that data entered into the field conforms to some business rule, such as "greater than zero," "date must occur after January 1, 2000," and so on.
- **Validation Text**. Displays a message when data fails validation.
- **Required**. Specifies whether you must enter a value into^a field.
- **Allow Zero Length**. Determines whether you may enter an empty string ("") into a text field type to distinguish it from a null value.
- **Indexed**. Speeds up data access and (if desired) limits data to unique values.
- **Unicode Compression**. Used For multilanguage applications. Requires about twice the data storage but enables Office documents including Access reports to be displayed correctly no matter what language or symbols are used. Generally speaking, Unicode is of no value unless the application is likely to be used in Asian environments.
- **IME Mode**. Also known as the Kanji Conversion Mode property, this mode is used to show whether the Kanji mode is maintained when the control is lost. The setting has no relevance in English or European-language applications.

- **IME Sentence Mode**. Used to determine the Sequence mode of fields of a table or con-trols of a form that switch when the focus moves in or out of the field. The setting has no relevance in English or European-language applications.
- **Smart Tags**. Used to assign a specific action to obtain data in this field, For example, the Financial Symbol Smart Tag obtains recent stock quotes on MSN Money Central.

Format

The Formal property specifies how the data contained in table fields appears whenever the data is displayed or printed. When set at the table level, the format is in effect throughout ihe application. There are different format specifiers for each data type.

Access provides built-in format specifiers for most field data types. The exact format used to dis-play field values is influenced by the Regional Sellings in the Windows Control Panel.

The Format property affects only the way a value is displayed and not the value itself or how the value is stored in the database. If you elect to build a custom format, construct a siring in the field's Fonnat property box. There are a number of different symbols you use for each data type. Access provides global format specifi-cations to use in any custom format specifier:

- **(space):** Display spaces as characters.
- **" SomeText":** Display the lext between the quotes as literal text.
- **! (exclamation mark):** Left-aligns the display.
- * **(asterisk):** Fills empty space with the next character.
- **\ (backslash):** Displays the next character as literal text. Use the backslash to display characters that otherwise have special meaning to Access.
- **[color]:** Displays the output in the color (black, blue, green, cyan, red, magenta, yellow, white) indicated between the brackets.

The Format property takes precedence when both a format specifier and input mask have been defined.

Number and Currency field formats

There is a wide variety of valid formats for Number and Currency fields. You can use one of ihe built-in formats or construct a custom format of your own:

- **General Number:** The number is displayed in the format in which it was entered (this is the default format for numeric data fields).
- **Currency:** Add a thousands separator (usually a comma), use a decimal point with two digits to the right of the decimal, and enclose negative numbers in parentheses.
- **Fixed:** Always display at least one digit with two digits to the right of the decimal point.
- **Standard:** Use the thousands separator with two digits to the right of the decimal point.
- **Percent:** The number value is multiplied by 100 and a percent sign is added to the right. Percent values are displayed with two decimal places to the right of the decimal point.
- **Scientific:** Scientific notation is used to display the number,
- **Euro:** Prepends the Euro currency symbol to the number and uses spaces instead of commas as the thousands delimiter.

The built-in numeric formats are summarized in Table 4-4.

TABLE 4-4 Numeric Format Examples

FormatType	*Number as Entered*	*Number as Displayed*	*Format Defined*
General	987654.321	987654.3	######.#
Currency	987654.321	$987,654.32	$###.##0.00
Euro	987654.321	€987,654.32	€###,##0.00
Fixed	987654.321	987654.32	######.##
Standard	987654.321	987,654.32	###,###.##
Percent	.987	98.7%	###.##%
Scientific	987654.321	9.88E+05	###E+00

All the formats above are the default formats based on setting the Decimal places property to AUTO.

Custom numeric formats

Custom formats are created by combining a number of symbols lo form a format specifier. The symbols used with Number and Currency fields are listed below:

- **. (period):** Specifies where the decimal point should appear.
- **, (comma):** The thousands separator.
- **0 (zero):** A placeholder for zero or a digit.
- **# (pound sign):** A placeholder for nothing or a digit.
- **$ (dollar sign):** Display the dollar sign character.
- **% (percent sign):** Multiply the value by 100 and add a percent sign.
- **E- or e-:** Use scientific notation to display the number. Use a minus sign to indicate a negative exponent and no sign for positive exponents.
- **E+ or e+:** Same as previous, but use a plus sign to indicate positive exponents.

You create custom formats by composing a string made up of one to four sections separated by semicolons. Each section has a different meaning to Access:

- **First section:** The format snerifipr for nn^mw w>in*-e
- **Second section:** The format specifier for negative values.
- **Third section:** The format specifier for zero (0) values.
- **Fourth section:** The format specifier for null values.

Each section is a combination of a numeric formatting string and an optional color specification. Here's an example of a custom format:

0,000.00 [Green]; (0, 000.00) [Red]; "Zero"; " -"

This format specifies showing the number with zeros in all positions (even if the number is less than 1,000), using the comma thousands separator, enclosing negative numbers in parentheses, using three pound signs to indicate a zero value, and using three dashes for null values.

Date/Time field formats

Access includes a wide variety of built-in and custom formats applicable to Dale/Time fields. You are able to create a custom format to display date and time data in virtually any format imaginable.

Built-in Date/Time formats

The following are the built-in Date/Time formats:

- **General Date:** If the value contains a date only, do not display a time value and vice versa. Dates are displayed in the built-in Short Date format, while time data is displayed in the Long Time format.
- **Long Date:** Sunday, May 13, 2010
- **Medium Date:** 13-May-07
- **Short Date:** V13/07
- **Long Time:** 9:21:17 AM
- **Medium Time:** 09:21AM
- **Short Time:** 9:21:17

Date and time formats are influenced by the Regional Settings in the Windows Control Panel.

Custom Date/Time formats

Custom formats are created by constructing the specifier as a string containing the following symbols:

- **: (colon):** Separates time elements (hours, minutes, seconds).
- **/ (forward slash):** Separates date elements (days, months, years).
- **c (lowercase c):** Instructs Access to use the built-in General Date format.
- **d (lowercase d):** Displays the day of the month as one or two digits, as necessary.
- **dd:** Displays the day of the month using two digits ("9" displays as "09").
- **ddd:** Displays the first three letters of the day of the week {Sun, Mon, Tue, Wed, Thu, Fri, Sat).
- **dddd:** Uses the full name of the day of the week (Sunday, Monday, Tuesday, Wednesday, Thursday, Friday, Saturday).
- **ddddd:** Uses the built-in Short Date format.
- **dddddd:** Uses the built-in Long Date format.
- **w:** Uses a number to indicate the day of the week.
- **ww:** Shows the week of die year (1 to 53).
- **m:** Displays the month of the year using one or two digits.
- **mm:** Displays the month of the year using two digits (with leading zero if necessary).
- **mmm:** Uses the first three characters of the month (Jan, Feb, Mar, Apr, May, Jun, Jul, Aug, Sep, Oct, Nov, Dec).
- **mmmm:** Displays the full name of the month (for example, January).
- **q:** Displays the date as the quarter of the year.
- **y:** Displays the day of the year (1 through 366).
- **yy:** Uses the last two digits of the year (for example, 07).
- **yyyy:** Uses the full four-digit year (2010).
- **h:** Displays the hour using one or two digits,
- **hh:** Displays the hour using two digits.
- **n:** Displays the minutes using one or two digits.
- **nn:** Displays the minutes using two digits.
- **s:** Displays the seconds using one or two digits.
- **ss:** Displays the seconds using two digits.
- **tttt:** Uses the built-in Long Time format.
- **AM/PM:** Uses a 12-hour format with uppercase AM or PM.
- **am/pm:** Uses a 12-hour format with lowercase am or pm.

- **A/P:** Uses a 12-hour format with uppercase A or E
- **a/p:** Uses a 12-hour format with lowercase a or p.
- **AMPM:** 12-hour format using the morning or after designator specified in the Regional Settings in the Windows Control Panel.

You must enclose a comma or other separator or text in quotation marks as part of the format specifier.

Text and Memo field formats

When applied to text fields, format specifiers clarify the data contained within the fields. tblContacts uses several formats. The State text field has a > in the Formal property to display the data entry in uppercase. The OrigCustDate field has an mmm dd yyyy formal to display ihe date of birth as the short month name, a space, the day and a four-digit year (May 13 2010). The Active field has a format of Yes/No with lookup Display Conirol property set to Text Box.

Text and Memo fields are displayed as plain text by default. If a panicular format is to be applied to Text or Memo field data, use the following symbols to construct the format specifier:

- **@ (at sign):** A character or space is required.
- **& (ampersand):** A character is optional (not required).
- **< (less than symbol):** Force all characters to iheir lowercase equivalents.
- **> (greater than symbol):** Force all characters to their uppercase equivalents.

The custom format specifier may contain as many as three different sections, separated by semi-colons:

- **First section:** Specifier for fields containing text
- **Second section:** Format for fields containing zero-length strings
- **Third section:** Format for fields containing Null values

If only two sections are given, the second section applies to both zero-length strings and null val-ues. For example, the following specifier displays "None" when no string data is contained in the field, "Unknown" when a null value exists in the field. Otherwise, the simple text contained in the field is displayed:

@;"None";"Unknown"

Several examples of custom text formats are presented in Table 4-5.

TABLE 4-5 Format Examples

Format Specified	*Data as Entered*	*Formatted Data as Displayed*
>	Adam Smith	ADAM SMITH
#,##0;(#,##0);"-0-";"None"	15 -15 0 No Data	15 (15) -0- None
Currency	12345.67	$12,345.67
"Acct No." 0000	3271	Acct No. 3271
mmm yy	9/17/08	Sep 08
Long Date	9/17/08	Thursday, September 17, 2008

Yes/No field formats

A Yes/No field displays the words "Yes," "No," "True," "False," "On," or "Off," depending on the value stored in the field and the setting of the Format property for the field. Access predefines these rather obvious format specifications for the Yes/No field type:

- **Yes/No:** Displays "Yes" or "No"
- **True/False:** Displays "True" or "False"

- **On/Off:** Displays "On" or "Off

Yes, True, and On all indicate the same "positive" value, while No, False, and Off indicate the opposite ("negative") value.

Access stores Yes/No data in a manner different from what you might expect. The Yes data is stored as -1, whereas No data is stored as 0. You'd expect it to be stored as 0 for No and 1 for Yes, but this isn't the case. Without a format setting, you must enter -1 or 0, and it will he stored and dis-played that way.

You are also able to specify a custom format for Yes/No fields. For instance, assume you've got a table with a field that indicates whether the employee has attended an orientation meeting. Although a Yes or No answer is appropriate, maybe you want to get a little fancy with the field's display. By default, a check box is used to indicate the value of the Yes/No field (checked means Yes). To customize the appearance of the Yes/No field, set its Format property according to the fol-lowing pattern:

."Text for Yes values";"Text for No values"

Notice the placeholder semicolon at the front of this string. Also notice that each text element must be surrounded by quotes. In the case of the employee table, you might use the following Format property specifier:

;"Attendance OK"; "Must attend orientation"

You must also set the Yes/No field's Display Control property to Text Box in order to change the default check box display to text.

Hyperlink data-type format

Access also displays and stores Hyperlink data in a manner different from what you would expect. The format of this lype is composed of up to three parts:

- **Display Text:** The text that is displayed as a hyperlink in the field or control
- **Address:** The path to a file {UNO or page (URL) on the Internet
- **Sub-Address:** A specific location within a file or page

The parts are separated by pound signs. The Display Text is visible in the field or control, while the address and sub-address are hidden. For example, Microsoft Net Home Paget#http://www.msn.com.

Input Mask

The Input Mask property makes it easier for users to enter the data in the correct format. An input mask limits the way the user inputs data into the table or a form. For instance, you can confine the user to only entering digits into phone number, Social Security number, and employee ID fields. An input mask for a Social Security number might look like "000-00-0000." This mask requires input into every space, restricts entry to digits only, and does not permit characters or spaces.

An input mask specified as part of the field's properties is used anywhere the field appears (query, form, report). The Input Mask property value is a string containing as many as three sections, each section separated by a semicolon.

- **First section:** Contains the mask itself, composed of the symbols shown below.
- **Second section:** Tells Access whether to store the literal characters included in the mask along with the rest of the data. For instance, the mask might include dashes to separate the pans of the Social Security number while a phone number may include parentheses and dashes. Using a 0 (zero) tells Access to store the literal characters as part of the data; a 1 tells Access to store only the data itself.
- **Third section:** Defines the "placeholder" character that tells the user how many charac-ters are expected in the input area. Many input masks use pound signs (#) or asterisks (*) as placeholders.

The following characters are used to compose the input mask string:

- 0: A digit is required, and plus (+) and (-) minus signs are not permitted.
- 9: A digit is optional, and plus (+) and (-) minus signs are not permitted.
- #: Optional digit or space. Spaces are removed when the data is saved in the table. Plus and minus signs are allowed.
- L: A letter from A to Z is required.
- ?: A letter from A to Z is optional.
- A: A character or digit is required.
- a: A character or digit is optional.
- &: Permits any character or space (required).
- c: Permits any character or space (optional).
- **."(period):** Decimal placeholder.
- **, (comma):** Thousands separator.
- **: (colon):** Date and time separator.
- **; (semicolon):** Separator character.
- **- (dash):** Separator character.
- **/ (forward slash):** Separator character.
- **< (less-than sign):** Convert all characters to lowercase.
- **> (greater-than sign):** Convert all characters to uppercase.
- **! (exclamation mark):** Display the input mask from right to left. Characters fill the mask from right to left.
- **\ (back slash):** Display the next character as a literal. The same specifiers are used on a field's property sheet in a query or form. Input masks are ignored when importing data or adding data 10 a table with an action query.

An input mask is overridden by the Format property assigned to a field. In this case, the input mask is in effect only as data is entered and reformatted according to the format specifier when entry is complete.

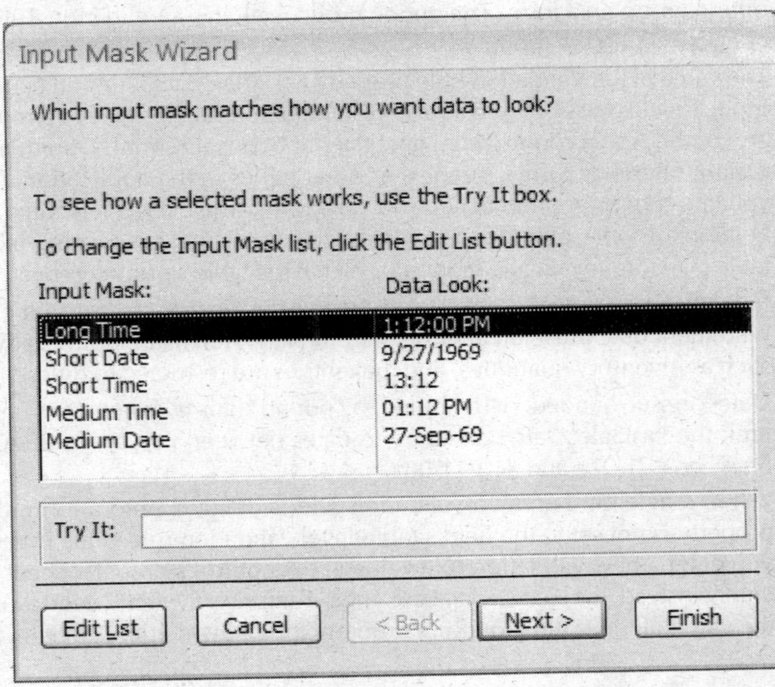

The Input Mask Wizard

Although you can manually enter an input mask, you can easily create an input mask for Text or Date/Time type fields with the Input Mask Wizard. When you click ihe Input Mask property, the builder button (three periods) appears. Click the Build button to start the Wizard. The figure here shows the dialog box of Input Mask Wizard.

The Input Mask Wizard shows not only the name of each

predefined input mask, but also an example for each name. You can choose from the list of predefined masks. Click in the Try It text box and enter a test value to see how data entry will look. After you choose an input mask, the next wizard screen enables you to refine the mask and specify the placeholder symbol (perhaps a pound sign [#] or "at" sign [@]). Another wizard screen enables you to decide whether to store special characters (such as the dashes in a Social Security number) with the data. When you com-plete the wizard, Access adds the input mask characters in the field's property sheet.

Enter as many custom masks as you need. You can also determine the international settings so' that you can work with multiple country masks.

Caption

The Caption property determines what appears in the default label attached to a control created by dragging the field from the field list onto a form or report. The caption also appears as the column heading in Datasheet views {table or query) that include the field.

Be careful using the Caption property. Because the caption text appears as the column heading in Datasheet view, you may be misled by a column heading in a query's Datasheet view. When the field appears in a query, you do not have immediate access to the field's properties, so you must be aware that the column heading is actually determined by the Caption property.

To be even more confusing, the caption assigned in the table's Design view and the caption assigned in a field's property sheet in the Query Design view are different properties and can contain different text.

Captions can be as long as 2,048 characters, more than adequate for all but the most verbose descriptions.

ValidationRule

The Validation Rule property establishes requirements for input into the field. Enforced by the Jet database engine, the validation rule ensures that data entered into the table conforms to the requirements of the application.

The Validation Rule property does not apply to check boxes, option buttons, or toggle buttons within an option group on a form. The option group itself has a Validation Rule property that applies to all of the controls within the group.

The value of the Validation Rule property is a string containing an expression that is used to test the user's input. The expression used as a field's Validation Rule property cannot contain user-defined functions or any of the Access domain or aggregate functions (DCount, DSum, and so on). A fields validation rule cannot reference forms, queries, or other tables in the application. (These restrictions do not apply to validation rules applied to controls on a form, however.) Field validation rules cannot reference other fields in the table, although a validation rule applied to a record in a table can reference fields in the same table (a record-level validation rule is set in the table's property sheet, rather than on an individual field).

Validation rules are often used to ensure that certain dates fall after other dates (for instance, an employee's retirement date must fall after his starting date), to ensure nonnegative numbers are entered for values such as inventory quantities, and that entries are restricted to different ranges of numbers or text.

Dates are surrounded, or delimited, by pound signs (#) when used in Access expressions. If you want to limit the LastSalesDate data entry to dates between January 1, 2010, and December 31, 2008, enter Between #I/1/07# and #12/31/08#.

When a field containing a validation rule is dragged onto a form, the new control's Validation Rule property is not set to the field's table-level validation rule value in the control's property sheet. Unless you enter a new validation rule value in the control's property sheet, the value in the property sheet is empty Instead, the Access database engine enforces the fields validation rule behind the scenes, based on the value of the Validation Rule property for the field at the table level.

Field and control validation rules are enforced when the focus leaves die table field or form control. Record-level validation rules are enforced when moving to another record. Validation rules applied to both a table field and a form control bound to the field are enforced for both entities. The table-level rule is applied as data is edited on the bound control and as focus leaves the control. You cannot create table-level validation rules for linked "foreign" tables, such as FoxPro, Paradox, or dBASE. Apply validation rules to controls bound to fields in linked foreign tables.

Validation Text

The Validation Text property contains a string that is displayed in a message box when the user's input does not satisfy the requirements of the Validation Rule property. The maximum length of the Validation Text property value is 255 characters.

When using the Validation Rule property, you should always specify a validation text value to avoid triggering the generic message box Access displays when the validation rule is violated. Use the Validation Text property to provide users with a helpful message that explains acceptable values for the field.

Required

The Required property directs Access to require input into the field. When set to Yes, input is required into the field within a table or into a control on a form bound to the field. The value of a required field cannot be Null.

The Required property is invalid for AutoNumber fields. By default, all AutoNurnber fields are assigned a value as new records are created.

The Access database engine enforces the Required property An error message is generated if the user tries to leave a text box control bound to a field with its Required property set to Yes.

The Required property can be used in conjunction with theAllow Zero Length property to determine when die value of a field is unknown or doesn't exist.

AllowZero Length

The Allow zero Length property specifies whether or not you want a zero-length string ("") to be a valid entry for a Text or Memo field. Allow Zero Length accepts the following values:

- **Yes:** A zero-length string is a valid entry.
- **No:** The table will not accept zero-length strings, and instead, inserts a Null value into the field when no valid text, data is supplied.
- **Using Visual Basic:** AllowZeroLength (with no spaces!) can be set from Visual Basic for Applications (VBA). Use the Allow Zero Length property of the TableDef object to determine its setting or change its value.

Appropriate combination if the Allow Zero Length and Required properties enables you to differentiate between data that doesn't exist (which you'll probably want to represent as a zero-length string) and data that is unknown (which you'll want to store as a null value). VBA determines the difference between null and zero-length string values and takes appropriate action based on this information. In some cases you'll want to store the proper value in the Text or Memo field.

An example of data that doesn't exist is the case of a customer who doesn't have an e-mail address. The e-mail address field should be set to an empty (zero-length) string indicating that no address exists. Another customer who you are sure is an e-mail user but who hasn't supplied an e-mail address should have a null value in the e-mail address field, indicating that we don't know whether the person has an e-mail address.

An input mask can help your application's users distinguish when a field contains a null value. For instance, the input mask could be set to display "None" when the field contains a zero-length string.

The Required property determines whether a null value is accepted by the field, while the Allow Zero

Length property permits zero-length strings in the field. Together, these independ-ent properties provide the means to determine whether a value is unknown or absent for the field.

The interaction between Required and Allow Zero Length can be quite complicated- Table 4-6 summarizes how these two properties combine to force the user to input a value, or to insert either a Null or zero-length string into a field.

TABLE 4-6 Required and Allow Zero Length Property Combinations

Allow Zero length	*Required*	*Data Entered by User*	*Value Stored in Table*
No	No	Null	Null
No	No	Space	Null
No	No	Zero-length string	Disallowed
Yes	No	Null	Null
Yes	No	Space	Null
Yes	No	Zero-length string	Zero-length string
No	"Yes	Null	Disallowed
No	Yes	Space	Disallowed
No	Yes	Zero-length string	Disallowed
Yes	Yes	Null	Disallowed
Yes	Yes	Space	Zero-length string
Yes	Yes	Zero-length string	Zero-length string

Indexed

The Indexed property tells Access you want to use a field as an index in the table. Indexed fields are internally organized to speed up queries, sorting, and grouping operations. If you intend to fre-quently include a certain field in queries (for instance, the employee ID or Social Security number), or if the field is frequently sorted or grouped on reports, you should set its Indexed property.

The valid settings for the Indexed property are as follows:

- **No:** The field is not indexed (default).
- **Yes (Duplicates OK):** The field is indexed and Access permits duplicate values in the column- This is the appropriate setting for values such as names, where it is likely that names like "Smith" will appear more than once in the table.
- **Yes (No Duplicates):** The field is indexed and no duplicates are permitted in the col-umn. Use this setting for data that should be unique within the table, such as Social Security numbers, employee IDs, and customer numbers.

Indexes are discussed in more detail later in this chapter.

In addition to the primary key, you are able to index as many fields as necessary to provide opti-mum performance. Access accepts as many as 32 indexes per table. Keep in mind that each index extracts a small performance hit as new records are added to the table. Access dynamically updates the indexing information each time a new record is added. If a table includes an excessive number of indexes, a noticeable delay may occur as each new record is added.

The Indexed property is set in the field's property sheet or on the table's property sheet. Using the table index's property sheet is discussed in the earlier section on assigning primary keys. You must use the tables property sheet to set multi-field indexes.

AutoIndex Option

The Access Options dialog box contains an entry (AutoIndex on Import/Create) that directs Access to automatically index certain fields as they are added to a table's design. By default, fields that begin or end with ID, key, code, or num (for instance, Employee ID or Task Code) are automatically indexed as the field is created. Every time a new record is added to the table, the fields data is incorporated into the field's index. If there are other fields you'd like Access to automatically index as they are created, add new values to the Auto Index on import/Create check box on the Object Designers tab in the Access Options dialog box, shown next.

When to Index

Generally speaking, you should index fields that are frequently searched or sorted. Remember that indexes slow down certain operations such as inserting records and some action queries. Memo and OLE Ob j ect fields cannot be indexed. It would be impossible for Access to maintain an index on these complete data types. An index should not be used if a field contains very few unique values. For instance, you will not see a significant benefit from indexing a field containing a person's sex or state, or Yes/No fields. Because there is a limited domain of values in such fields, Access easily sorts the data in these fields.

Use a multiple-field index in situations where sorts are often simultaneously performed on multi-ple fields (for instance, first and last names). Access will have a much easier time sorting such a table.

Setting the Primary Key

Every table should have a primary key—one or more fields with a unique value for each record. (This principle is called entity integrity in the world of database management.) In tblContacts, the ContactID field is the primary key. Each contact has a different ContactID value so that you can identify one from the other. ContactID 17 refers to one and only one record in the Contacts table. If you don't specify a primary key (unique value field), Access can create one for you.

Understanding unique values

Without the ContactID field, you'd have to rely on another field or combination of fields for uniqueness. You couldn't use the LastName field because two customers could easily have the same last name. In fact, you couldn't even use the FirstName and LastName fields together (multi-field key), for the same reason — two people could be named James Smith. You need to come up with a field that makes every record unique. Looking at the table, you may think that you could use a combination of the LastName, FirstName, and Company fields, but theoretically, its possible that two people working at the same company have the same name. The easiest way to solve this problem is to add an AutoNumber field for the express purpose of using it as the tables primary key. This is exactly the situation with the Contacts table. The pri-mary key of this table is ContactID, an AutoNumber field.

If you don't designate a field as a primary key, Access can add an AutoNumber field and designate it as the tables primary key. This field contains a unique number for each record in the table, and Access maintains it automatically.

Generally speaking, you may want to create and maintain your own primary key, even if you always use AutoNumber fields as primary keys:

- A primary key is always an index.
- An index maintains a presorted order of one or more fields that greatly speeds up queries, searches, and sort requests.
- When you add new records to your table, Access checks for duplicate data and doesn't allow any duplicates for the primary key field.
- By default, Access displays a table's data in the order of its primary key

By designating a field such as ContactID as the unique primary key, you can see your data in a meaningful order. In our example, because the ContactID field is an AutoNumber, its value is assigned automatically by Access in the order that a record is put into the system.

Choosing a primary key

Although all of the tables in the Access Auto Auctions application use AutoNumber fields as their primary keys, you should be aware of the reasons why AutoNumbers make such excellent primary keys. The characteristics of primary keys include the following:

- The primary key must uniquely identify each record.
- The primary key cannot be null.
- The primary key must exist when the record is created.
- The primary key definition must remain stable — you should never change a primary key value once it is established.
- The primary key must be compact and contain as few attributes as possible.

The ideal primary key is, then, a single field that is immutable and guaranteed to be unique within the table. For these reasons, the Access Auto Auctions database uses the AutoNumber field exclusively as the primary key for all tables.

Creating the primary key

The primary key can be created in any of three ways. With a table open in Design View:

- Select the field to be used as the primary key and select the Primary Key button (ihe key icon) in the Tools group in the ribbons Design tab.
- Right-click on the field to display the shortcut menu and select Primary Key
- Save the table without creating a primary key, and allow Access to automatically create an AutoNumber field.

After you designate the primary key, a key icon appears in the gray selector area to the left of the field's name to indicate that the primary key has been created.

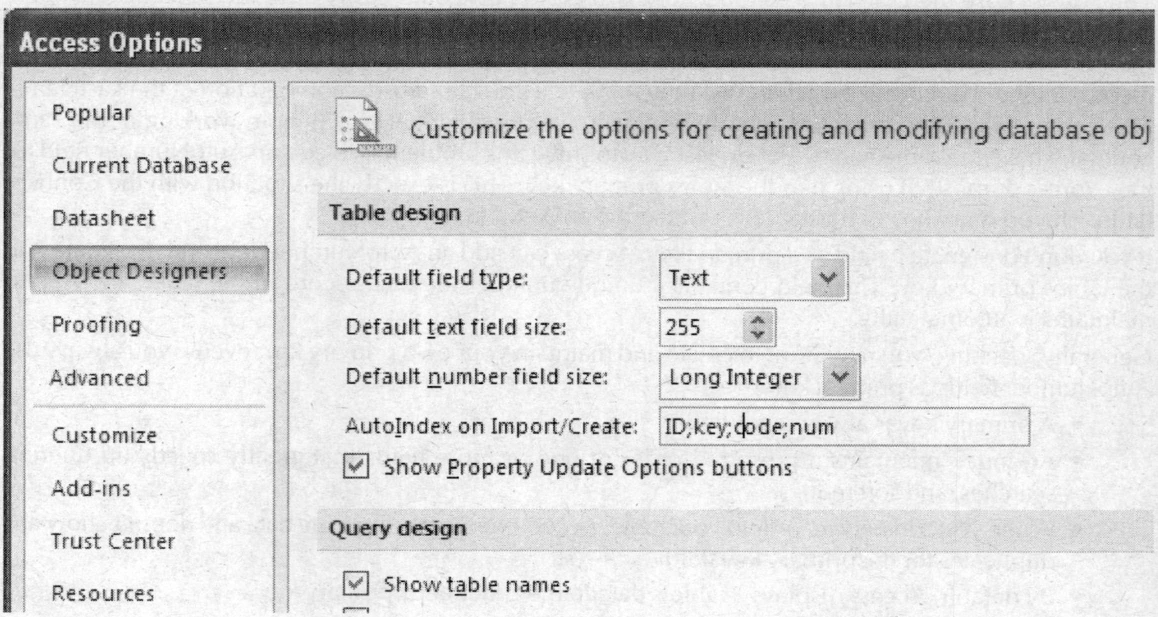

Indexing Access Tables

Data is rarely, if ever, entered into tables in a meaningful order. Usually records are added to tables in totally random order (with the exception of time-ordered data). For instance, a busy order entry system will gather information on a number of different customer orders in a single day Most often this data will be used to report orders for a single customer for billing purposes or for extracting order quantities for inventory management. The records in the Orders table, however, are in chronological order, which is not necessarily helpful when preparing reports detailing customer orders. In that case, you'd rather have data entered in customer ID order.

To further illustrate this concept, consider the Rolodex card file many people use to store names, addresses, and phone numbers. Assume for a moment that the cards in the file were fixed in place. You could add new cards, but only to the end of the card file. This limitation would mean that "Jones" might follow "Smith," and in turn be followed by "Baker." In other words, there is no particular order to the data stored in this file.

An unsorted Rolodex like this would be very difficult to use. You'd have to search each and every card looking for a particular person, a painful and time-consuming process. Of course, this is not how we use address card files. When we add a card to the file, we insert it into the Rolodex at the location where it logically belongs. Most often, this means inserting the card in alphabetical order, by last name, into the Rolodex.

Records are added to Access tables as described in the "fixed" card file example earlier. New records are always added to the end of the table, rather than in the middle of the table where they may logically belong. However, in an order entry system you'd probably want new records inserted next to other records on the same customer. Unfortunately, this isn't how Access tables work. The natural order of a table is the order in which records were added to the table. This order is sometimes referred to as entry order or physical order to emphasize that the records in the table appear in the order in which they were added to the table.

Using tables in natural order is not necessarily a bad thing. Natural order makes perfect sense if the data is rarely searched or if the table is very small. Also, there are situations where the data being added to the table is highly ordered to start with. If the tabie is used to gather sequential data (like readings from an electric meter) and the data will be used in the same sequential order, there is no need to impose an index on the data.

But for situations where natural order does not suffice, Microsoft Access provides indexing to help you find and sort records faster. You specify the logical order for the records in a table by creating an index on that table. Access uses the index to maintain one or more internal sort orders for the data in the table. For instance, you may choose to index the LastName field that will frequently be included in queries and sorting routines.

Microsoft Access uses indexes in a table as you use an index in a book: To find data, Access looks up the location of the data in the index. Most often, your tables will include one or more simple indexes. A simple index is one that involves a single field in the table. Simple indexes may arrange the table's records in ascending or descending order. Simple indexes are created by setting the field's Indexed property to one of the following values:

- Yes (Duplicates OK)
- Yes (No Duplicates)

By default, Access fields are not indexed. However, it is hard to imagine a table that does not require some kind of index. The next section discusses why indexing is important to use in Access tables. Once you've read the following section, we're sure you'll agree that it's difficult to imagine an Access table that would not benefit from an index or two.

Multiple-field indexes

Multiple-field indexes (also called composite indexes) are easy to create. In Design view, click on the Indexes toolbar button or select the Indexes command on the View menu. The Indexes dialog box opens, allowing you to specify the fields to include in the index.

The index properties are quite easy to understand:

- **Primary:** When set to Yes, Access uses this index as the table's primary key. More than one field can be designated as the primary key, but keep the rules governing primary keys in mind, particularly those requiring each primary key value to be unique and that no field in a composite primary key can be empty The default for the Primary property is No.
- **Unique:** When set to Yes, the index must be unique within a table. When applied to composite keys, the combination of field values must be unique — each field within the composite key can duplicate fields found within the table. A Social Security number field is a good candidate for a unique index, but a last name field should not be uniquely indexed.
- **Ignore Nulls:** If a record's index field contains a null value (which happens in a com-posite index only if all fields in the composite index are null) the record's index won't contribute anything to the overall indexing. In other words, unless a record's index contains some kind of value, Access doesn't know where to insert the record in the table's internal index sort lists. Therefore, you may want to instruct Access to ignore a record if the index value is null. By default, the Ignore Nulls property is set to No, which means Access inserts records with a null index values into the indexing scheme along with any other records containing null index values.

You should test the impact of the index properties on your Access tables and use the properties that best suit the data handled by your databases.

A field can be both the primary key for a table and part of a composite index. You should index your tables as necessary to yield the highest possible performance without worrying about over-indexing or violating some arcane indexing rules.

CHAPTER 6

Creating a Form in Microsoft Access 2010

Introduction

Forms are the easiest way of entering data into the tables. Microsoft Access 2010 allows you to create these forms with ease.

Introduction

The biggest problem with Datasheet view is that it can be confusing to find a field for a specific record. Because most people are familiar with paper forms or index cards that arrange related data (fields) on a page, Access offers you Form view. Form view simply displays the fields of a single record onscreen. To use Form view, you must first create a form and arrange your fields on that form. After you create a form, you can add, edit and view data through that form.

Creating a Form

The simplest way to create a form to let Access desing one for you, which you can modify.

To create a form quickly, follow these steps:

1. Click the Office Button and then choose Open.
   The Open dialog box appears.
2. Click the Access database file you want to add or edit data. Then click Open.
   Access displays your chosen database.
3. In the All Tables pane on the left of the screen, double-click a table.
   Access displays the Datasheet view of your database.
4. Click the Create tab.
5. Click the Form icon in the Forms group.
   Access creates a form. Notice that the form name automatically uses the name of the database table you choose in Step 3.
6. Click the Office Button and then choose Save (or click the Save icon on the Quick Access toolbar).
   The Save As dialog box appears, asking you to type a name for your form.
7. Type a descriptive name for your form in the Form Name text box and then click Ok.
   Acess displays your form's name underneath the All Tables pabe. The next time you open this database and want to view the form, you can double-click the form's name in the left pane.

Searching a Database

The simplest type of search ooks for a specific record. To search for a record, you need to know the data stored in at least one of its fields, such as a phone number and e-mail address. The more information you already know, the more likely Access will find the one record you want. If you search for all records that contain the first name, Access could find dozens of records. But, if you feed in the name and surname, your search would narrow down to just few records.

To search for a specific record in a database table, follow these steps:

1. In the All Tables pane on the left of the screen, double-click the name of the databse table you want to search.
   Access displays the Datasheet view of your database.
2. Click the Home tab.
3. Click the Find icon in the Find group.
   The Find and Replace dialog box appears.
4. Click in the Find What text box and type in the data you know is stored in the record in the record you want to find.
   For example, if you want to find the phone number of a person but you know only that person's last name in the Find What text box.

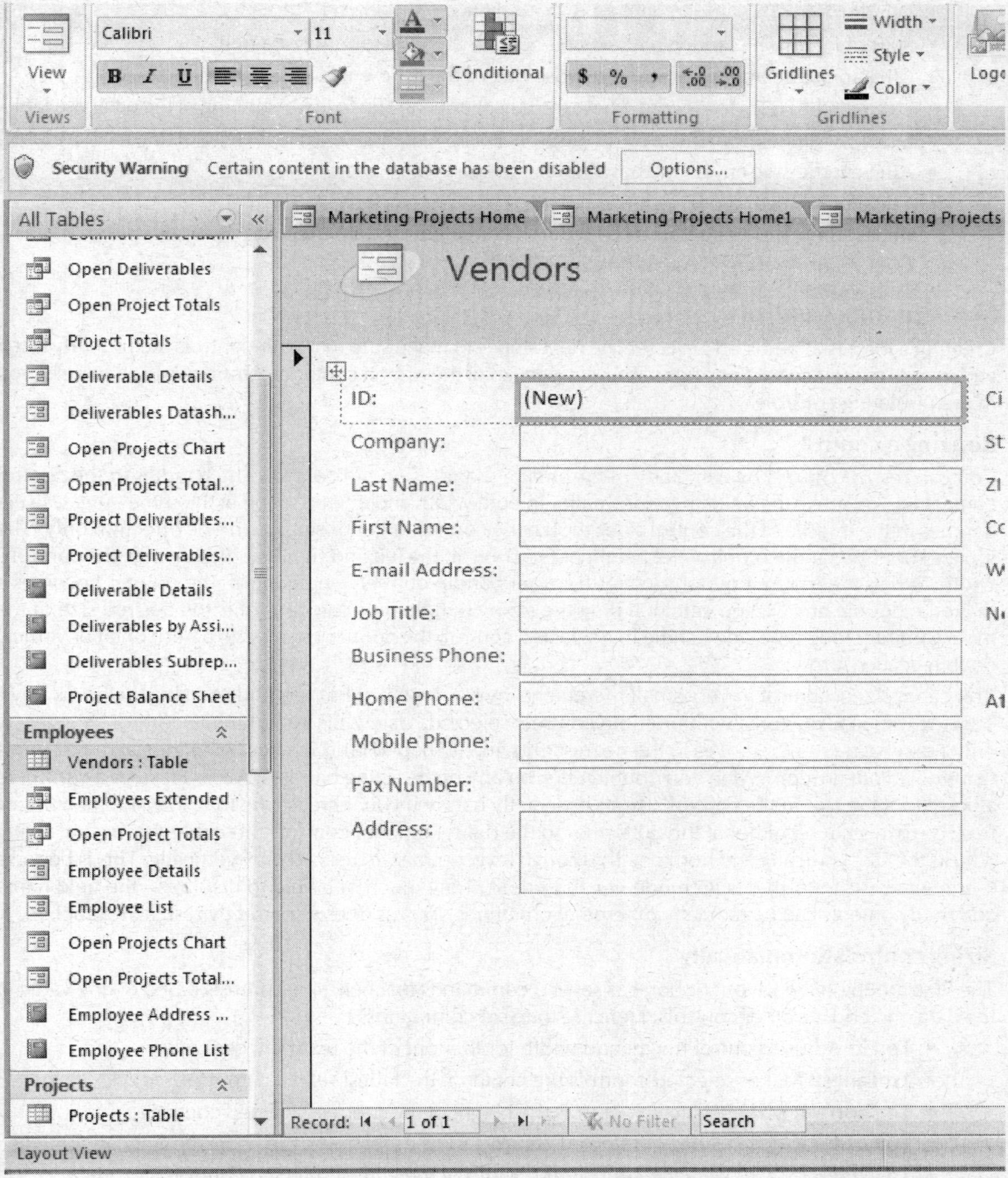

5. Click the Look In list box and choose the name of the entire databse table.
6. Click in the Match list box and choose one of the following:

- Any Part of Field: The Find What text can appear in any part of a field.

- Whole Field: The Find What text is the only text stored in a field.
- Start of Field: The Find What text can be only at the beginning of a field.

7. Click in the Search list box and choose one of the following:.
   - Up: Searches from the record where the cursor appears, up to the beginning of the database table.
   - Down: Searches from the record where the cursor appears, down to the end of the database table.
   - All: Searches the entire database table.
8. Click Find Next.
9. Repeat Step 8 to search for more records that might contain the text you typed in Step 4.
10. Click Cancel or the Close button.

Manipulating Controls

Creating a form is a multistep process. The next step is to make sure that your controls are properly sized and moved to their correct positions. The Arrange tab of the ribbon contains commands used to assist you in manipulating controls.

Resizing a control

You can resize controls by using any of the smaller handles on the control. The bandies in the control corners let you make the field larger or smaller in both width and height — and at the same time. Use the handles in the middle of the control sides to size the control larger or smaller in one direction only. The lop and bottom handles control the height of the control; the left and right handles change the control's width. When the mouse pointer touches a corner handle of a selected control, the pointer becomes a diagonal double arrow. You can then drag the sizing handle until the control is the desired size. If the mouse pointer touches a side handle in a selected control, the pointer changes to a horizontal or vertical double-headed arrow.

You can resize a control in very small increments by holding ihe Shift key and pressing the arrow keys. This technique also works with multiple controls selected. Using this technique, a control changes by only t pixel at a time (or moves to the nearest grid line if Snap to Grid is selected in the Layout ribbon's Control Layout group). When you double-click on any of the sizing handles, Access resizes a control to a best fit for the text in the cofltrol. This is especially handy if you increase the font size and then notice that the text is cut off either at the bottom or to the right. For label controls, note that this best-fit sizing adjusts the size vertically and horizontally, though text controls are resized only vertically. This is because when Access is in form-design mode, it can't predict how much of a field to display — the field name and field contents can be radically different. Sometimes, Access doesn't correctly resize the label.

Sizing controls automatically

The Size group on the Layout ribbon has several commands that help size controls based on the value of the data, the grid, or other controls. Here are the Size commands:

- **To Fit:** Adjusts control height and width for the font of the text they contain.
- **To Tallest:** Makes selected controls the height of the tallest selected control.
- **To Shortest**: Makes selected controls the height of the shortest selected control.
- **To Grid:** Moves all sides of selected controls in or out to meet the nearest points on the grid.
- **To Widest:** Makes selected controls the width of the widest selected control.
- **To Narrowest:** Makes selected controls the height of the narrowest selected control.

You can access many commands by right-clicking after selecting multiple controls. When you right-click on multiple controls, a shortcut menu displays choices to size and align controls.

Moving a control

After you select a control, you can easily move it, using either one of these methods:

- Click on the control and hold the mouse button down; the cursor changes to a four-directional arrow. Drag the mouse to move the control to a new location.
- Click once to select the control and move the mouse over any of the highlighted edges; the cursor changes to a four-directional arrow. Drag the mouse to move the control to a new location.
- Select the control and use the arrow keys on the keyboard to move the control. Using this technique, a control changes by only 1 pixel at a time (or moves to the nearest grid line if Snap to Grid is selected in the Layout ribbon's Control Layout group).

When an attached label is created automatically with another control, it is called a compound control If a control has an attached label, the label and control move together; it doesn't matter whether you click the control or the label. You can move a control separately from an attached label by pointing to the Move handle of the control and then dragging it. Move the label control separately from the other control by pointing to the Move handle of the label control and dragging it separately.

Aligning controls

You may want to move several controls so that they are all aligned {lined up). The Layout ribbons Control Alignment group has several options described in the following list:

- **Left:** Aligns the left edge of the selected controls with that of the leftmost selected control.
- **Right:** Aligns the right edge of the selected controls with that of the rightmost selected control.
- **Top:** Aligns the top edge of the selected controls with that of the topmost selected control.
- **Bottom:** Aligns the bottom edge of the selected controls with that of the bottommost selected control.
- **To Grid**: Aligns the top-left comers of the selected controls to the nearest grid point.

You can align any number of selected controls by selecting a command from the Control Alignment group. When you choose one of the commands, Access uses the control that is the closest to the desired selection as the model for the alignment. For example, suppose that you have three con-trols and you want to left-align them. They are aligned on the basis of the control farthest lo the left in the group of the three controls. Use the Snap to Grid command in the Layout ribbons Control Layout group to align new controls to the grid as you draw or place them on a form. It also aligns existing controls to the grid when you move or resize them. Snap to Grid is on when it appears selected in the ribbon.

When Snap to Grid is on and you draw a new control by clicking on the form and dragging to size the control, Access aligns the four corners of the control to points on the grid. When you place a new control by clicking the control in the Field List and then dragging it to the form, only the upper-left comer is aligned. As you move or resize existing controls, Access 2010 lets you move only from grid point to grid point. When Snap to Grid is off, Access 2010 ignores the grid and lets you place a control any-where on the form or report.

You can temporarily turn Snap to Grid off by pressing the Ctrl key before you create a control (or while sizing or moving it). You can change the grid's fineness (number of dots) from form to form by using the Grid X and Grid Y Form properties. (Higher numbers indicate greater fineness.) The Layout ribbon's Position group contains commands to adjust the space between multiple controls. These commands change the space between controls on the basis of the space between the first two selected controls. If the controls are across the screen, use horizontal spacing. If they are down the screen, use vertical spacing. These commands are as follows:

- **Equal Horizontal:** Makes the horizontal space between selected controls equal. You must select three or more controls for this command to work,

- **Increase Horizontal:** Increases the horizontal space between selected controls by one grid unit.
- **Decrease Horizontal:** Decreases the horizontal space between selected controls by one grid unit.
- **Equal Vertical:** Makes the vertical space between selected controls equal. You must select three or more controls for this command to work.
- **Increase Vertical:** Increases the vertical space between selected controls by one grid unit.
- **Decrease Vertical:** Decreases the vertical space between selected controls by one grid unit.

Aligning controls aligns the control boxes only. If you want to align the text within the controls (also known as justifying the text), you must use the Design ribbon's Font group and select the Left, Right, or Center commands.

Modifying the appearance of a control

To modify the appearance of a control, select the control and click on commands that modify that control, such as commands in the Font group or Controls group. To change the text color and font of the Description label, follow these steps:

1. Click Description label on the form.
2. In the Design ribbon's Font group, change the Font Size to 14, click the Bold command, and change the Font Color to blue.
3. Resize the Description label so the larger text fits (remember, you can double-click any of the sizing handles to autosize the label).

Modifying the appearance of multiple controls

To modify the appearance of multiple controls at once, select the controls and click on commands to modify the controls, such as commands in the Font group or Controls group. To change the text color and font of the Description, Category, and Cost labels and text boxes, follow these steps:

1. Select the three labels and three text boxes by dragging a selection box through them.
2. In the Design ribbon's Font group, change the Font Size to 14, click the Bold command, and change the Font Color to blue.
3. Resize the labels and text boxes so the larger text fits (remember, you can double-click any of the sizing handles to autosize the controls).

When multiple controls are selected, you can also move the selected controls together. When the cursor changes to the four-directional arrow, click and drag to move the selected controls. You can also change the size of all the controls at once by resizing one of the controls in the selection. All the selected controls increase or decrease by the same number of units.

Grouping controls

If you routinely change properties of multiple controls, you may want to group them together. To group controls together, select the controls by holding down the Shift key and clicking them or dragging the selection box through them. After the desired controls are selected, select the Group command from the Layout ribbon's Control Layout group. A box appears around the selected controls, indicating they're grouped together.

After you've grouped the controls together, whenever you click any of the controls inside the group, the entire group is selected. Double-click on a control to select just that one control. After a single control in the group is selected, you can click on any other control to select it.

To resize the entire group, put your mouse on the side you want to resize. After the double arrow appears, click and drag until you reach the desired size. Every control in the group changes in size. To move the entire group, click and drag the group to its new location. With grouped controls, you don't have to select all the controls every time you change something about them. To remove a group, select the group by clicking any field inside the group, then select the Ungroup command from the Layout ribbon's Control Layout group.

Deleting a control

You can delete a control by simply selecting it in the form's Design View and pressing the Delete key on your keyboard. The control and any attached labels will disappear. You can bring them back by immediately selecting Undo from the Quick Access toolbar. You can also select Cut from the Home ribbon's Clipboard group or Delete from the Home ribbon's Records group.

You can delete more than one control at a time by selecting multiple controls and pressing Delete. You can delete an entire group of controls by selecting the group and pressing Delete. If you have a control with an attached label, you can delete only the label by clicking the label itself and then selecting one of the delete methods. If you select the control, both the control and the label are deleted. To delete only the label of the Description control, follow the next set of steps (this exam-ple assumes that you have the Description text box control in your Form Design window):

1. Select the Description label control only.
2. Press Delete to remove the label from the form.

Attaching a label to a control

If you accidentally delete a label from a control, you can reattach it. To create and then reattach a label to a control, follow these steps:

1. Click the Label button on the Controls group.
2. Place the mouse pointer in the Form Design window.
   The mouse pointer becomes the Text Box button.
3. Click and hold down the mouse button where you want the control to begin; drag the"mouse to size the control.
4. Type Description: and click outside the control.
5. Select the Description label control.
6. Select Cut from the Home ribbon's Clipboard group.
7. Select the Description text box control.
8. Select Paste from the Home ribbon's Clipboard group to attach the label control to the text box control.

Another way to attach a label to a control is to click the informational icon next to the label. This informational icon lets you know that this label is unassociated with a control. Click the Associate Label with a Control command from the menu, and then select the control you want to associate the label with.

Copying a control

You can create copies of any control by copying it to the Clipboard and then pasting the copies where you want them. If you have a control for which you have entered many properties or speci-fied a certain format, you can copy it and revise only the properties (such as the control name and bound field name) to make it a different control. This capability is useful with a multiple-page form when you want to display the same values on different pages and in different locations, or when copying a control from one form to another.

Changing the control type

The Complete control is a check box. Although there are times you may want to use a check box to display a Boolean (Yes/No) data type, there are other ways to display the value, such as a toggle button. A toggle button is raised if it's true and depressed (or at least very unhappy) if it's false.

Use these steps to turn the check box into a toggle button:

1. Select the Complete label control (just the label control, not the check box).
2. Press the Delete key to delete the label control because it is not needed.
3. Right-click the Complete check box, and choose Change To > Toggle Button from the pop-up menu.
4. Resize the toggle button and click inside it to get the blinking cursor; then type Complete on the button as its caption.

Understanding Properties

Properties are named attributes of controls, fields, or database objects that are used to modify the characteristics of a control, field, or object. Examples of these attributes are the size, color, appearance, or name of an object. A property can also modify the behavior of a control, determining, for example, whether the control is read-only or editable and visible or not visible. Properties are used extensively in forms and reports to change the characteristics of controls. Each control on the form has properties. The form itself also has properties, as does each of its sections. The same is true for reports; the report itself has properties, as does each report section and individual control. The label control also has its own properties, even if it is attached to another control.

Everything from moving and resizing controls to changing fonts and colors that you do with the ribbon commands can be done by setting properties. In fact, all these commands do is change properties of the selected controls.

CHAPTER 7

Creating a Query in Microsoft Access 2010

Introduction

Queries are used to get information from the database in Microsoft Access 2010. This information can be any form.

Creating a Query

A query is nothing more than a saved version of your sort or filter criteria. By saving the particular sort or filter criteria as a query, you can select that query by name later.

Creating a Simple Query

If your databse table contains dozens of different fields, you may find it confusing to make sense of all your information. As an aid, a simple query strips away fields so you see only the fields containing data you want to see, such as a person's name and phone number but not her hire date or employee number.

To create a query, follow these steps:

1. Click the Create tab.
2. Click the Query Wizard icon in the Other group.

   The New Query dialog box appears.

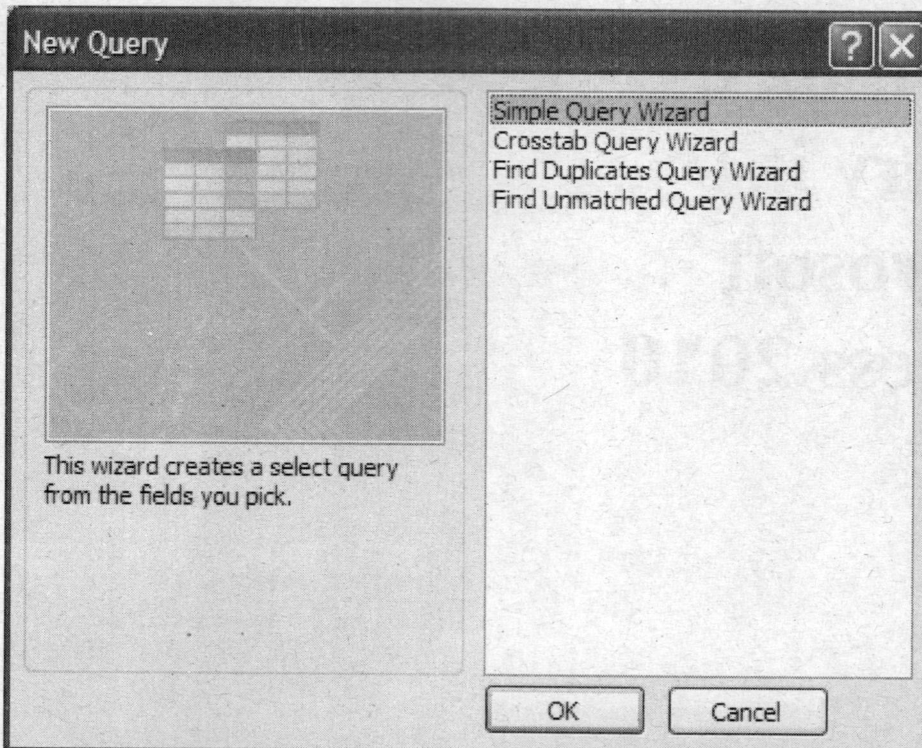

3. Click Simple Query Wizard and then click Ok.

   The Simple Query Wizard dialog box appears.
4. Click a field name listed in the Available Fields box and then click the > button.

   Access displays your chosen filed in the Selected Fields box.
5. Repeat Step 4 for each field you want to use in your query.
6. Click Next.

   Another dialog box appears. This dialog box asks whether you want to display a Detail or Summary (shows numerical information such as the total number of records found, the average value, and the minimum/maximum value) view of your data.

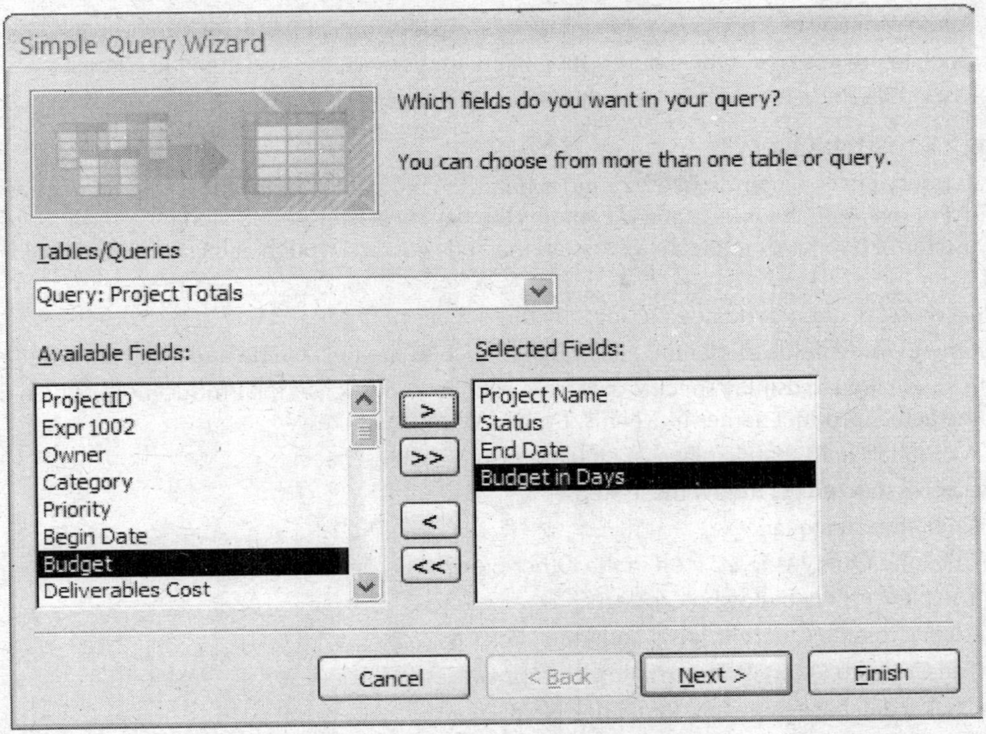

7. Select the Detail or Summary radio button and then click Next.

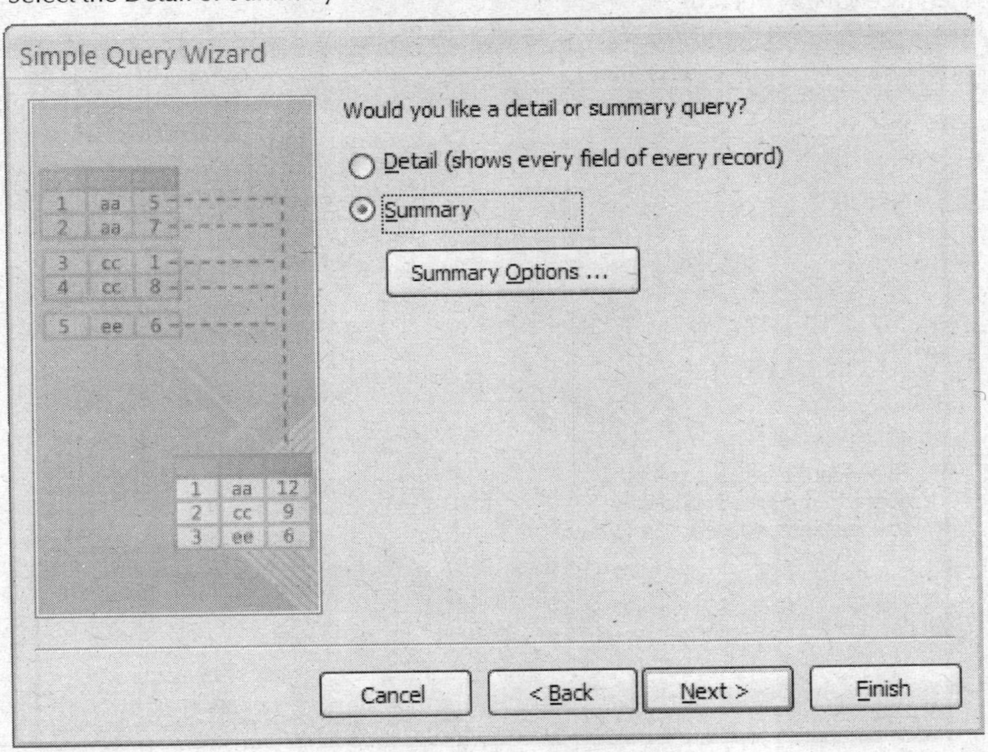

Another dialog box appears, asking you to type a descriptive name for your query.

8. Click to the text box, type a descriptive name for your query, and then click Finish.
9. Click the Office Button and then choose Save to save your query.

Creating a Crosstab Query

A crosstab query lets you combine tow or more fields to calculate and display a calculation based on a third field. For example, if your database contains the names of salespeople and the products they sold, you can use those two fields to create a crosstab that tells you how much each salesperson sold of each product.

To create a crosstab query, you need to identify three types of fields.

- One to three fields to identify each record (such as the First Name and Last Name fields)
- A single field to dsiplay specific data from each record (such as the Product field, which displays the actual product names like Nails, Barbed Wire, and Screws)
- A crosstab field that dsiplays a calculate result (such as Sales)

To create a crosstab query, follow these steps:

1. Click the Create tab.
2. Click the Query Wizard icon in the Other group.

   The New Query dialog box appears.
3. Click Crosstab Query Wizard and then click Ok.

   The Crosstab Query Wizard dialog box appears.
4. Click a database table and then click Next.

   Another Crosstab Query Wizard dialog box appears that asks for between one and three fields to identify each row (record).

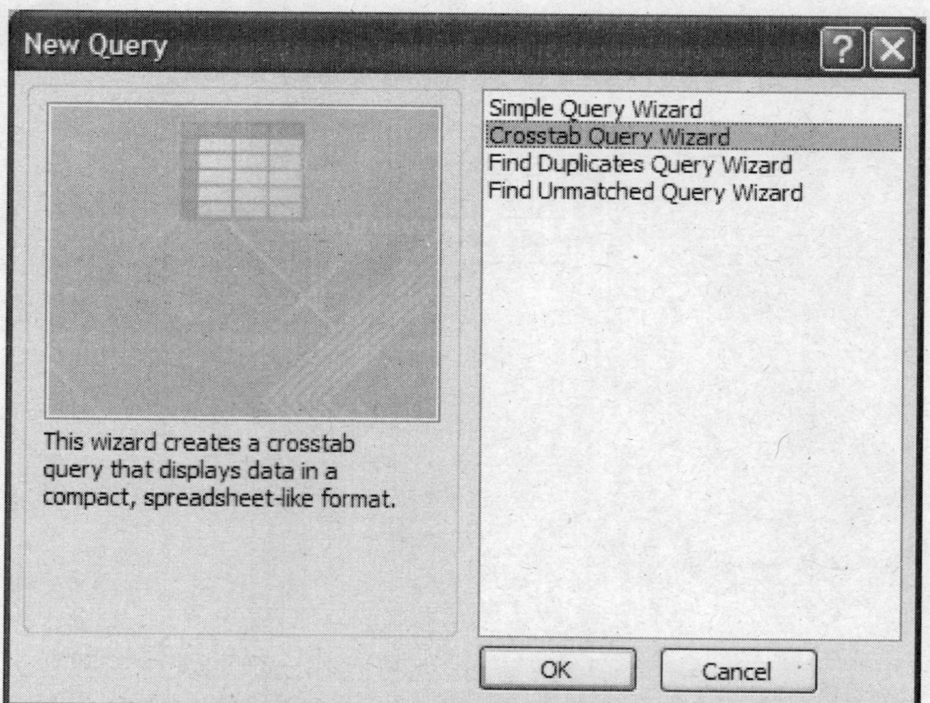

5. Click a field in the Available Fields box and then click the > button to move your chosen field to the Selected Fields box.
6. Repeat Step 5 for each additional field you want to include.
7. Click Next.

   Another dialog box appears, asking for a single field to use to crosstabular data with the fields you choose in Steps 5 and 6.
8. Click a field name and then click Next.
9. Click a field that contains numerical data and then click a matematical function that you want Access to calculate, such as Sum, Avg., or Count.
10. Click Next.

    Another dialog box appears.
11. Type a descriptive name for your query in the text box at the top of the dialog box and then click Finish.
12. Click the Office Button and choose Save to save your query.

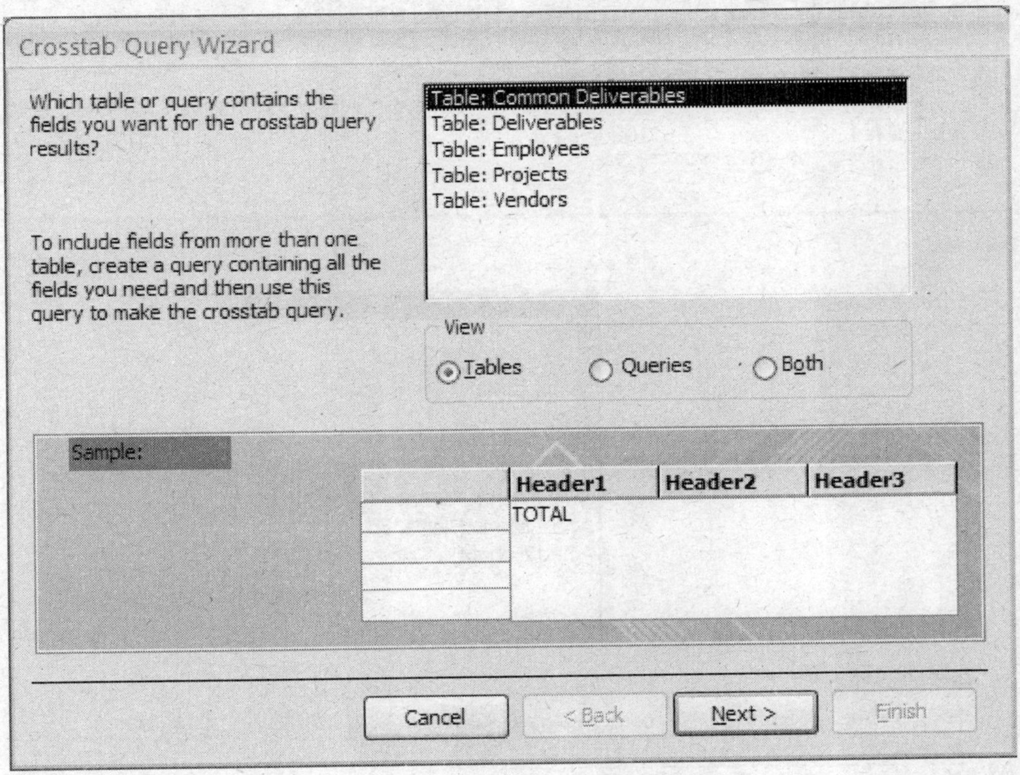

Working with the Table/Query Pane

A join line connects tables in the Query Designer. The join line connects ihe primary key in one table to the foreign key in another table.

The join line

A. join line represents the relationship between two tables in the Access database. In this example, a join

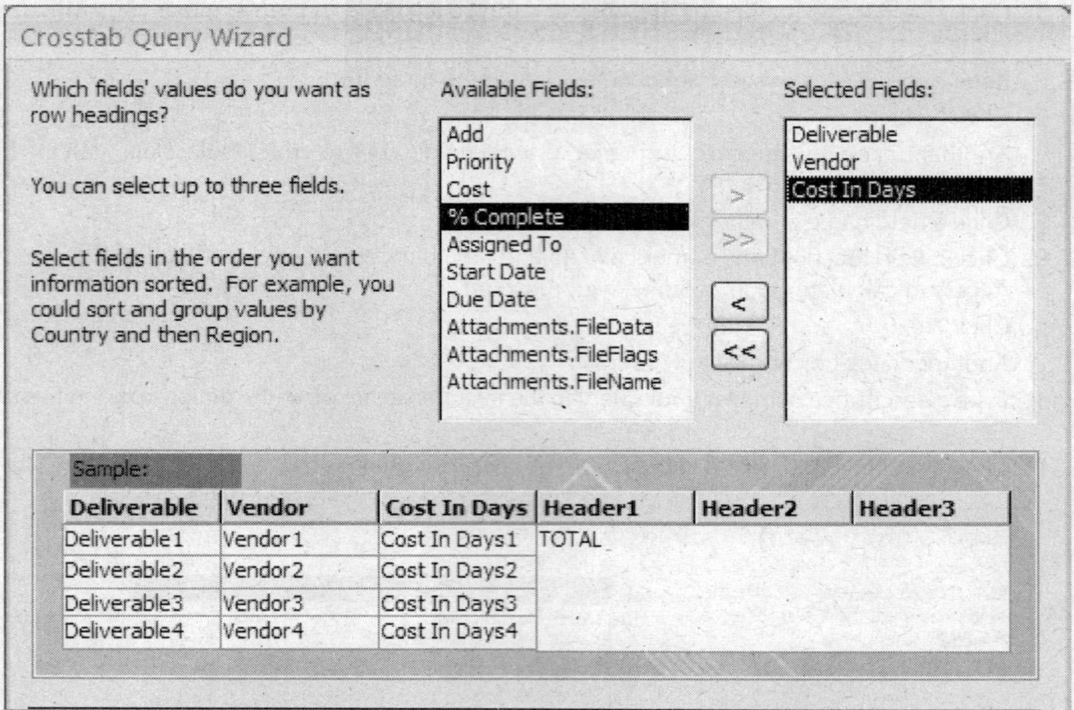
Crosstab Query Wizard
Which fields' values do you want as row headings?
You can select up to three fields.
Select fields in the order you want information sorted. For example, you could sort and group values by Country and then Region.
Available Fields:
Add
Priority
Cost
% Complete
Assigned To
Start Date
Due Date
Attachments.FileData
Attachments.FileFlags
Attachments.FileName
Selected Fields:
Deliverable
Vendor
Cost In Days
Sample:
Deliverable
Vendor
Cost In Days
Header1
Header2
Header3
Deliverable1
Vendor1
Cost In Days1
TOTAL
Deliverable2
Vendor2
Cost In Days2
Deliverable3
Vendor3
Cost In Days3
Deliverable4
Vendor4
Cost In Days4

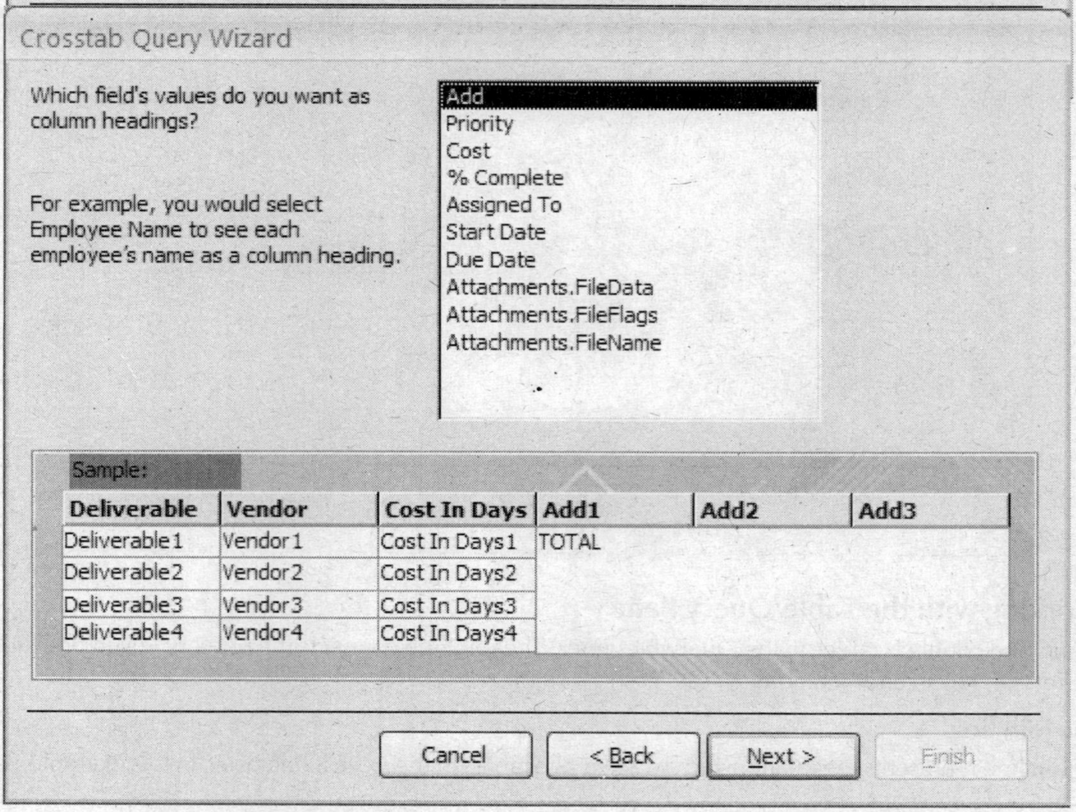
Crosstab Query Wizard
Which field's values do you want as column headings?
For example, you would select Employee Name to see each employee's name as a column heading.
Add
Priority
Cost
% Complete
Assigned To
Start Date
Due Date
Attachments.FileData
Attachments.FileFlags
Attachments.FileName
Sample:
Deliverable
Vendor
Cost In Days
Add1
Add2
Add3
Deliverable1
Vendor1
Cost In Days1
TOTAL
Deliverable2
Vendor2
Cost In Days2
Deliverable3
Vendor3
Cost In Days3
Deliverable4
Vendor4
Cost In Days4
Cancel
< Back
Next >
Finish

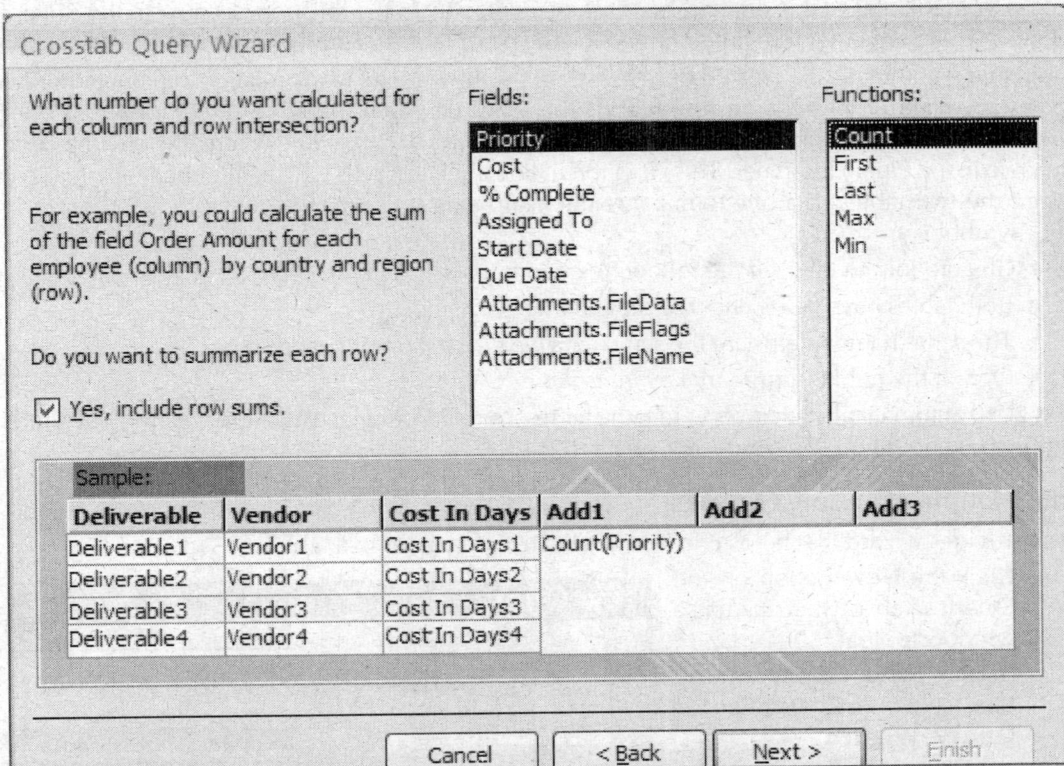
Crosstab Query Wizard
What number do you want calculated for each column and row intersection?
For example, you could calculate the sum of the field Order Amount for each employee (column) by country and region (row).
Do you want to summarize each row?
Yes, include row sums.
Fields:
Priority
Cost
% Complete
Assigned To
Start Date
Due Date
Attachments.FileData
Attachments.FileFlags
Attachments.FileName
Functions:
Count
First
Last
Max
Min
Sample:
Deliverable
Vendor
Cost In Days
Add1
Add2
Add3
Deliverable1
Vendor1
Cost In Days1
Count(Priority)
Deliverable2
Vendor2
Cost In Days2
Deliverable3
Vendor3
Cost In Days3
Deliverable4
Vendor4
Cost In Days4
Cancel
< Back
Next >
Finish

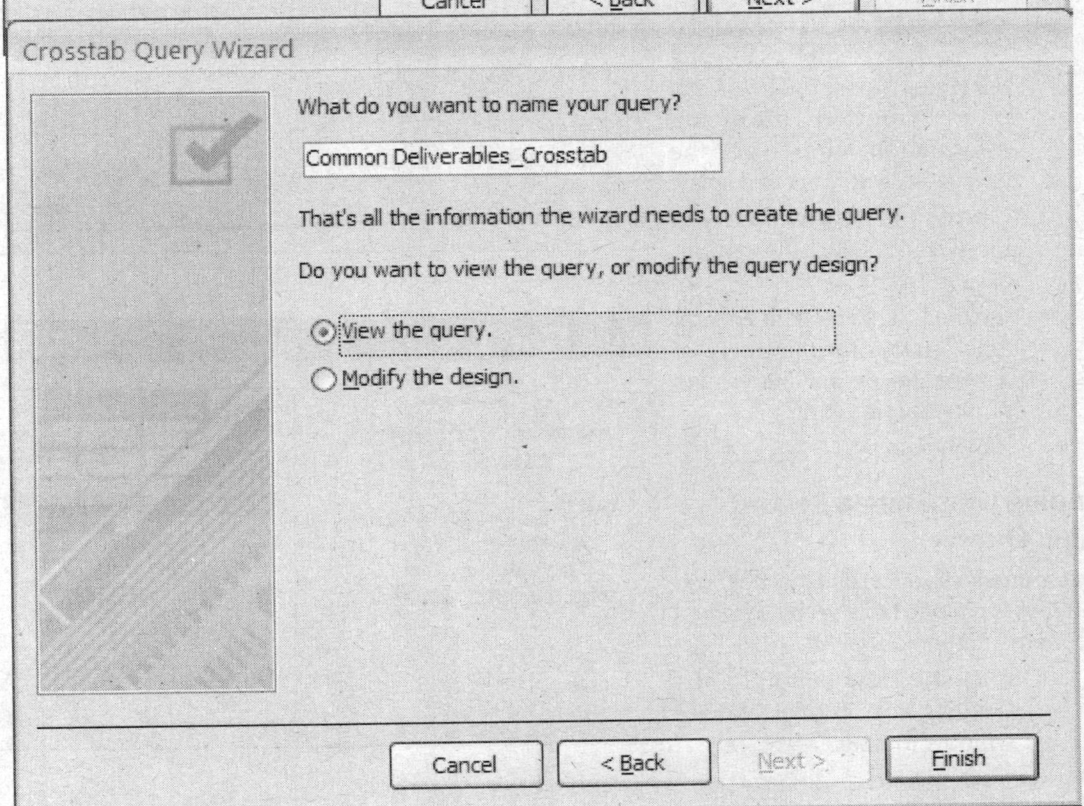
Crosstab Query Wizard
What do you want to name your query?
Common Deliverables_Crosstab
That's all the information the wizard needs to create the query.
Do you want to view the query, or modify the query design?
View the query.
Modify the design.
Cancel
< Back
Next >
Finish

line goes from tblSales to tblContacts, connecting ContactID in the tblContacts table to the Buyer field in tblSales. There are other join lines connecting the other tables in this query

The join line is automatically created because relationships were set in the relationship builder. If Access already knows about the relationship, it adds the join line when the tables are added to a query. If Referential Integrity is set on the relationship, Access displays a thicker line where the join line connects to the table in the Query Designer. This variation in line thickness tells you that Referential Integrity is set between the two tables. If a one-to-many relationship exists, the many-side table is indicated by an infinity symbol (∞).

Access will auto join to tables if the following conditions are met:

- Both tables have fields with the same name.
- The same-named fields are the same data type (text, numeric, and so on).
- One of the field is a primary key in its table.

Access 2010 automatically attempts to join the tables if a relationship exists. Access cannot set referential integrity on the join line.

Finding Duplicate using Queries

Access provides wizard that helps you find duplicate field values in a table.

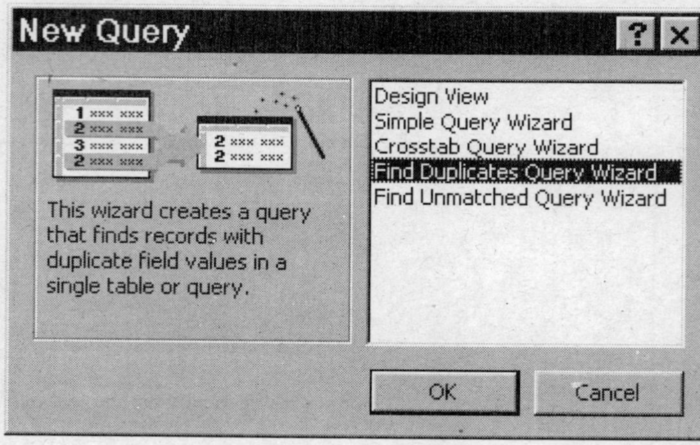

1. Click the **New** button on the Queries tab of the Database window toolbar.
2. In the **New Query** dialog box, select **Find Duplicates Query Wizard**.
3. Click Ok.
4. Follow the wizard steps to select the table, choose the fields that might contain duplicate information, and select the other fields you want to display.
5. On the first two windows of the wizard, select the options as required.
6. On the last page of the wizard, type a name for the query or accept the default name and click **Finish**.
7. Run the query.

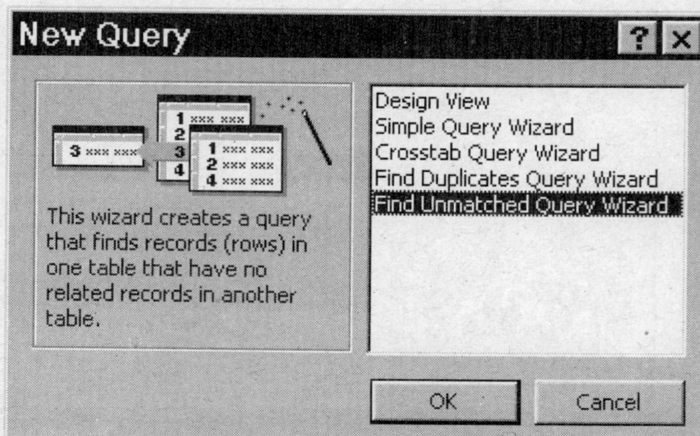

Finding Unmatched Records using Query

Access provides you wizard that help you find records in one table with no related record in another table.

1. Click the **New** button on the Queries tab of the Database window toolbar.

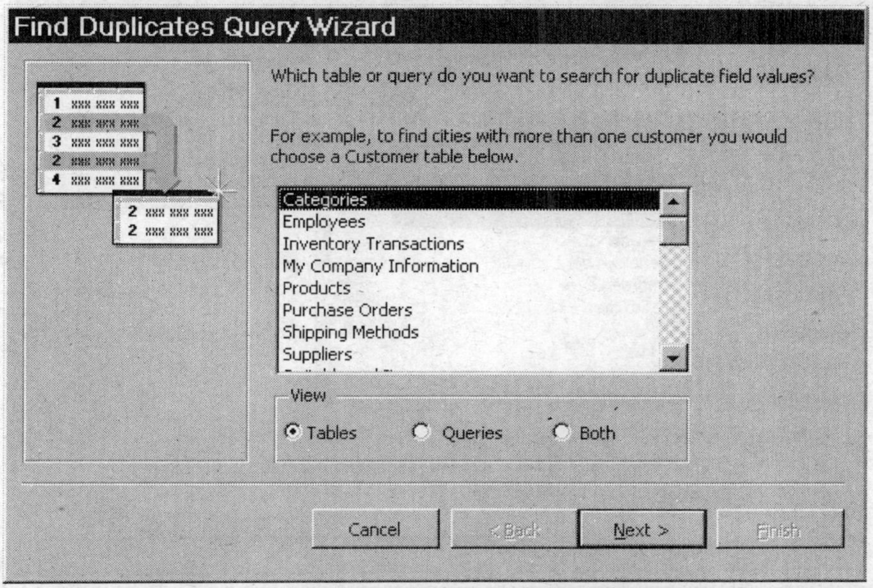

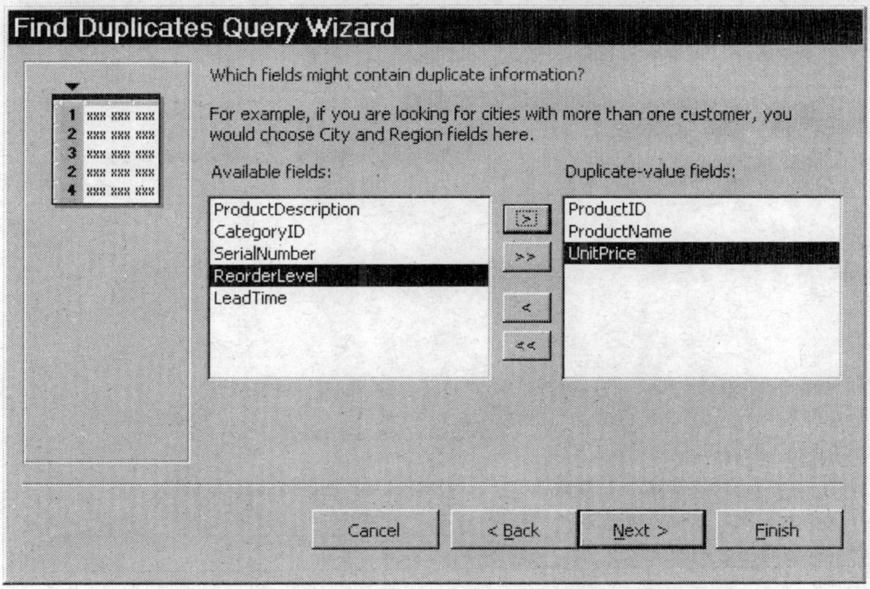

2. In the New Query dialog box, select **Find Unmatched Query Wizard**.
3. Click Ok.
4. Follow the wizard steps to select the first table, select the table with the related records, choose the field in each record containing the same information, and select the fields you want to display.
5. On the last page, type a name for the query or accept the default name and click **Finish**.
6. Run the query.

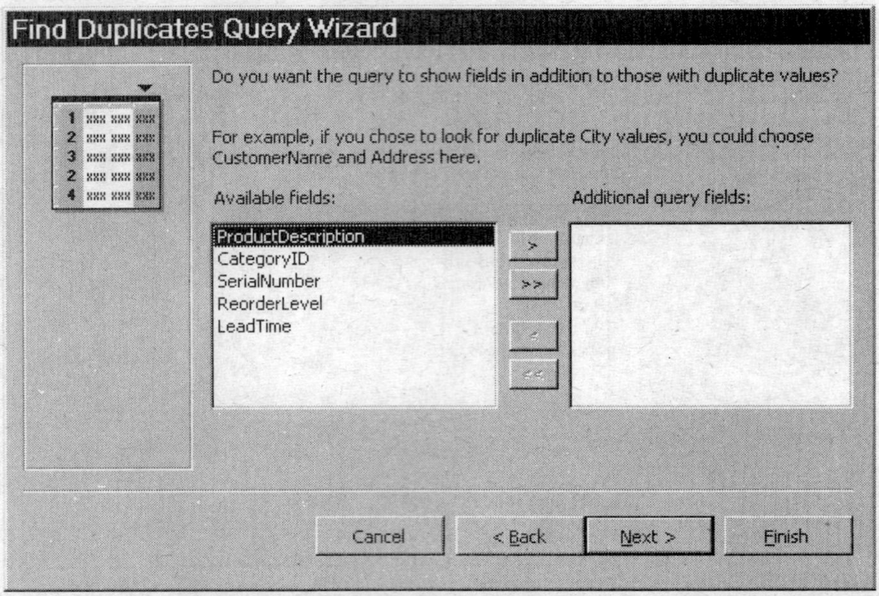

Manipulating the Field List window

Each Field List window begins at a fixed size, which shows approximately four fields and perhaps 12 characters for each field. Each Field List is a resizable window and can be moved within the Query Designer. If there are more fields than will show in the Field List window, a scroll bar enables you to scroll through the fields in the Field List.

When you're working with many tables, ihese join lines can become confusing as they cross or overlap. As you scroll through the table, the line eventually becomes visible, and the field it is linked to becomes obvious.

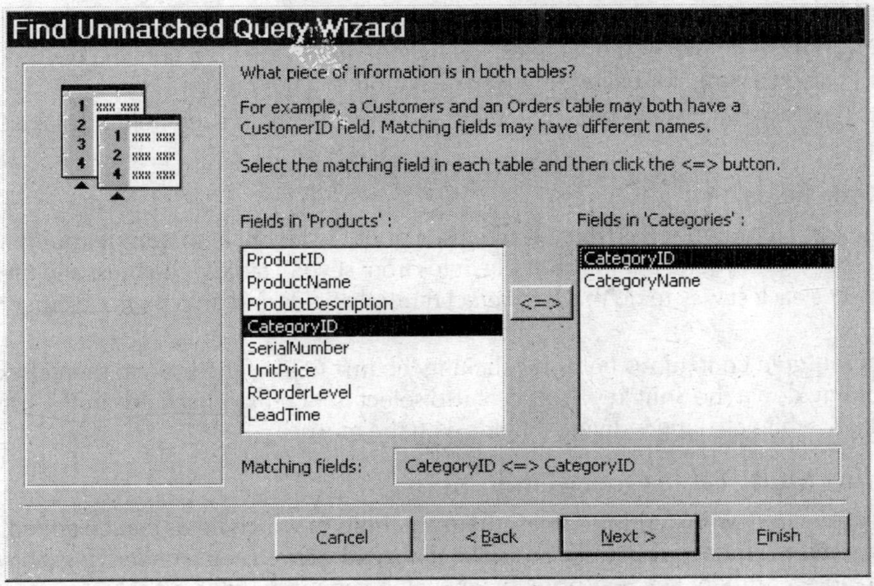

Moving a table

Move the Field Lists by grabbing the title bar of a Field List (where the name of the table is) with the mouse and dragging the Field List to a new location. You may want to move the Field Lists for a better working view or to clean up a confusing query diagram. You can move and resize the Field Lists anywhere in the top pane. Access saves the arrangement when you save and close the query. Generally speaking, the Field Lists will appear in the same configuration the next time you open the query.

Removing a table

There are times when you need to remove tables from a query. Any table can be removed from the Query window. Use the mouse to select the table you want to remove in the top pane of the Query window and press the Delete key. Or right-click on the Field List and choose Removed Table from the shortcut menu.

Adding more tables

You may decide to add more tables to a query or you may accidentally delete a table and need to add it back. You accomplish this task by clicking on the Show Table button on the Query Setup group in the Design ribbon. The Show Table dialog box appears in response to this action.

Adding Fields from More Than One Table

You add fields from more than one table to the query in exactly the same way as when you're working with a single table. You can add fields one at a time, multiple fields as a group, or all the fields from a table.

If you select the field from the drop-down list in the Field cell, you see the name of the table first, followed by a period and the field name. For example, the ProductID in tblsalesLineItems is displayed as tblsalesLineItems.ProductID. This helps you select the right field name. Using ihis method, you can select a common field name from a specific table-The easiest way to select fields is still to double-click the field names in the top half of the Query Designer. To do so, you may have to resize the Field Lists to see the fields that you want to select.

Viewing the table names

When you're working with two or more tables, the field names in the QBE grid can become confusing. You may find yourself asking, for example, just which table the field is from.

Access automatically maintains the table name that is associated with each field displayed in the QBE grid.

Adding multiple fields

The process of adding multiple fields in a multi-table query is identical to adding multiple fields in a single-table query. When you're adding multiple fields from several tables, you must add them from one table at a lime. The easiest way to do this is to select multiple fields and drag them together down to the QBE grid.

You can select multiple contiguous fields by clicking the first field of the list and then clicking the last field while holding down the Shift key. You can also select noncontiguous fields in the list by holding down the Ctrl key while clicking individual fields with the mouse.

Understanding Multi-Table Query Limitations

When you create a query with multiple tables, there are limits to which fields can be edited. Generally, you can change data in a query's recordset, and your changes are saved in the underlying tables. The main exception is a table's primary key — a primary key value cannot be edited if referential integrity is in effect and if the field is part of a relationship.

To update a table from a query, a value in a specific record in the query must represent a single record in the underlying table. This means that you cannot update fields in a query that transforms data because most transformations group records and fields display aggregate information. Each field in a transformed recordset represents multiple fields in the underlying tables. There is no way to change the data in a transformed field and have it reflected in the underlying tables.

Updating limitations

In Access, the records in your tables may not always be updateable. Table 6-1 shows when a field in a table is updateable. As Table 6-1 shows, queries based on one-to-many relationships are updateable in both tables (depending on how the query was designed).

TABLE 6-1 Rules for Updating Queries

Type of Query or Field	*Updateable*	*Comments*
One table	Yes	
One-to-one relationship	Yes	
Results contains Memo field	Yes	Memo field updateable
Results contain Hyperlink	Yes	Hyperlink updateable
Results contain an OLE object	Yes	OLE object updateable
One-to-many relationship	Mostly	Restrictions based on design methodology {see text)
Many-to-one-to-many	No	Can update data in a form or data access page if RecordType = Recordset
Two or more tables with no join line	No	Must have a join to determine updateability
Crosstab	No	Creates a snapshot of the data
Totals Query (Sum, Avg, and so on)	No	Works with grouped data creating a snapshot

Unique Value property is Yes	No	Shows unique records only in a snapshot
SQL-specific queries	No	Union and pass-through work with ODBC data
Calculated field	No	Will recalculate automatically
Read-only fields	No	If opened read-only or on read-only drive
Permissions denied	No	Insert, replace, or delete are not granted
ODBC tables with no primary key	No	A primary key (unique index) must exist
Paradox table with no primary key	No	A primary key file must exist
Locked by another user	No	Cannot be updated while a field is locked by another

Overcoming query limitations

The above table shows that there are times when queries and fields in tables are not updateable. As a general rule, any query that performs aggregate operations or uses an ODBC (Open DataBase Connectivity) data source is not updateable. Most other queries can be updated. When your query has more than one table and some of the tables have a one-to-many relationship, there may be fields that are not updateable (depending on the design of the query).

Updating a unique index (primary key)

If a query uses two tables involved in a one-to-many relationship, the query must include the pri-mary key from the one-side table. Access must have the primary key value so that they can find the related records in the two tables.

Replacing existing data in a query with a one-to-many relationship

Normally, all the fields in the many-side table (such as the tblsales table) are updateable in a one-to-many query. All the fields (except the primary key) in the one-side table (tblCustorners) can be updated. Normally, this is sufficient for most database application purposes. Also, the primary key field is rarely changed in the one-side table because it is the link to the records in the joined tables.

Design tips for updating fields in queries

If you want to add records to both tables of a one-to-many relationship, include the foreign key from the many-side table and show the field in the datasheet. After doing this, records can be added starling with either the one-side or many-side table. The one side's primary key field is auto-matically copied to the many side's join field.

If you want to add records to multiple tables in a form (covered in Chapters 7 and 8), remember to include all (or most) of the fields from both tables. Otherwise, you will not have a complete record of data in your form.

Creating and Working with Query Joins

By default, an Access query returns only records where data exists on both sides of a relationship. This means, for instance, that a query that extracts data from the Contacts table and the Sales table only returns records where contacts have actually placed sales, and will not show contacts who haven't yet placed a sale. If a contact record is not matched by at least one sales record, the contact data is not returned by the query. This means that, sometimes, the query does not return all of the records that you expect it to produce.

The situation described in the preceding paragraph is called an inner join, or an equi-join. Although this is the most common join type between tables in a query, there are instances where users want to see all of the data in a table (like the tblcontacts table in the preceding example), whether or not those records are matched in another table.

In fact, users often want to specifically see records that are not matched on the other side of the join. Consider a sales department that wants to know all the contacts who have not made a sale in the last year. You must modify the default query join characteristics in order to process this type of query. You can create joins between tables in these three ways:

- By creating relationships between the tables when you design the database.
- By selecting two tables for the query that have a field in common that has the same name and data in both tables. The field is a primary key field in one of the tables.
- By creating joins in the query designer at the time you create the query.

The first two methods occur automatically in the Query Design window. Relationships between tables are displayed in the Query Designer when you add the related tables to a query It also creates an automatic join between two tables that have a common field, provided that field is a primary key in one of the tables and the Enable Auto Join choice is selected (by default) in the Options dialog box. If relationships are set in the relationship builder, you may add a table to a query and it will not automatically be related to another table, as in these examples:

- The two tables have a common field, but it is not the same name.
- A table is not related and cannot be logically related to the other table (for example, tblcontacts cannot directly join the tblSalesLineItems table).

If you have two tables that are not automatically joined and you need to relate them, you join them in the Query Design window. Joining tables'in the Query Design window does not create a perma-nent relationship between the tables. Rather, the join (relationship) applies only to the tables while the query operates.

Tables in a query have to be joined in some fashion or other. Including two tables with nothing in common (for instance, a query based on tblcontacts and tblProducts, with nothing in between them) means that Access has no way to know which records in the tblcontacts table match which records in the tblProducts table. Unless there is some way to relate the tables to one another, the query returns unusable data.

CHAPTER 8

Creating a Report in Microsoft Access 2010

Introduction

Reports are used to print information extracted from the database in Microsoft Access 2010. This report can be printed in various styles, as would read in the chapter.

Creating a Report

Each software has its own method of giving the output in the form of a print out, which can either be on printer or on screen. Access also has the same. But for this you have to first create a report design and then send it either to printer or monitor.

Creating Report using Wizard

The easiest way to create a report is to use the Report Wizard, which guides you step by step through arranging and selecting which data to print on a report along with sorting your data at the same time.

To use the Report Wizard, follow these steps:

1. Click the Create tab.
2. Click the Report Wizard icon in the Reports group.

   The Report Wizard dialog box appears.
3. Click in the Tables/Queries list box and choose the table or query that contains the data you want to print in a report.
4. Click a field in the Available Fields box and then click this > button. Report this step for each additional field you want to display in your report.
5. Click Next.

   Another dialog box appears, asking whether you want to group your data by a speecific field such as Last Name or Employee Number.
6. Click a field name displayed in the box and then click the > button. Repeat this step for each additional field you want to use to group your data on the report.
7. Click Next.

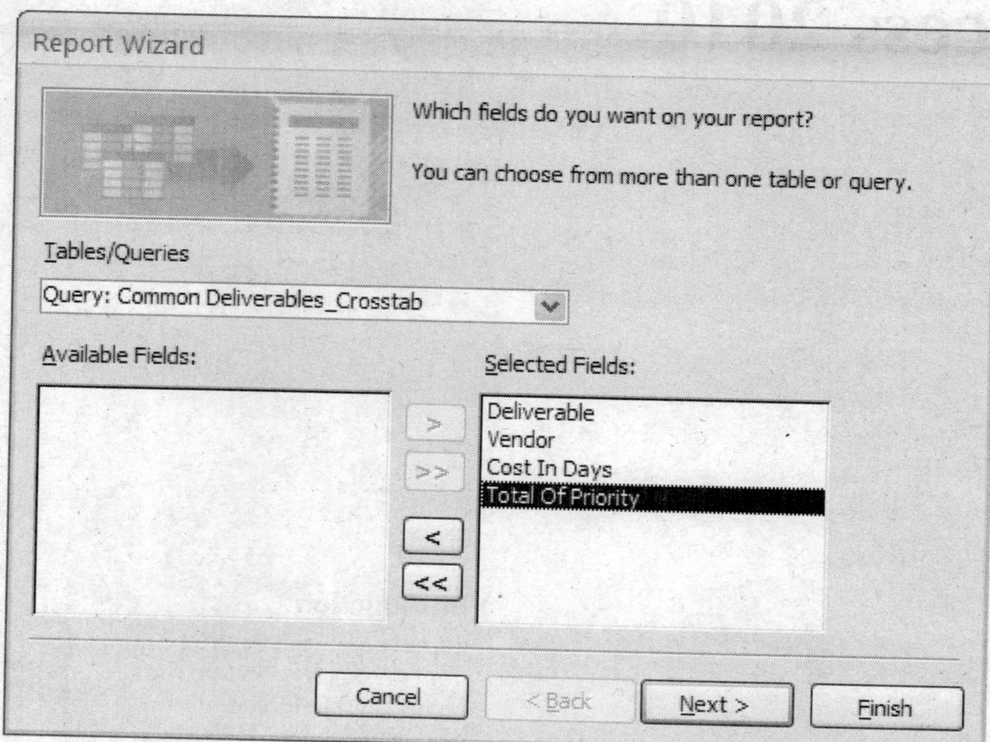

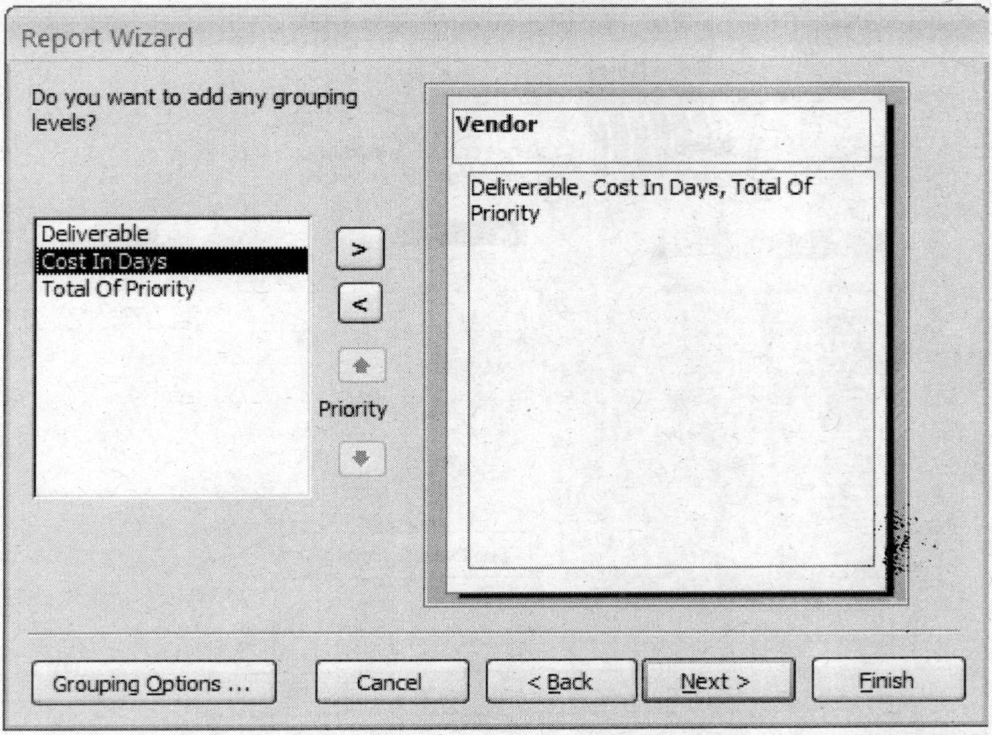

Another dialog box appears, asking you to choose up to four fiels to use for sorting your data in your report.

8. Click in a list box and choose a field to sort your data.

   Data will be sorted by the order chosen here for each additional field you sort on.

9. Click the Ascending button to change the soring criteria from Ascending to Descending and vice versa.

10. Click Next.

    Another dialog box appears.

11. Select a radio button under the Layout group, such as Stepped or Outline.

12. Select on a radio button in the Orientation group, such as Portrait or Landscape.

13. Click Next.

    Another dialog box appears, asking you to choose a style for your report. The preview to the left will give you an indication of what the printed report will look like.

14. Click Next.

    Another dialog box appears, asking you for a descriptive name for your report.

15. Type a descriptive name for your report and then click Finish.

    Access displays your report.

16. Right-click the Report tab.

    A pop-up menu appears.

17. Click Close.

    A dialog box appears.

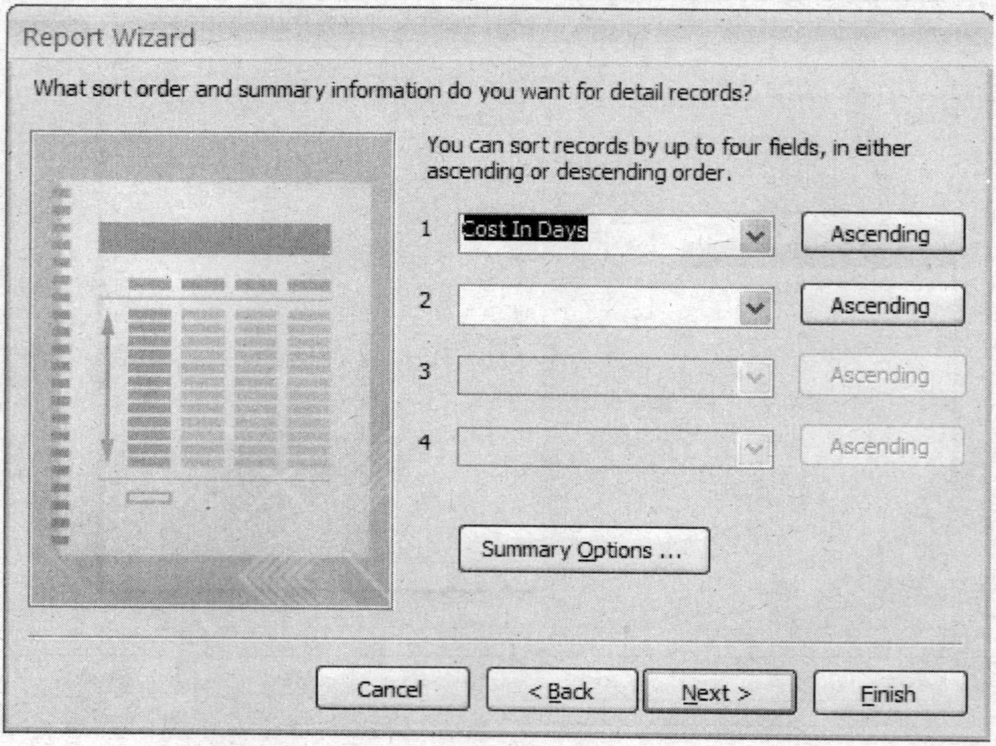
Report Wizard
What sort order and summary information do you want for detail records?
You can sort records by up to four fields, in either ascending or descending order.
1 Cost In Days
Ascending
2
Ascending
3
Ascending
4
Ascending
Summary Options ...
Cancel
< Back
Next >
Finish

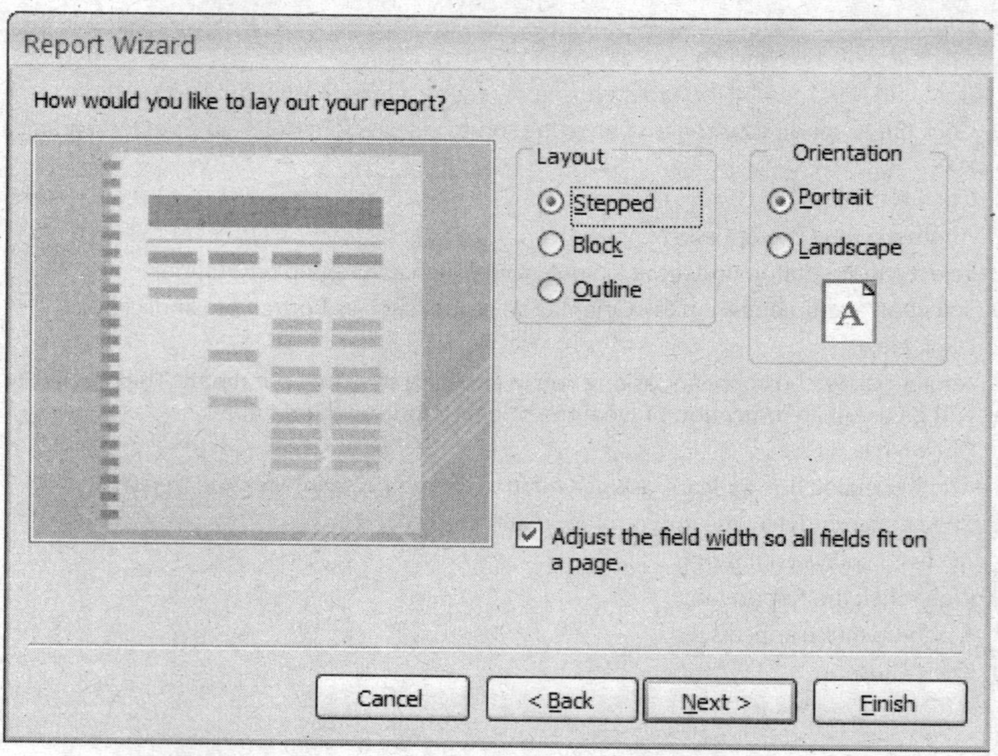
Report Wizard
How would you like to lay out your report?
Layout
Stepped
Block
Outline
Orientation
Portrait
Landscape
A
Adjust the field width so all fields fit on a page.
Cancel
< Back
Next >
Finish

18. Click Yes.

    Access saves your report for future use and removes it from view.

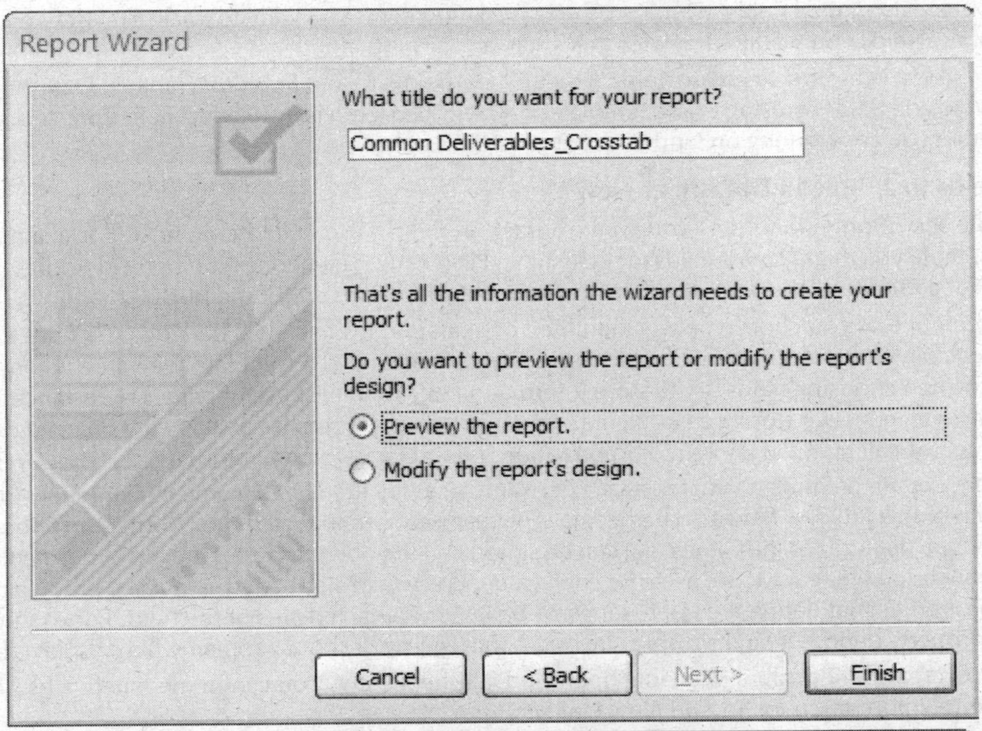

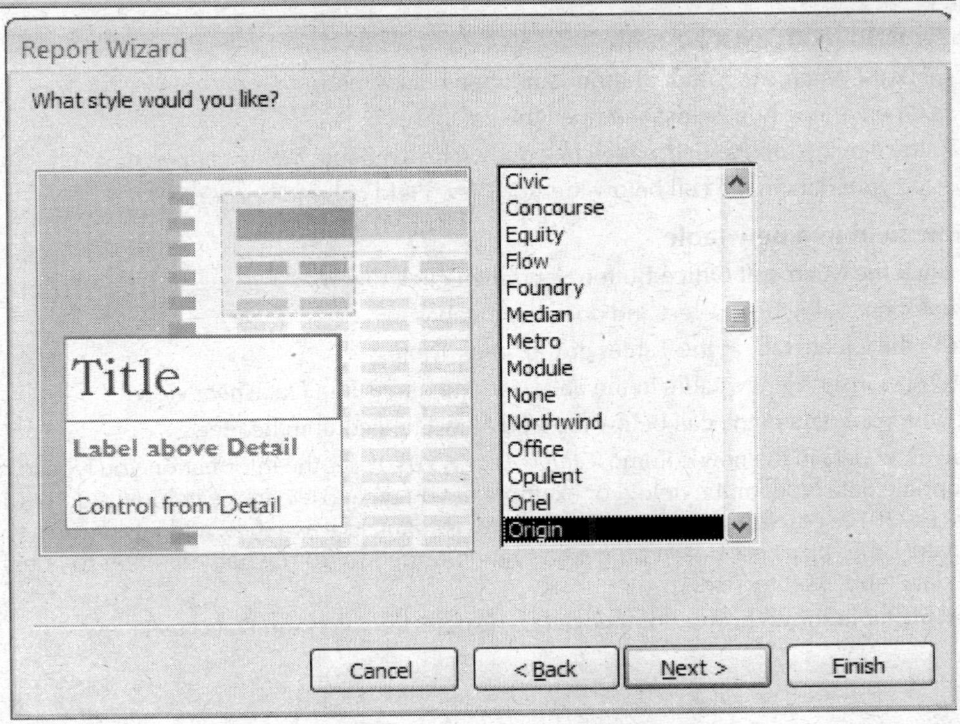

Insert, add, or create a new field in a table

When you create a database you store your data in tables — subject-based lists of rows and columns. Columns are also called fields, which are the information items you want to track. You define a table in terms of the fields you want to track for that subject.

This article explains how to create fields. You will learn how to add fields to a table in Datasheet view, and how to add fields by using a field template. You will also learn how to add a field from another table to the table you are working on, and how to set a field's data type.

Add fields to a table in Datasheet view

You store the information items you want to track in fields (also called columns). For example, in a Contacts table you might create fields for LastName, FirstName, Telephone Number and Address, among others. For a Products table you might create Product Name, Product ID and Price.

It is important that you choose fields carefully. For example, it's usually a bad idea to create a field to store a calculated value. You can usually have Office Access 2010 calculate the value when needed instead. When choosing fields, try to store information in its smallest useful parts. For instance, instead of a FullName, consider storing a LastName and a FirstName. Generally speaking, if you need to report, sort, search or calculate on an item of information, put it in a column by itself.

A field has certain defining characteristics. For example, every field has a Name that uniquely identifies the field within a table. A field also has a data type that's chosen to match the information to be stored. The data type determines the values that can be stored and the operations that can be performed, as well as how much storage space to set aside for each value. Every field also has an associated group of settings called properties that define the appearance or behavior characteristics of the field. For example, the Format property defines a field's display layout — that is, how it should appear when displayed.

When you create a new table, the table opens in Datasheet view. You can immediately add a field by typing some information in the Add New Field column.

Add a new field to an existing table

1. Click the Microsoft Office Button , and then click Open.
2. In Open dialog box, select and open the database.
3. In the Navigation Pane, double-click one of the available tables to open it.
4. Type your data in the cell below the Add New Field column header.

Add a new field to a new table

1. Click the Microsoft Office Button , and then click Open.
2. In Open dialog box, select and open the database.
3. On the Create tab, in the Tables group, click Table.

   Access inserts a new table in the database and opens it in Datasheet view.
4. Type your data in the cell below the Add New Field column header.

When you enter data in the new column, Office Access 2010 uses the information you type to recognize the appropriate data type for the field. For example, if you type a date in the column, such as 1/1/2006, Office Access 2010 sees the information you entered, recognizes it as a date, and sets the data type for the field to Date/Time. If Access doesn't have enough information from what you enter to guess the data type, the data type is set to Text.

The following table shows how automatic data type detection works in Datasheet view.

If you type:	*Office Access 2010 creates a field with a data type of:*
John	Text
http://www.contoso.com	Hyperlink
	You can use any valid Internet protocol prefix. For example, http://, https://, and mailto: are valid prefixes.
50000	Number, Long Integer
50,000	Number, Long Integer
50,000.99	Number, Double
50000.389	Number, Double
12/31/2006	Date/Time
The date and time formats recognized are those of your user locale.	
December 31, 2006	Date/Time
10:50:23	Date/Time
10:50 am	Date/Time
17:50	Date/Time
$12.50	The currency symbol recognized is that of your user locale. Currency
21.75	Number, Double
123.00%	Number, Double
3.46E+03	Number, Double

In addition to determining the data type, Office Access 2010 may set the Format property, depending on what you enter. For example, if you type 10:50 am, Access sets the data type Date/Time and the Format property to Medium Time.

If you want to explicitly set the data type and format for a field, overriding the choice that Office Access 2010 makes, you can do so by using the commands in the Data Type & Formatting group on the Home tab.

Explicitly set the data type

1. On the Datasheet tab, in the Data Type & Formatting group, click the arrow in the drop-down list next to Data Type, and then select a data type.
2. Click the data type you want.

Explicitly set the format

1. On the Datasheet tab, in the Data Type & Formatting group, click the arrow in the drop-down list next to Format, and then select a format.
2. Click the format you want.

When you add a field by typing information into the cell below the Add New Field header, Office Access 2010 automatically assigns a name to the field. These names start with Field1 for the first field, Field2 for the second field, and so on. It is a good practice to use more descriptive field names. You can rename the field by right-clicking its header, and then clicking Rename Column on the shortcut menu.

Field names can consist of up to 64 characters (letters or numbers), including spaces. You should try to give fields descriptive names so that you can easily identify them when you view or edit records. For example, you might use field names such as Last Name, Address, and Home Phone.

Add fields by using field templates

Sometimes it is easier to choose from a predefined list of fields than to manually create a field. You can use the Field Templates task pane to choose from a list of predefined fields. Office Access 2010 comes with a set of built-in field templates that can save you considerable time when you create fields. To create a new field using a field template, you display the Field Templates pane, and then drag and drop one or more templates to the table that is opened in Datasheet view.

A field template is a predefined set of characteristics and properties that describes a field. The field template definition includes a field name, a data type, a setting for the field's format property, and also a number of other field properties that, when taken together, form a model that serves as the basis for creating a new field.

1. Ensure that your table is in Datasheet view.
2. On the Datasheet tab, in the Fields & Columns group, click New Field.
3. The Field Templates pane appears.
4. Select one or more fields in the Field Templates pane and drag them to the table. When the insertion line appears, drop the fields in position.
5. The fields appear in the datasheet.

Field templates are models. They provide a basis from which you can create a new field. But it is not the only basis from which you can create a new field. In addition to creating a new field from a field template, you can also create a new field from an existing field in another table.

Add a field from an existing table

If you are using a database that contains multiple tables, you can add a field from another table. In fact, chances are good that some of those tables are related. In a relational database, you store information in separate subject-based tables, and then define relationships to provide your database management system with what it needs to bring the information together as needed. Office Access 2010 allows you to create a new field by adding it from another related table, or by adding it from another table for which you have not created a relationship. You add the field by using the Field List, which shows you fields available in other tables in your database.

Open the Field List pane

- On the Datasheet tab, in the Fields & Columns group, click Add Existing Fields.

The Field List pane appears.

The Field List pane lists all of the other tables in your database, grouped into categories. When you work with a table in Datasheet view, two categories appear in the Field List pane: Fields available in related tables, and Fields available in other tables. The first category lists all of the tables with which the table you have open has a relationship. The second category lists all of the tables with which your table does not have a relationship.

When you click the plus sign (+) next to a table to, you see a list of all of the fields available in that table. To add a field to your table, drag and drop the field you want from the Field List pane to the table in Datasheet view.

Add a field from the Field List pane

1. On the Datasheet tab, in the Fields & Columns group, click Add Existing Fields.
2. The Field List pane appears.
3. Click the plus sign (+) next to a table to display the list of fields in that table.
4. Drag the field you want from the Field List pane to the table in Datasheet view.

5. When the insertion line appears, drop the field in position.
6. The Lookup Wizard starts.
7. Follow the instruction to complete the wizard.
8. After you have completed the wizard, the field appears in the table in Datasheet view.

When you drag and drop a field from an unrelated table and then complete the Lookup Wizard, a new one-to-many relationship is automatically created between the table in the Field List pane and the table you have open.

Set a field's data type in Datasheet view

Office Access 2010 does a good job of automatically detecting the data type for a field that you create in Datasheet view. Sometimes, however, you will need to override the decision that Access makes. For example, you might have existing products IDs that serve to identify the products you sell. If you type a numeric ID, such as 1003, into a table in Datasheet view, the automatic data type detection feature sets a numeric data type for the field. However, you should only use a numeric data type for fields that will be involved in arithmetic calculations. Normally, identifiers such as a product ID should be stored as the Text data type.

If you want to explicitly set the data type and format for a field, overriding the choice that Office Access 2010 makes, you can do so by using the commands in the Data Type & Formatting group on the Home tab.

Explicitly set the data type

On the Datasheet tab, in the Data Type & Formatting group, click the arrow in the drop-down list next to Data Type, and then select a data type.

1. Click the data type you want.
2. Use the following table to determine the correct data type.

Explicitly set the format

1. On the Datasheet tab, in the Data Type & Formatting group, click the arrow in the drop-down list next to Format, and then select a format.
2. Click the format you want.

The following table describes the data types available for fields in Office Access 2010.

Data type	***Stores***	***Size***
Text	Alphanumeric characters Use for text, or text and numbers that are not used in calculations (for example, a product ID).	Up to 255 characters.
Memo	Alphanumeric characters (longer than 255 characters in length) or text with rich text formatting. Use for text greater than 255 characters in length, or for text that uses rich text formatting. Notes,	Up to 1 gigabyte of characters, or 2 gigabytes of storage (2 bytes per character), of which you can display 65,535 characters in a control.

	lengthy descriptions, and paragraphs with formatting such as bold or italics are good examples of where you would use a Memo field.	
Number	Numeric values (integers or fractional values). Use for storing numbers to be used in calculations, except for monetary values (use the Currency for data type for monetary values).	1, 2, 4, or 8 bytes, or 16 bytes when used for replication ID.
Date/Time	Dates and times. Use for storing date/time values. Note that each value stored includes both a date component and a time component.	8 bytes.
Currency	Monetary values. Use for storing monetary values (currency).	8 bytes.
AutoNumber	A unique numeric value that Office Access 2010 automatically inserts when a record is added. Use for generating unique values that can be used as a primary key. Note that AutoNumber fields can be incremented sequentially, by a specified increment, or chosen randomly.	4 bytes or 16 bytes when used for replication ID.
Yes/No	Boolean values. Use for True/False fields that can hold one of two possible values: Yes/No or True/False, for example.	1 bit (8 bits = 1 byte).
OLE Object	OLE objects or other binary data. Use for storing OLE objects from other Microsoft Windows applications.	Up to 1 gigabyte.
Attachment	Pictures, Images, Binary files, Office files. This is the preferred data type for storing digital images and any type of binary file.	For compressed attachments, 2 gigabytes. For uncompressed attachments, approximately 700k, depending on the degree to which the attachment can be compressed.

Hyperlink	Hyperlinks. Use for storing hyperlinks to provide single-click access to Web pages through a URL (Uniform Resource Locator) or files through a name in UNC (universal naming convention) format. You can also link to Access objects stored in a database.	Up to 1 gigabyte of characters, or 2 gigabytes of storage (2 bytes per character), of which you can display 65,535 characters in a control.
Lookup Wizard	Not actually a data type; instead, this invokes the Lookup Wizard. Use to start the Lookup Wizard so you can create a field that uses a combo box to look up a value in another table, query or list of values.	Table or query based: The size of the bound column. Value based: The size of the Text field used to store the value.

For phone numbers, part numbers, and other numbers that you don't intend to use for mathematical calculations, you should select the Text data type, instead of the Number data type.

For the Text and Number data types, you can specify the field size or data type more specifically by setting the FieldSize property.

Working with text boxes and their attached label controls

So far, you added controls bound to fields in the tables and unbound label controls used to display titles in your report. There is another type of text box control that is typically added to a report: unbound text boxes that are used to hold expressions such as page numbers, dates, or a calculation.

Adding and using text box controls

In reports, text box controls serve two purposes. First, they enable you to display stored data from a particular field in a query or table. Second, they display the result of an expression. Expressions can be calculations that use other controls as their operands, calculations that use Access functions (either built-in or user-defined), or a combination of the two. You learned how to use a text box control to display data from a field and how to create that control.

Entering an expression in a text control

Expressions enable you to create a value that is not already in a table or query. They can range from simple functions (such as a page number) to complex mathematical computations.

A function is a small program that, when run, returns a single value. The function can be one of many built-in Access functions or it can be user-defined. For example, earlier in this chapter you saw the Now () function used to return the current date and time for a text box located in a report's page footer. The following steps show you how to use an unbound text box to add a page number to your report:

1. Click in the middle of the Page Footer section, resize the page footer so that it is a ½ inch in height
2. Drag a text box control from the Controls group on the Design ribbon tab and drop it into the Page Footer area. Make the text box about three-quarters of the height of the Page Footer section and about Yi-inch wide.
3. Select the text box's attached label and change its contents to say Page:.

4. Select the text box control (it says "Unbound") and enter = Page directly into the text box. Alternatively, you could open the Property sheet (press F4) and enter = [Page] as the text box's ControlSource property.
5. Drag the new text box control until it is near the right edge of the report's page.

You may want to also move the text box's label so that it is positioned close to the text box. The upper-left handle on the label moves the label independently of the text box.

You can always check your result by clicking the Print Preview button on the toolbar and zooming in on the Page Footer section to check the page number.

Sizing a text box control or label control

You select a control by clicking it. Depending on the size of the control, from three to seven sizing handles appear — one on each corner except the upper-left corner and one on each side. Moving the mouse pointer over one of the sizing handles changes the mouse pointer to a double-headed arrow. When the pointer changes, click the control and drag it to the size you want. Notice that, as you drag, an outline appears indicating the size the label control will be when you release the mouse button.

If you double-click any of the sizing handles, Access resizes a control to best fit for text in the control. This feature is especially handy if you increase the font size and then notice that the text no longer fits the control.

Note that, for label controls, the best-fit sizing resizes both vertically and horizontally, although text controls resize only vertically. The reason for this difference is that in Report Design mode, Access doesn't know how much of a field's data you want to display. Later on, the field's name and con-tents might be radically different. Sometimes label controls are not resized correctly, however, and have to be adjusted manually.

Before continuing, you should check how the report is progressing. You should also save the report frequently as you make changes to it. You could send a single page to the printer, but is probably easier to view the report in Print Preview. Right-click the report's title bar, and select Print Preview from the shortcut menu.

The page header information is at the very top of the page, and the first product record appears below the header.

As you move the mouse over the print preview, the cursor changes to a magnifying glass. Click any portion of the view to zoom in so that can closely examine the report's layout. Only one record per page appears on the report because of the vertical layout. In the next section, you move the con-trols around and create a more horizontal layout.

Deleting and cutting attached labels from text controls

To create the report, you must move the text box labels from the Detail section to the Page Header section. Once moved, these controls appear as headings above each column of data and are repeated on each page of the report.

It's easy to delete one or more attached controls in a report. Simply select the desired controls and press Delete. However, if you want to move the label to the Page Header section (rather than simply deleting it), you can cut the label instead of deleting it. When removing attached controls, there are two choices:

- Delete only the label control.
- Cut the label control to the Clipboard.
- Delete or cut the label and the text box control.

Oddly enough, you cannot simply drag a label from the Detail section to the page header. Dragging an attached label from the Detail section drags its text box along with it. You must cut the label from the Detail section and paste it into the page header.

If you select the label control and cut it by pressing Ctrl+X or the Delete key, only the label control is removed. If you select the text box control and cut or delete it, the label and the text box con-trols are removed. To cut an attached label control (in this case, the Product ID controls and their attached label), follow these steps:

1. Click the Close button on the toolbar to exit Print Preview mode.
2. Select the Product ID label control only in the Detail section.
3. Press Ctrl+X (Cut).

After you have cut the label, you may want to place it somewhere else. In this example, plate it in the Page Header section.

Pasting labels into a report section

It is as easy to cut labels from controls placed in the Detail section and paste them into the page header as it is to delete the labels and create new ones in the page header. Regardless, you now paste the label you cut in the previous steps:

1. Click anywhere in or on the Page Header section.
2. Press Ctrl+V (Paste).

   The Product ID label appears in the page header.
3. Repeat for the Description, Category, and Quantity in Stock labels.
4. Delete the remaining label controls in the Detail section, leaving all the text box controls.

If you accidentally selected the data text box control and both controls are cut or deleted, click the Undo toolbar button, or press Ctr!+Z, to undo the action.

If you want to delete only the text box control and keep the attached label control, right-click the label control and then select Copy from the shortcut menu. Next, to delete the text box control and the label control, press the Delete key. Finally, right-click anywhere on the form and select Paste from the shortcut menu to paste only the copied label control to the report.

Moving label and text controls

Before discussing how to move label and text controls, it is important to review a few differences between attached and unattached controls. When an attached label is created automatically with a text control, it is called a compound control. In a compound control, whenever one control in the set is moved, the other control moves along with it. This means that, moving either the label or the text box also moves the related control. To move both controls in a compound control, select either of the pair of controls with the mouse. As you move the mouse pointer over either of the objects the pointer turns into a hand. Click the controls and drag them to their new location. As you drag, an outline for the compound control moves with your pointer.

To move only one of the controls in a compound control, drag the desired control by its move handle (the large square in the upper-left corner of the control). When you click a compound control, it looks like both controls are selected, but if you look closely, you see that only one of the two controls is selected (as indicated by the presence of both moving and sizing handles). The unse-lected control displays only a moving handle. A pointing finger indicates that you have selected the move handles and can now move only one control. To move either control individually, select the control's move handle and drag it to its new location.

To make a group selection, click with the mouse pointer anywhere outside a starting point and drag the pointer through (or around) the controls you want to select. A gray, outlined rectangle appears, showing the extent of the selection. When you release the mouse button, all controls the rectangle surrounds are selected. You can then drag the group of controls to a new location.

Make sure you also resize all the controls as shown in the figure. Change the size and shape of the Features memo field and the OLE picture field Picture. The OLE picture field displays as a rectangle with no field name in design view. Place all the controls in their proper position to complete the report layout. You make a series of block moves by selecting several controls and positioning them close to where you want them. Then, if needed, you fine-tune their position. This is the way most reports are done.

Modifying the appearance of multiple controls

The next step is to apply bold formatting to all the label controls in the Page Header section directly above the section separator. The following steps guide you through modifying the appear-ance of text in multiple label controls:

1. **Select all label controls in the bottom of the Page Header section by individually clicking them while holding down the Shift key.**

   Alternatively, click in the vertical ruler immediately to the left of the labels in the Page Header. There are four label controls to select.

   Alternatively, you can drag a bounding box around the label controls in the page header.

2. **Click the Bold button on the toolbar.**

   After you make the final modifications, you are finished, except for fixing the picture con-trol. To do this, you need to change properties, which you do in the next section.

Changing label and text box control properties

To change the properties of a text or label control, you need to display the control's Property Sheet. If it is not already displayed, perform one of these actions to display it:

- Double-click the border of the control (anywhere except a sizing handle or move handle).
- Press F-4
- Right-click the mouse and select Properties.

The Property Sheet enables you to look at a control^ property settings and provides an easy way to edit them. Using tools, such as the formatting windows and text-formatting buttons, on the Design ribbon also changes the property settings of a control. Clicking the Bold button, for example, sets the controls Font 'Weight property to Bold. It is usually easier and more intuitive to use the con-trols on the Design ribbon, but some properties are not accessible this way. In addition, sometimes objects have more options available through the Property Sheet.

The Size Mode property of an OLE object (bound object frame), with its options of Clip, Stretch, and Zoom, is a good example of a property that is available only through the Property Sheet.

The image control, which is a bound object frame, presently has its Size Mode property set to Clip, which is the default. With Clip, the picture is displayed in its original size and may be too large to fit in the frame. In this exercise, you change the setting to Stretch so that the picture is sized auto-matically to fit the picture frame.

Follow these steps to change, the property for die bound object frame control that contains the picture:

1. Click the frame control of the picture bound object.
2. Click the Size Mode property and Click the arrow to display the drop-down list box.
3. Select Stretch.

You might also consider changing the Border Style property to Transparent. When set to Transparent, no boxes drawn around the picture on the report.

Growing and shrinking text box controls

When you print or print-preview controls that can have variable text lengths, Access provides options for enabling a control to grow or shrink vertically, depending on the exact contents of a record. The Can Grow and Can Shrink properties determine whether a text control resizes its verti-cal dimension to accommodate the amount of text contained in.its bound field. Although these properties are usable for any text control, they are especially helpful for text box controls.

Table 7-1 explains the acceptable values for these two properties.

TABLE 7-1 Text Control Values for Can Grow and Can Shrink

Property	*Value*	*Description*
Can Grow	Yes	If the data in a record uses more lines than the control is defined to display, the control resizes to accommodate additional lines.
Can Grow	No	If the data in a record uses more lines than the control is defined to display, the control does not resize; it truncates the data display.
Can Shrink	Yes	If the data in a record uses fewer lines than the control is defined to display, the control resizes to eliminate blank lines.
Can Shrink	No	If the data in a record uses fewer lines than the control is defined to display, the control does not resize to eliminate blank lines.

To change the Can Grow settings for a text control, follow these steps:

1. Select the Features text box control.
2. Display the Property window.
3. Click the Can Grow property; then click the arrow and select Yes.

Sorting and grouping data

You can often make the data on the report more useful to users by grouping the data in informative Ways. Suppose that you want to list your products first by category and then by description within each category. To do this, you use the Category and Description fields to group and son the data.

Creating a group header or footer

Grouping on a field in the report's data adds two new sections (Group Header and Group Footer) to the report. In the following steps, you use the group header to display the name of the product category above each group of records. You won't use the Category group footer in this example because there are no totals by category or other reasons to use a group footer.

Follow these steps to create a Category group header:

1. Click the Grouping button in the Grouping and Totals group of the Design ribbon tab.

   You should see that the report's data already sorted by Description and Category.
2. Click the Add a group button in the Group, Sort, and Total area.
3. Select Category from the field list, and Access adds Group on Category with A on top of the Group, Sort, and Total area.

Access adds Category Header and Category Footer sections to the report's design as soon as you select the Category field for grouping. The Category Header section appears between the Page Header and Detail sections. If you define a group footer, it appears below the Detail section. If a report has multiple groupings, each subsequent group becomes the one closest to the Detail section. The groups defined first are farthest from the Detail section.

The Group Properties pane (displayed at the bottom of the Sorting and Grouping box) contains these properties:

- **Group Header:** Yes creates a group header. No removes the group header.
- **Group Footer:** Yes creates a group footer. No removes the group footer.
- **Group On:** Specifies how you want the values grouped. The options you see in the drop-down list box depend on the data type of the field on which you're grouping. If you group on an expression, you see all grouping options as listed below.

For Text dam types, there are two choices:

- **Each Value:** The same value in the field or expression
- **Prefix Characters:** The same first n number of characters in the field

For Date/Time data types, there are additional options:

- **Each Value:** The same value within the field or expression
- **Year:** Dates within the same calendar year.
- **Qtr:** Dates within the same calendar quarter
- **Month**: Dates within the same month
- **Week:** Dates within the same week
- **Day:** Dates on the same dale
- **Hour:** Times within the same hour
- **Minute:** Times within the same minute

Currency, or Number data types provide three options:

- **Each Value:** Includes the same value in the field or expression
- **Interval:** Includes values falling within the interval you specify
- **Group Interval:** Specifies any interval that is valid for the values in the field or expres-sion you're grouping on. The Group Interval has its own options:
    - **Keep Together:** Controls widows and orphans so that you don't have a header at the bottom of a page without detail until the next page
    - **Whole Group:** Prints header detail and group footer on one page
    - **With First Detail:** Prevents the contents of the group header from printing without any following data or records on a page
    - **No:** Does not keep data together

Sorting data within groups

Sorting enables you to determine the order in which the records are viewed on the report, based on the values in one or more controls. This order is important when you want to view the data in your tables in a sequence other than that of your input. For example, new products are added to tblProducts as they are needed on an invoice. The physical order of the database reflects the date and time a product is added. Yet, when you think of the product list, you probably expect it to be in alphabetical order by Product ID, and you want to sort it by Description of the cost of the product.

By sorting in the report itself, you don't have to worry about the order of the data. Although you can sort the data in the table by the primary key or in a query by any field you want, there are good reasons to do it in the report. This way, if you change the query or table, the report is still in the correct order.

In the case of the products report, you warn to display the records in each category group sorted by description.

Follow these steps to define a sort order based on the Description field within the Category grouping:

1. Click the Grouping button in the Design ribbon tab to display tbe Group, Sort and Total area, if it is not already open.
   You should see that the Category group already exists in the report.
2. Click the Add a Sort button in the Group, Sort and Total area.
3. Select Description in the field list. Notice that Sort Order defaults to Ascending.
4. Close the Group, Sort and Total area by clicking the X in the upper-right corner.

Removing a group header or footer

To remove a Page or Report Header/Footer section, display the Group, Sort and Total area, select the group or sort specifier to delete, and press the Delete key.

Hiding a section

Access also enables you to hide headers and footers so that you can break data imo groups without having to view information aboul the group itself. You can also hide the Detail section so that you see only a summary report.

To hide a section, follow these steps:

1. Ctick the section you want to hide.
2. Display the section's Propertv Sheet.
3. Click the Visible property's text box.
4. Click the drop-down list arrow on the right side of the text box.
5. Select No from the drop-down list box.

Sizing a section

Now that you have created the group header, you might want to put some controls in the section, move some controls around, or even move controls between sections. Before you start manipulating controls within a section, you should make sure the section is the proper height. To modify the height of a section, drag the top border of the section below it. If, for example, you have a report with a page header, Detail section, and page footer, change the height of the Detail section by dragging the top of the Page Footer section's border. You can make a section larger or smaller by dragging the bottom border of the section.

For this example, change the height of the group header section to % inch with these steps:

1. Move your mouse pointer to the bottom of the Category section.
   The pointer changes to a horizontal line split by two vertical arrows.
2. Select the top of the detail section (which is also the bottom of the Category Header section).
3. Drag the selected band lower until three dots appear in the vertical ruler (%").
   The gray line indicates where the top of the border will be when you release the mouse button.
4. Release the mouse button.

Moving controls between sections

You now want to move the Category control from the Detail section to the Category Header section. You can move one or more controls between sections by simply dragging the control with your mouse from one section to another or by cutting it from one section and pasting it to another section.

Follow these instructions to move the Category control from the Detail section to the Category section:

1. Select the Category control in the Detail section.
2. Drag the Category control up to the Category Header section and drop it close to the vertical ruler.

You should now perform the following steps to complete the report design.

3. Delete the Category label from the page header.
4. Move the ProductID control and its associated label after the Description control and its associated label.
5. Move the Description control and its associated label to the left so that it starts just to the right of the start of the Category control in the Category Header control.

   By offsetting the first control in the Detail section slightly to the right of the start of the control in the Group Header section, you show the hierarchy of the data presented in the report. It now shows that each group of products is for the category listed in the group header.
6. Lengthen the Description control so tbat it approaches the Product ID control.

Adding page breaks

Access enables you to force page breaks based on groups. You can also insert forced breaks within sections, except in Page Header and Footer sections. In some report designs, it's best to have each new group begin on a different page. You can achieve this effect easily by using the Force New Page property of a group section, which enables you to force a page break every time the group value changes.

The four Force New Page property settings are listed here:

- **None:** No forced page break (the default)
- **Before Section:** Starts printing the current section at ihe top of a new page every time there is a new group
- **After Section:** Starts printing the next section at the top of a new page every time there is a new group
- **Before & After:** Combines the effects of Before Section ancPAfter Section

To create the report you want, force a page break before the Category group with rhe Force New Page property in the Category header:

1. Click anywhere in the Category header, or click the Category Header bar above the section.
2. Display the Property Sheet.
3. Select the Force New Page property, and select Before Section from the drop-down list in the property's box.

Sometimes, you don't want to force a page break on the basis of a grouping, but you still want to force a page break. For example, you may want to split a report title across several pages. The solution is to use the Page Break tool from the Controls group on the ribbon. Just drag the control and drop it on the report where you want a page break to occur every time the page prints.

CHAPTER 9

Expressions in Microsoft Access 2010

Introduction

An expression consists of a number of elements that you use, alone or in combination, to produce a result.

About expressions

In Office Access 2010, an expression is the equivalent of a formula in Office Excel 2010. Those elements can include:

- Identifiers — the names of table fields or controls on forms or reports, or the properties of those fields or controls.
- Operators, such as + (plus) or - (minus).
- Functions, such as SUM or AVG, and the arguments that are used with them.
- Constants — values that do not change — such as strings of text, or numbers that are not calculated by an expression.

You use an expression to perform a calculation, retrieve the value of a field or control, supply criteria to a query, define rules, create calculated controls and calculated fields, and define a grouping level for a report.

You use an expression when you need to create values that do not reside directly in your data. For example, you might need to calculate sales tax on an order, or calculate the total value of the order itself. At other times, you'll need to add criteria to a query or filter — information that determines which records the query returns or that appear when a filter is applied. In other cases, you might want to set a default value or a validation rule for a field or control. In all of these cases, you use an expression.

The following table shows some sample expressions and how they are typically used:

Expression	*Purpose*
=[RequiredDate]-[ShippedDate]	Calculates the difference between the date values in two text box controls (called RequiredDate and ShippedDate) on a report.
Date()	Sets the default value for a Date/Time table field to the current date.
ExtendedPrice: CCur([Order Details].Unit Price*[Quantity]*(1-[Discount])/100)*100	Creates a calculated field in a query.
Between #1/1/2005# And #12/31/2005#	Used to enter criteria for a Date/Time field in a query.
=[Orders Subform].Form!OrderSubtotal	Returns the value of the OrderSubtotal control on the Orders subform that is on the Orders form.
> 0	Sets a validation rule for a numeric field in a table — users must enter values greater than zero.

As you can see from the preceding examples, an expression in Access is not just a mathematical calculation. Instead, expressions serve a variety of purposes. You will also notice that the sample expressions differ from each other in some ways. For example, some expressions start with the = (equal) operator. When calculating a value for a control on a form or report, you use the = operator to start the expression. In other instances, you don't use the = operator. For example, when you type an expression in a query or in the DefaultValue or ValidationRule property of a field or control, you don't use the = operator unless you're adding the expression to a Text field in a table. In some cases, such as adding expressions to queries, Access removes the = operator automatically.

The following sections describe the various parts of an expression in more detail. The examples in the sections also provide brief descriptions of the syntax that expressions use.

Identifiers

An identifier is the name of a field, property, or control. You use an identifier in an expression to refer to the value that is associated with a field, property, or control. For example, consider the expression

=[RequiredDate]-[ShippedDate]. This expression subtracts the value of the ShippedDate field or control from the value of the RequiredDate field or control. In this expression, both RequiredDate and ShippedDate serve as identifiers.

Operators

Access supports a variety of operators, including the expected arithmetic operators such as +, -, * (multiply), / (divide). You can also use comparison operators for comparing values, text operators for concatenating (combining) text, logical operators for determining true or false values, and other operators specific to Access.

Functions and arguments

Functions are built-in procedures that you can use in your expressions. You use functions for a wide variety of operations, such as calculating values, manipulating text and dates, and summarizing data. For example, one commonly used function is Date, which returns the current date. You can use the Date function in a variety of ways, such as an expression that sets the default value for a field in a table. That way, whenever someone adds a new record, the value for the field defaults to the current date.

Some functions require arguments. An argument is a value that provides input to the function. If a function requires more than one argument, you separate the arguments with a comma. For example, consider the Date function in the following example expression:

=Format(Date(),"mmmm d, yyyy")

This example uses two arguments. First, the Date function supplies the current date. The second argument, separated from the first by a comma, is a text string that tells the Format function how to format the date value. Note that the text string is enclosed in quotation marks. As a general rule, when you need to supply text, you place it inside quotation marks. This expression also illustrates a principle that you should remember as you proceed: You can often use the value returned by one function as an argument to yet another function.Finally, Access supports a large number of built-in functions.

Constants

A constant is a named item whose value remains constant while Access is running. Typically, you use the True, False, and Null constants most often in your expressions. You can also define your own constants in Visual Basic for Applications (VBA) code that you can use in VBA procedures. VBA is the programming language that Access uses.

Note You cannot use Microsoft Visual Basic constants in custom functions that you use in your expressions. For example, Visual Basic has constants for the days of the week: vbSunday represents Sunday, vbMonday represents Monday, and so on. Each of these constants has a corresponding numeric value: The numeric value for vbSunday is 1, vbMonday is 2, and so on. You cannot use these constants in a custom function that is called from within an expression. You must instead use the numeric values.

Values

You can employ literal values in your expressions, such as the number 1,254 or the string "Enter a number between 1 and 10." Numeric values can be a series of digits, including a sign and a decimal point, if needed. In the absence of a sign, Access assumes a positive value. To make a value negative, include the minus sign (-). You can also use scientific notation. To do so, include "E" or "e" and the sign of the exponent (for example, 1.0E-6).

When you use text strings as constants, place them within quotation marks. In some circumstances, Access will supply the quotation marks for you. For example, when you type text in an expression for a validation rule or for query criteria, Access surrounds your text strings with quotation marks automatically. For example, if you type the text Paris, Access displays "Paris" in the expression. If you want an expression to produce a string that is actually enclosed in quotation marks, you can enclose the nested string either in single (') quotation marks or within three sets of double (") quotation marks. For example, the following expressions are equivalent:

Forms![Contacts]![City].DefaultValue = ' "Paris" '

Forms![Contacts]![City].DefaultValue = " " "Paris" " "

To use date/time values, you enclose them in pound signs (#). For example, #3-7-07#, #7-Mar-07#, and #Mar-7-2010# are all valid date/time values. When Access sees a valid date/time value enclosed by # characters, it automatically treats the value as a Date/Time data type.

Why you use expressions?

In Access, you use expressions when you need to do any of the following:

- Calculate values that do not exist directly in your data. You can calculate values for table fields, for queries, and for controls on forms and reports.
- Set a default value for a table field or a control on a form or report. Your default values then appear whenever you open a table, form, or report for use.
- Create a validation rule. Validation rules control what values users can and cannot enter into a field or control.
- Set criteria for a query.

The figure here illustrates some typical expressions used in the scenarios described here:

For example, suppose that you need to calculate the total dollar amount for a line item in an invoice. Typically, you do not store the line item total in the database. Instead, you calculate it as needed from two items that you *should* store in the database — quantity and price. You then use an expression such as this one to calculate the value:

=CCur([Quantity]*[Price])

This expression multiplies quantity times price and then uses the CCur function (convert to currency) to convert the result to the Currency data type. You can also calculate a discount for each order.

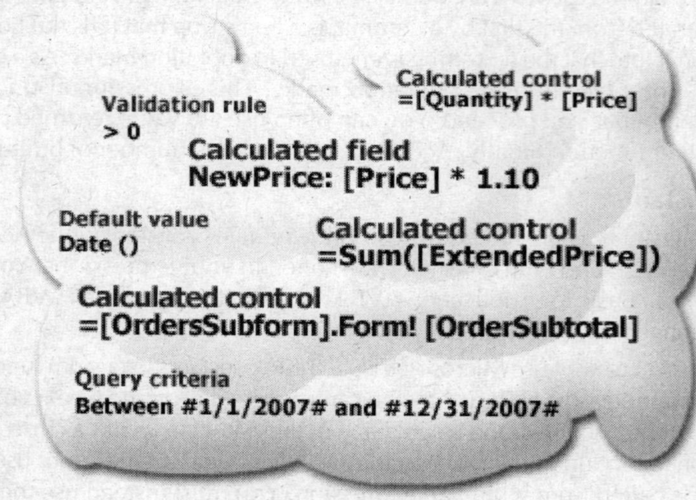

You can also create a field in a query that calculates a line item total, and then use that value in a form or report. A column in a query that results from such a calculation is called a *calculated field*. For example, the following expression in a query calculates the line item totals with an applied discount:

ExtendedPrice: CCur([Order Details].[Unit Price]*[Quantity]*(1-[Discount])/100)*100

The expression gives the resulting column the name ExtendedPrice. You create a calculated field whenever you need to calculate or perform operations on the data in two or more table fields. For example, many tables store first and last names in separate fields. If you want to combine those first and last names and display them in a single field, you create a calculated field in a query. Some users try to create those types of calculated fields directly in tables, but by default, tables do not support that type of operation — they do not provide a field or property in which you can add the necessary expression.

A calculated field that combines first and last names would look like this: [FirstName] & " " & [LastName]. In this case, the ampersands combine the values in the FirstName and LastName fields with a space — the double quotes with a space between them.

You can also use expressions to provide a default value for a field in a table or for a control. For example, if you have a date field that you want to default to the current date, you can type Date() in the Default Value property box for that field.

You can also use an expression to set a validation rule. For example, you might use a validation rule that requires the date that is entered to be greater than or equal to the current date. In that case, you set the value in the Validation Rule property box to >= Date().

Finally, you can also use an expression to set criteria for a query. For example, suppose you want to see product sales for the orders that were shipped within a certain time frame. You can enter criteria to define a date range, and Access returns only the rows that match the criteria:

Between #1/1/2010# And #12/31/2010#

When you add criteria to the query and then run the query, it returns only those values that match the specified dates.

Where and how to use expressions

You can use an expression in many places in a database. For example, tables, queries, forms, reports, and macros all have properties that accept an expression. For example, you can use expressions in the Control Source and Default Value properties of controls. You can also use them in the Validation Rule property in table fields. In addition, when you write VBA code for an event procedure or for a module, you often use expressions that are similar to those that you use in an Access object, such as a table or query.

A brief look at expression syntax

Expressions often use the data in your tables and queries and also data stored in controls on forms and reports. To use those data, expressions reference the names of the fields in your tables and queries, and the names of your controls. To use field and control names in expressions, you enclose them in brackets ([ ]). For example, if you want to use a table field called Unit Price in an expression, you enter it as [Unit Price]. If you enter a name that doesn't include spaces or special characters, Access automatically encloses it in brackets. If a name includes spaces or special characters, you must type the brackets yourself.

Using expressions in form and report controls

You can give a name to a calculated control by setting the control's Name property. The name must be unique among all the control names on the form or report. It also must be different from any field or control name that is used in the expression for that control, and it should be different from any field name in the underlying table or query. You can use this name when you want to refer to the value in the control in other expressions on the form or report.

The most common places where you use expressions include the following:

- In a text box control on a form or report This creates a calculated control. For example, suppose you want to create a subtotal that sums all of the line items on an order form. The subtotal might look something like this on your form:

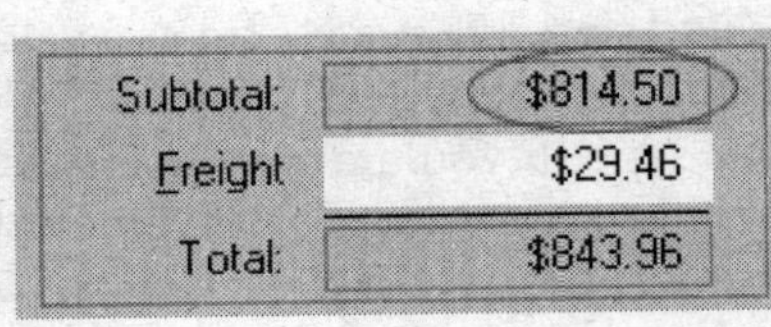

To calculate the subtotal, you place a text box control on the form and set the ControlSource property of the text box to the following expression:

=Sum([*table_field*])

In this case, *table_field* is the name of the field that contains your subtotal values. That field can reside in a table or a query. The Sum function calculates the total for a set of values from your record source.

The following steps explain how to enter an expression in a text box control.

Enter an expression in a text box control

1. In the Navigation Pane, right-click the form that you want to change and click Design View.
2. Right-click the text box that you want to change, and click Properties to display the property sheet for the control.

   -or-

   On the Design tab, in the Tools group, click Property Sheet.

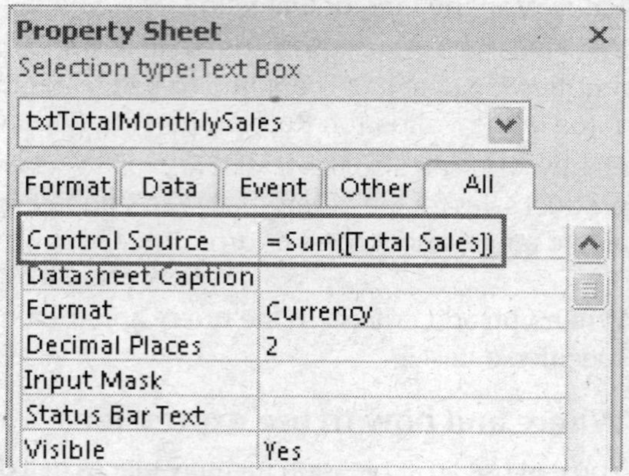

3. On the Data tab or the All tab of the property sheet, click the ControlSource property of the text box, and then enter = and the rest of your expression. For example, to calculate the subtotal shown above, you type =Sum([*table_field*]), being sure to substitute the name of your field with *table_field*.

   -or-

   Click the Build button to the right of the property box to create an expression by using the **Expression Builder.**

   Your property sheet will look something like the illustration here:
4. Close the property sheet and save your changes.

Using expressions in query criteria

You use an expression to define criteria in a query. Access then returns only those rows that match the criteria. For example, suppose you want to see all orders whose shipped date occurs in the year 2004. To enter the criteria, you enter the following expression in the Criteria cell for the Date/Time column in your query. This example uses a Date/Time column called ShippedDate. To define a date range, enter the following criteria:

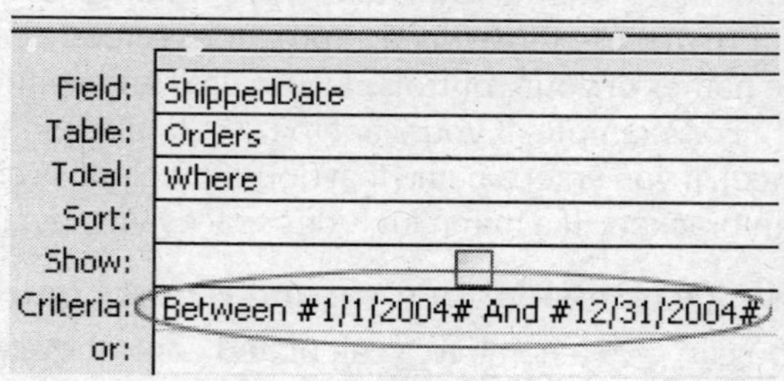

Between #1/1/2004# And #12/31/2004#

The ShippedDate column will look something like the following illustration.

The expression determines whether the values in the ShippedDate column fall in the date range that you specify. Note that you surround the dates with pound signs (#). Access treats a value within the pound signs as a Date/Time data type. If you are new to Access, treating those values as date/time data enables you to perform calculations on those values.

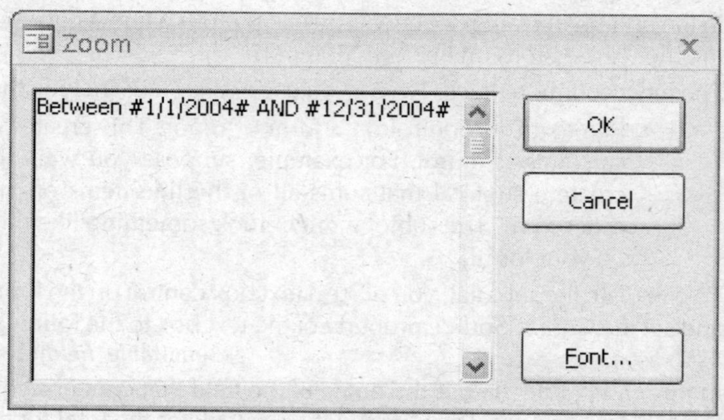

Enter criteria in the query design grid

1. In the Navigation Pane, right-

click the query that you want to change, then and click Design View on the shortcut menu.

2. Click in the Criteria cell in the column for which you want to enter your criteria.
3. Type your criteria expression.

   -or-

   On the Design tab, in the Query Setup group, click Builder to start the **Expression Builder** and build your criteria.

   If you want a larger area in which to enter an expression, press SHIFT + F2 to display the Zoom dialog box.

Using expressions to create calculated fields in of a query

You use an expression to create a calculated field in a query. For example, suppose you want to display the year that an order was shipped as part of a query. To create the calculated field, you place the following expression in a blank cell in the Field row in your query:

Year Shipped: Format([ShippedDate],"yyyy")

In this case, the expression uses the Format function to extract the year from the values in a field called ShippedDate. The Format function then formats the year as four digits. Prefacing the expression with Year Shipped: names the resulting column Year Shipped.

Enter a calculated field in query Design view

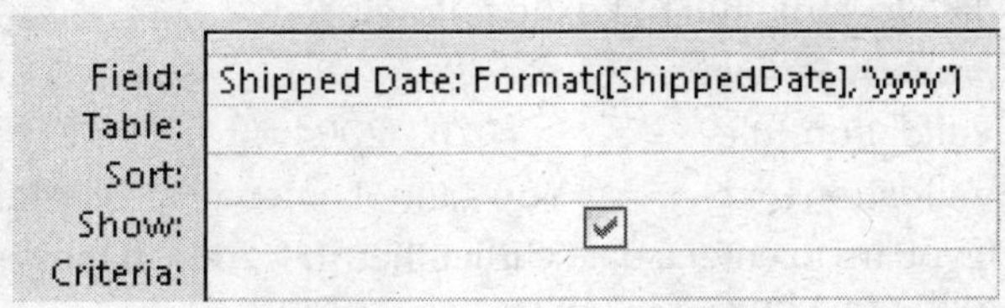

1. In the Navigation Pane, right-click the query that you want to change, and then click Design View on the shortcut menu.
2. Click the Field cell in the column where you want to create the calculated field.
3. Type your expression.

   -or-

   On the Design tab, in the Query Setup group, click Builder to start the Expression Builder and build your criteria.

   Do not precede the criteria expression with the = operator, but do start the expression with a name followed by a colon. For example, you type ExtendedPrice: to start an expression that creates a calculated field called ExtendedPrice.

Using expressions in the Validation Rule property of a table field

Another place where an expression comes in handy is the Validation Rule property of a field in a table. Suppose you have a table called Inventory with a field called Units On Hand, and you want to set a rule that forces users to enter a value greater than or equal to zero. In other words, inventory can never be a negative number. You can do this by using the expression shown in the following illustration.

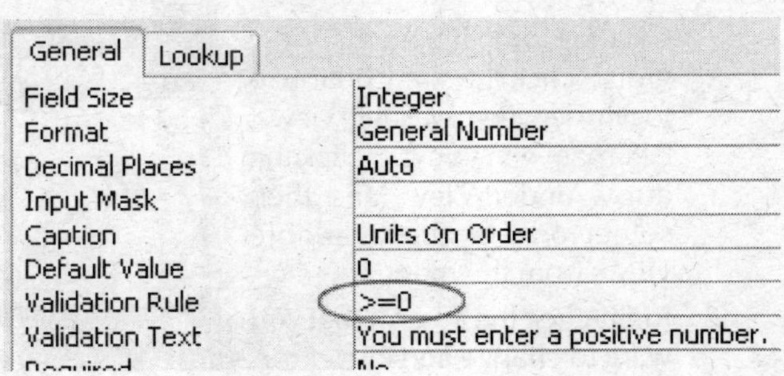

Enter a validation rule for a field in a table

1. In the Navigation Pane, right click the table that you want to change, and then click Design View on the shortcut menu.
2. In the Field Name column, click the field that you want to change.

3. On the General tab, click the Validation Rule property box.
4. Type your expression.

   -or-

   Click the Build button to the right of the property box to start the **Expression Builder** and create your expression.

   -or-

   On the Design tab, in the Tools group, click Builder to start the **Expression Builder.**

Do not precede the expression with the = operator when you create a validation rule.

The key point to remember when you work with validation rule expressions is that they must resolve to True for the value to be accepted. So, in this example, the value for [Units On Hand] must be > =0. If it isn't, Access displays the text shown in the Validation Text property box. If you haven't entered any text in the Validation Text property box, Access displays its own message to indicate that the value you entered is prohibited by the validation rule for the field.

Using expressions in the Validation Rule property of a control

You can also set the Validation Rule property for a control. For example, suppose you use a form to enter the date range for a report, and you want to ensure that the beginning date isn't earlier than 1/1/2004. You can set the Validation Rule and ValidationText properties for the text box where you enter the beginning date to something like the following.

Property	***Setting***
ValidationRule	> =#1/1/2004#
ValidationText	You cannot enter a date earlier than 1/1/2004.

If you try to enter a date earlier than 1/1/2004, a message appears. After you click OK, Access returns you to the text box.

Enter a validation rule for a control

1. In the Navigation Pane, right-click the form or report that you want to change and click Design View on the shortcut menu.

   -or-

   If you already have the form or report open, right-click the document tab and click Design View on the shortcut menu.

   -or-

   On the Home tab, in the View group, click the View button to toggle between available views. Alternatively, you can click the arrow under View, and then select one of the available views from the menu.

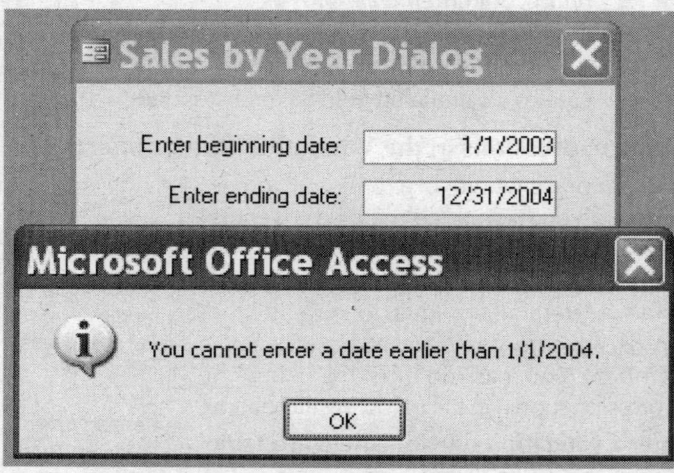

2. Right-click the control that you want to change and click Properties.

   -or-

   On the Design tab, in the Tools group, click Property Sheet.

   Access displays the property sheet for the control.

3. Click the All tab, and then click the Validation Rule property box.
4. Type the expression, or click the Build button to the right of the property box to create an expression by using the **Expression Builder**.

   Do not precede the expression with the = operator when you create a validation rule.
5. Optionally, change the Validation Text property.
6. Close the property sheet and save your changes.

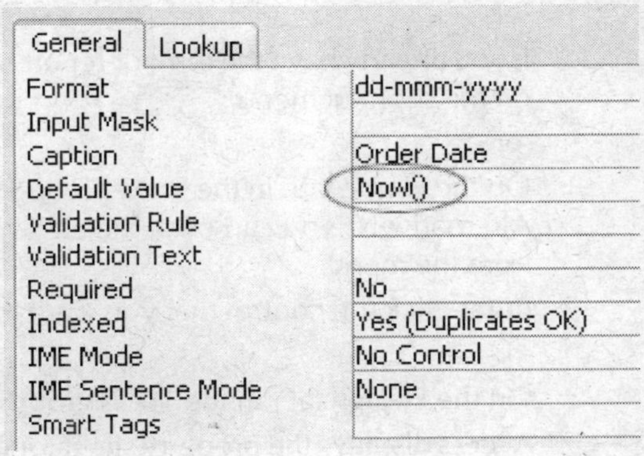

When you enter a value that the validation rule prohibits, you can press ESC while the cursor is in the control to restore the original or default value. You can then enter a value that satisfies the validation rule.

If the Control Source property for your control is a field in a table, it's usually best to set the field's Validation Rule property, in addition to that of the control. That way, the rule is enforced all the time, no matter which form or query is used to update the field.

Using expressions to set default values for a table field

You can use an expression to store a default value for a field in a table. For example, suppose you want to automatically insert the date and time into a field called OrderDate when you add a new record. You can use an expression like the following.

The expression uses the Now function to insert the date and time into the OrderDate field.

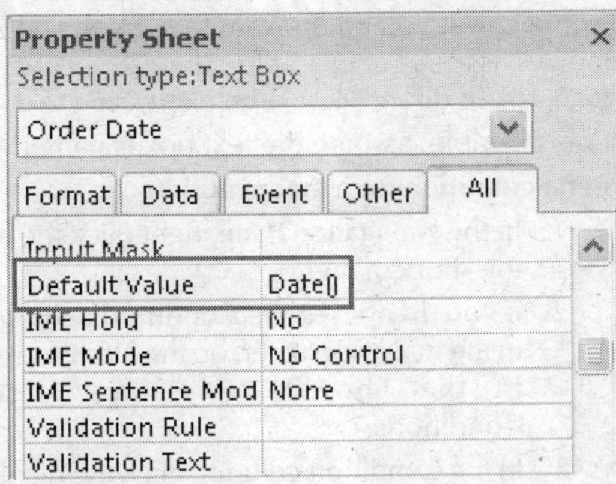

Enter a default value for a field in a table

1. In the Navigation Pane, right-click the table that you want to change and click Design View on the shortcut menu.
2. In the Field Name column, click the field that you want to change.
3. On the General tab, click the Default Value property box.
4. Type your expression, or click the Build button to the right of the property box to create an expression by using the **Expression Builder**.
5. If you bind a control to a table field, and the control and field have a default value, the control's default value takes precedence.

Using expressions to set default values for controls

Another common place to use an expression is in the Default Value property of a control. The Default Value property of a control behaves similarly to the Default Value property of a field in a table. For example, if you want to enter the current date as the default value for a text box named OrderDate, you can use an expression like the following.

This expression uses the Date function to return the current date, but not the time. If you bind the text box to a table field, and the field has a default value, the control's default value takes precedence. It often makes better sense to set the Default Value property for the field in the table, because the default value is always applied to the control unless the control overrides it.

Enter a default value for a control

1. In the Navigation Pane, right-click the form or report that you want to change and click Design View on the shortcut menu.

   -or-

   If you already have the form or report open, right-click the document tab and click Design View on the shortcut menu.

   -or-

   On the Home tab, in the View group, click the View button to toggle between available views. Alternatively, you can click the arrow under View, and then select one of the available views from the menu.
2. Right-click the control that you want to change, and then click Properties.

   -or-

   On the Design tab, in the Tools group, click Property Sheet.

   Access displays the property sheet for the control.
3. Click the All tab, and then click the Default Value property box.
4. Type the expression, or click the Build button to the right of the property box to create an expression by using the **Expression Builder**.
5. Close the property sheet.

Using expressions to carry out macro actions

In some cases, you might want to carry out an action or series of actions in a macro only if a particular condition is true. For example, suppose you want a macro action to run only when the value in a text box equals 10. To do so, you use an expression to define the condition in the Condition column of the macro. In this example, assume the text box is named "Items."

Enter a condition for a macro action

1. In the Navigation Pane, right-click the macro that you want to change and click Design View on the shortcut menu.
2. If you do not see the Condition column in the macro designer, on the Design tab, in the Show/Hide group, click Conditions.
3. In the Condition column, click the blank cell next to the macro action that you want to change, and then type your conditional expression.

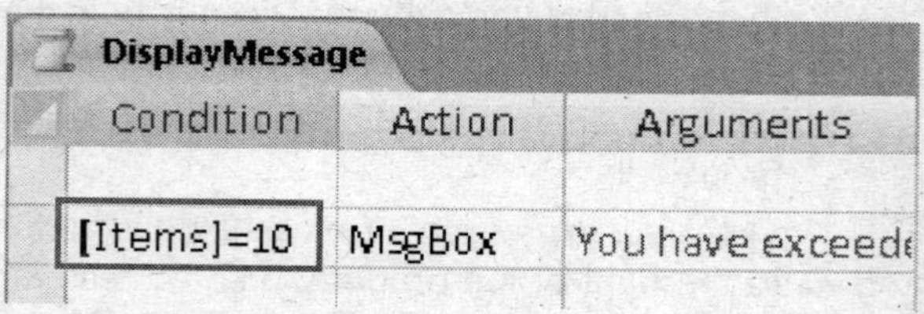

4. Save your changes and then close the macro.

As with the Validation Rule property, the expression in the Condition column must resolve to either True or False. The macro action runs only when the condition is True.

Using expressions to group and sort data in reports

You use the Group, Sort, and Total pane to define grouping levels and sorting orders for the data in a report. The pane replaces the Sorting and Grouping dialog box provided by earlier versions of Access. You can display and use the pane only when you open a report in Design view — the pane appears in the same window as your report.

The figure here illustrates the pane as it appears when it first opens:

If you are new to Access, grouping is the process of combining columns that contain duplicate values. For example, suppose your database contains sales information for offices in different cities. One of the most common reports in that type of database is "Sales by City," and the query that provides the data for the report groups the data by your city values. Grouping can make your information easier to read and understand.

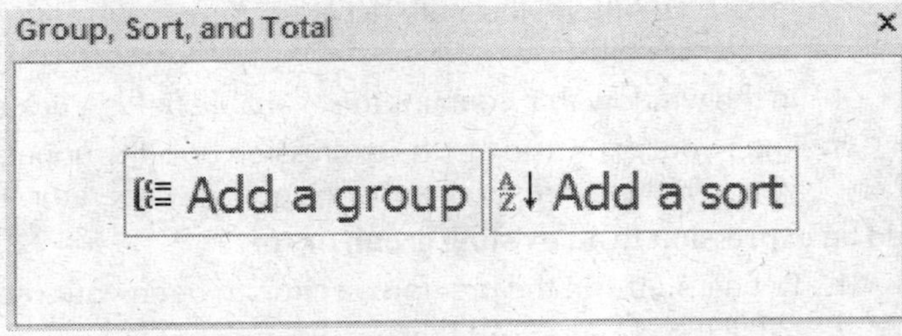

In contrast, sorting is the process of imposing an order on the rows (the records) in your query results. For example, you can sort records by their primary key values (or another set of values in another field) in either ascending or descending order, or you can sort them by one or more characters in (for example) alphabetical order. As you proceed, remember that, by default, queries in Access return records by the fastest means possible. When you first create a query, Access might return your data in a way that makes sense, such as by the sequence of primary key values. However, as users change data and add or remove rows, Access might return your data in a different sequence because that new sequence is faster. You impose a sort order when you need your queries to return data in the same sequence, regardless of changes to that data.

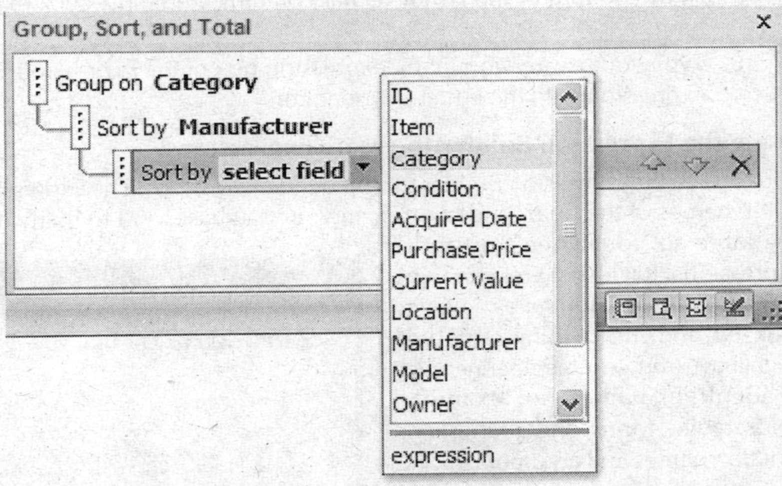

Add grouping and sorting to a report

1. In the Navigation Pane, right-click the report that you want to change and click Design View on the shortcut menu.

   -or-

   If you already have the report open, right-click the document tab and click Design View on the shortcut menu.

   -or-

   On the Home tab, in the View group, click the View button to toggle between available views. Alternatively, you can click the arrow under View, and then select one of the available views from the menu.

2. On the Design tab, in the Grouping & Totals group, click Group & Sort.

   The Group, Sort, and Total pane appears at the bottom of the working area.

3. Click Add a group to add a grouping level to the report.

   -or-

   Click Add a sort to add a sort order to the report.

   A new group or sort order appears in the pane, plus a list of the fields that provide data for the report. This figure illustrates a typical new group and sort order, plus a window that contains the available fields:

4. In the window that contains the available fields, click expression to start the Expression Builder.
5. Enter your expression in the expression box (the upper box) of the Expression Builder. Make sure you start the expression with the equal (=) operator.

Add an expression to an existing group or sort

1. Repeat step 1 in the previous section to open your report in Design view.
2. Click the group or sort that you want to change.
3. Click the down arrow next to Group on (for grouping levels) or Sort by (for sort orders).
4. A window that contains the available fields appears.
5. At the bottom of the window that contains the fields, click expression to start the Expression Builder.
6. Type your expression in the expression box of the Expression Builder. Be sure to preface your expression with the equal (=) operator.

Using the Expression Builder to create expressions

You can use the Expression Builder to help build expressions. The Expression Builder provides easy access to the names of the fields and controls in your database, and to many of the built-in functions that are available to you when you write expressions. If it helps, you can think of the Expression Builder as a way to look up and insert things that you might have trouble remembering, such as identifier names (for example, fields, tables, forms, and queries) and function names and arguments.

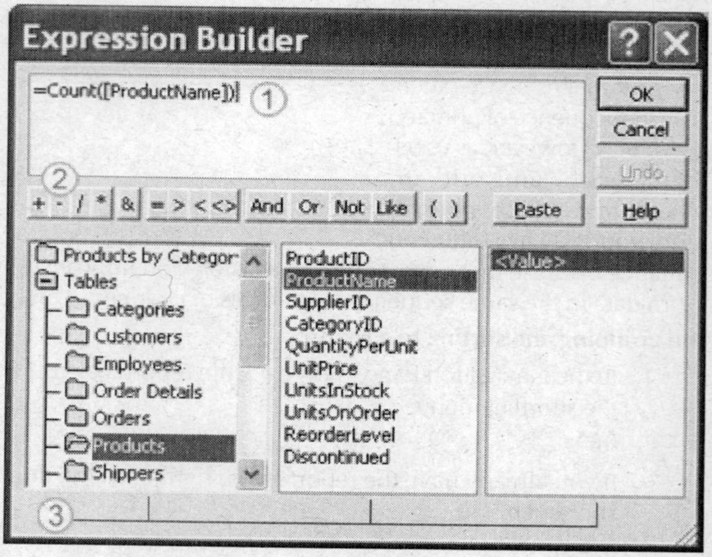

You can use the Expression Builder to create an expression from scratch, or you can select from some prebuilt expressions for displaying page numbers, the current date, and the current date and time.

You can start the Expression Builder from most of the places where you would write expressions manually, such as the Control Source property of a control or the Validation Rule property of a table field. As a rule, if you see the Build button ( ), you can click it to start the Expression Builder.

This figure and the text that follows illustrate the Expression Builder:

Expression box

The upper section of the builder contains an *expression box* where you construct your expression. You can type your expression in the box manually, or you can select elements from the three columns in the lower section of the Expression Builder and add them to your expression box. To add an element, double-click it or select it from one of the columns and then click Paste.

Operator buttons

The middle section of the Expression Builder displays buttons for inserting common arithmetical and logical operators into your expression. To insert an operator in the expression box, click the appropriate button. To display a longer list of operators that you can use in expressions, click the Operators folder in the lower-left column, and then click the category that you want in the middle column. The right column then lists all of the operators in the selected category. To insert an operator, double-click the operator, or select it and then click Paste.

Expression elements

The lower section contains three columns:

- The left column displays folders that list the tables, queries, forms, and reports in your database, as well as the available built-in functions and user-defined functions, constants, operators, and common expressions.
- The middle column lists specific elements or categories of elements for the folder that is selected in the left column. For example, if you click Built-In Functions in the left column, the middle column lists function categories.
- The right column lists the values, if any, for the elements that you selected in the left and middle columns. For example, if you click Built-In Functions in the left column and then click a function category in the middle column, the right column lists all of the built-in functions in the selected category.

You construct your expression by typing text in the expression box and pasting elements from the other areas in the Expression Builder. For example, you can click in the lower-left column to see any of the objects in your database, and also the functions, constants, operators, and common expressions. When you click an item in the left column, the other columns change accordingly. For example, when you click the name of a table in the left column, the middle column lists the fields in that table. When you double-click *Functions* and then click Built-In Functions, the middle column lists all of the function categories, and the right column lists the functions in those categories. When you double-click a function to insert it into your expression, the function and the text that indicates the needed arguments for that function appear as placeholder text in the expression box. You can then replace that text with the argument values.

When you paste an identifier (the name of a table field or control) into your expression, the Expression Builder inserts only the parts of the identifier that are required in the current context. For example, if you start the Expression Builder from the property sheet of a form called Customers, and then paste an identifier for the Visible property of the form in your expression, the Expression Builder pastes only the property name Visible. If you use this expression outside of the context of the form, you must include the full identifier: Forms![Customers].Visible.

Start the Expression Builder in a table, form, or report

In the Navigation Pane, right-click the table, form, or report that you want to change and click Design View on the shortcut menu.

1. If you open a table, in the Field Name column, click the field that you want to change, and then on the General tab, click the property that will contain the expression and click the Build button next to the property.

   -or-

   If you open a form or report, right-click the control that you want to change, click Properties, locate the property that will contain the expression, and then click the Build button next to the property.

Start the Expression Builder in a query

1. In the Navigation Pane, right-click the query that you want to change and click Design View on the shortcut menu.

   -or-

   If you have the query open, right-click the document tab for the query and click Design View on the shortcut menu.
2. Click the cell in the design grid that will contain the expression. For example, click the Criteria cell for the column where you want to supply criteria, or click the Field cell for the column where you want to create a calculated field.
3. On the Design tab, in the Query Setup group, click Builder.

Use expressions for practical purposes

This section introduces some of the ways that you can use expressions to solve problems and calculate needed information for your forms, reports, and tables.

"Stamping" a new record with the current date and time

In some tables, it is important to keep track of ("stamp") the date or the date and time when you add a record. To have Access automatically fill in that value for you, you can create a field with the Date/Time data type and set the DefaultValue property for the field to Date() or Now(). The Date function returns the current date, as stored in your computer's system clock. The Now function returns the current date and time.

The following steps explain how to add a new field to a table, set the data type for the field to Date/Time, and then add the Now or Date functions to the field.

Add a Date/Time field and time stamp field

1. In the Navigation Pane, double-click the table that you want to change.

   Access opens the table in Datasheet view.
2. Click the first blank column, located at the far side of the table. If you can't find the blank column, look for the words Add New Field in the column header.
3. Double-click in the column header and type a name for the field, such as Date Added, and then press ENTER.

   -or-

   Right-click the column, click Rename, type a name for the field, and then press ENTER.
4. On the Datasheet tab, in the Data Type & Formatting group, click the down arrow next to the Data Type list and select Date/Time.
5. Save your changes, keep the table open, and go to the next set of steps.

Add a date expression to a Date/Time field

1. Right-click the document tab for the table, and then click Design View on the shortcut menu.
2. In the Field Name column, click your new field.
3. On the General tab, click in the Default Value property box.
4. Type **Now()** or **Date()**.
5. Click the Show Date Picker property box and set the value to Never.
6. Save your changes and then close the table.

Now, when you add a new record to the table, Access automatically inserts the date or the date and time into the Date Added field.

Combining text values

When you want to combine the values in two or more text fields, you use the ampersand (&) operator. For example, suppose you have a form called Employees. You enter the employees first and last name in separate fields, but you want to display the employee's full name in the form header.

To display the full name, you can use this expression:

=[FirstName] & " " & [LastName]

The expression uses the & operator to combine the values in the FirstName and LastName fields. The expression also uses a pair of double quotation marks separated by a space character to insert a space between the first and last names. Remember that the spaces between the field names and the ampersand operators do not affect the appearance of your data (they only make the expression easier to read). When you want to insert something between fields, such as a space, punctuation, or literal text, you must enclose that additional value in quotation marks.

As another example, you can use this expression to display last names and first names, separated by a comma:

=[LastName] & ", " & [FirstName]

In this case, the values surround by quotation marks insert a comma and a space between the names.

The steps in this section assume you have a form, and they assume you have a table with fields called FirstName and LastName. If not, you can alter the expression in these steps to suit your own data.

Add a text box with an expression for full names

1. In the Navigation Pane, right-click the form or report that you want to change, and then click Design View on the shortcut menu.
2. On the Design tab, in the Controls group, click Text Box.
3. Drag the pointer on the form or report to create the text box.
4. Right-click the text box and click Properties.

   -or-

   On the Design tab, in the Tools group, click Property Sheet.
5. Click the Data tab.
6. Change the value in the ControlSource property box to =[FirstName] & " " & [LastName], and then press TAB.
7. Close the property sheet and save your changes.

At times, you may try to combine records that do not have a value entered in a field. The absent value is called a null value. When you use the & operator, and a field has no value, Access returns a zero-length string for that field. For example, if an employee's record has only a last name, the expression in the previous example returns a zero-length string for the First Name field, a space character, and the value in the Last Name field.

When you combine values, you might want to include a value, such as a comma, only when data exists in a particular field. To do that, you use the + operator instead of the & operator.

For example, suppose you have a table called Customer, and the table contains fields called City, Region, and Postal Code. You want to combine those fields for a report, and some records might not have a value in the Region field. In that case, you end up with an unwanted comma before the postal code value if you use the & operator.

To eliminate the unwanted comma, you can use the plus (+) operator, as shown in the following sample expression:

=([City] & (", " + [Region]) & " " & [PostalCode])

The + operator combines text in the same way as the & operator. However, the + operator also supports what is called *Null propagation*. This means that if any component of an expression is null, the entire expression is also null. In the previous example, consider the section that reads (", " + [Region]). Because the + operator is used, the expression within the inner parentheses includes a comma only if a value exists in the Region field. If a value does not exist, Null propagation goes into effect, and the entire expression within the inner parentheses evaluates to a null value, thus "hiding" the comma.

Creating calculated controls to perform arithmetic calculations

You can use expressions to add, subtract, multiply, and divide the values in two or more fields or controls. For example, suppose you record the date that a customer needs to receive an order and the date that the order is shipped. You can find out how many days early (or late) an order was shipped by subtracting the value in the ShippedDate field from the value in the RequiredDate field. You can do this because Access can perform arithmetic calculations on dates.

The result of a date calculation is called an *interval*. This value contains a days component on the left side of the decimal point, and a time component on the right side. If the value returned is a positive number, you know how many days early the order was shipped. If the value is negative, you know how many days late it was shipped. If the value is 0, you know the order was shipped on time.

The steps in this section assume that you have a form, and that form is bound to a table of data containing orders. In turn, the Orders table contains fields called RequiredDate and ShippedDate. You can alter the expression in the following steps to work with your database.

Add a text box that contains an expression to calculate the number of days early or late

1. In the Navigation Pane, right-click the form or report that you want to change and click Design View on the shortcut menu.
2. On the Design tab, in the Controls group, click Text Box.
3. Drag the pointer on the form or report to create the text box.
4. Right-click the text box and then click Properties.

   -or-

   On the Design tab, in the Tools group, click Property Sheet.
5. Click the Data tab.
6. In the ControlSource property box, type **=[RequiredDate]-[ShippedDate]**, and then press TAB. Remember to replace the RequiredDate and ShippedDate identifiers with the names of your own table fields.
7. Save your changes and then close the property sheet.

When you use the +, –, *, /, or \ operators to perform a calculation on two values, and one of the values is null (that is, no value has been entered), the value of the expression evaluates to a null value. For example, if one of the dates in the previous expression is null, the value of the entire expression is also null. On a report, that results in blank space. If you want to replace the null value with 0, you can use the Nz function to convert the null value to zero. For example:

=Nz([RequiredDate]-[ShippedDate],0)

You can also set the fields in your table so that users can't enter null values. When you design the table, set the Required property for that field to Yes. You should also set the DefaultValue property for that field to a non-null value.

Adding the values in two controls

Often, you may want to add the values in two controls. For example, to calculate the total cost of an order, you add the values in the Subtotal and Freight controls, as shown in the following illustration.

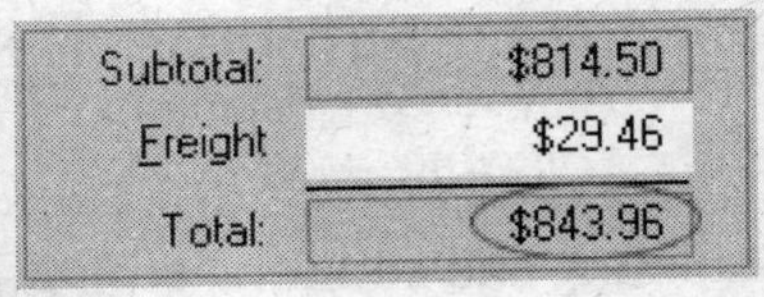

The following steps assume you have a form with two controls that contain numeric data. In this case, the controls are called Subtotal and Freight. You can alter the control names in the following expression to work with your own data.

Add a text box with an expression that calculates a total

1. In the Navigation Pane, right-click the form or report that you want to change and click Design View on the shortcut menu.
2. On the Design tab, in the Controls group, click Text Box.
3. Drag the pointer on the form or report to create the text box.
4. Right-click the text box and click Properties.

   -or-

   On the Design tab, in the Tools group, click Property Sheet.
5. Click the All tab.
6. Set the property values as shown in the following table.

Property	***Setting***
Name	Total
ControlSource	=[Subtotal]+[Freight]
Format	Currency

   Remember to change the identifiers in the expression (Subtotal and Freight) to match the control names on your form.
7. Save your changes and then close the property sheet.

Multiplying two values to calculate the sales tax or value-added tax

Suppose you need to calculate the sales tax or value-added tax for an order. You can do this by using an expression that multiplies two existing values — the sales tax rate and the subtotal amount of each order. You can place your expression in a text box control and display the results on a form or report.

For this exercise, assume that you have two table fields, SalesTaxRate and Subtotal. You could also store these values in other controls on a form or report, but for this exercise, assume they reside in a table.

Add a text box with an expression to calculate a tax amount

1. In the Navigation Pane, right-click the form or report that you want to change and click Design View on the shortcut menu.
2. On the Design tab, in the Controls group, click Text Box.
3. Drag the pointer on the form or report to create the text box.
4. Right-click the text box and click Properties.

   -or-

   On the Design tab, in the Tools group, click Property Sheet.
5. Click the All tab.
6. Set the property values as shown in the following table.

Property	***Setting***
Name	SalesTax
ControlSource	=[Subtotal]*[SalesTaxRate]
Format	Currency

Remember to change the field identifiers (Subtotal and SalesTaxRate) to match the field names in your own database.

7. Close the property sheet.

Summing and counting groups of records

Often, you need to calculate a sum of the values stored in a group of records. For example, you might need to calculate a group total for the group footer in a report, or an order subtotal for the line items on a form. At other times, you might need to count the number of items, rather than sum them. To calculate a sum for a group of records, you use the Sum function, and to count a group of records, you use the Count function.

For example, to count the number of orders in a report that shows orders grouped by customer, you can use the following expression:

=Count([OrderID])

You can use field names in the argument expression for the Sum and Count functions, but not control names. The field names can come from a table or a query. You can even use the name of a calculated field from a query. However, when you want to total the values in a calculated control, you must repeat the expression that is used in the calculated control in the function.

When you want to refer to the same expression more than once on a form, or if you are going to use a function, such as Sum, you should consider whether you can include the expression in the form's underlying query. That way, the calculation can be performed in the query instead of on the form. It is often faster to perform a calculation in a query.

Create a calculated control on one form and reference that control from another form

At times, you may need to create a calculated control — a control that uses an expression as its data source — and then reference the values in that control from a separate control located on another form. The steps in this section explain how to use the SUM function in a calculated control, and then reference that control from another form.

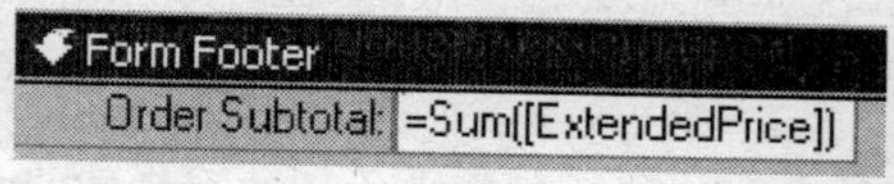

The steps assume the use of an orders database and an order-entry form made up of two components — a main form and a subform. The main form contains data about the entire order such as such as "bill to" and "ship to" information. The subform contains details about the line items in the order, such as products, quantities of each product, and the unit prices of each product.

Separate queries supply data to each component, and the query for the subform has a calculated field called ExtendedPrice. In this example, the "extended price" is the quantity of product in each line item multiplied by the number of items, any discounts, and so on.

To calculate the subtotal amounts for each order, you need to sum the values in the ExtendedPrice field. You do that by adding the following expression to a text box. In this example, the text box is located in the footer of the subform:

The following steps explain how to add the calculated control to the subform. Information after these steps explains how to reference the control from another control.

Add a text box with an expression that calculates subtotals on a subform

1. In the Navigation Pane, right-click the subform that you want to change and click Design View on the shortcut menu.
2. If you cannot see the form footer section of the form, click the Form Footer bar, and then drag the lower edge of the bar downward.

3. On the Design tab, in the Controls group, click Text Box.
4. In the form footer section, drag the pointer on the form to create the text box.
5. Right-click the text box and then click Properties.

   -or-

   On the Design tab, in the Tools group, click Property Sheet.
6. Click the All tab, and then set the property values as shown in the following table.

Property	***Setting***
Name	OrderSubtotal
ControlSource	=Sum([Extended Price])
Format	Currency

   If you are adapting these steps to work with your own data, remember to change the field name (ExtendedPrice) to match the field name in your own database.
7. Click the box in the upper left or right corner of the subform — the box next to the ruler — to display the properties for the entire subform.
8. Locate the Default View property box and change its value to Datasheet.
9. Save your changes, close the property sheet, and go to the next steps.

Although the text box on the subform calculates the order subtotal, you might not want to display the resulting values in the subform because subforms often appear as datasheets. Adding a subtotal would, at the least, mean that users see the same value many times. For example, you could see this type of result:

Product	***Quantity***	***Unit Price***	***Discount***	***Extended Price***	***Subtotal***
Product 1	4	$8.00	0.00%	$32.00	$137.00
Product 2	5	$9.00	0.00%	$45.00	$137.00
Product 3	6	$10.00	0.00%	$60.00	$137.00

As you can see, a piece of summary data belongs in a single field, and it often makes sense to put that field on a main form. To do that, you add a control to the main form that references the control on the subform. The following illustration shows how you can do this:

1. The name of the subform control on the main form
2. The Form property, which provides access to the subform's controls and properties
3. The name of the text box control on the subform

The following steps explain how to create a text box that references the values in another control.

Create the control

1. In the Navigation Pane, right-click the main form that you want to change and click Design View on the shortcut menu.
2. On the Design tab, in the Controls group, click Text Box.
3. Locate the area on the form to which you want to add the control, and then drag the pointer on the form to create the text box.
4. Right-click the text box and click Properties.

   -or-

On the Design tab, in the Tools group, click Property Sheet.

5. Click the All tab.
6. Set the property values as shown in the following table.

Property	***Setting***
Name	Subtotal
ControlSource	=[Orders Subform].Form![OrderSubtotal]
Format	Currency

If you are adapting these steps to work with your own data, remember to change the identifiers (the form and control names between the square brackets) to match the names in your own database.

7. Save your changes and then close the property sheet.

Looking up a value in a table

When you design a form, you might want to display a value from a table or query other than the one that your form is bound to. For example, suppose that you have a Products form that is bound to a Products table. After you design the form, however, you decide that you want the form to display the name of the supplier contact for each product — data that resides in a table called Suppliers.

Access provides two ways to do that type of task. You can use the Lookup Wizard to create a lookup field (the most common technique), or you can create an expression. To create an expression that looks up values in another table, you use the DLookup function. You supply three arguments to the DLookup function:

- The name of the field whose value you want to look up
- The table or query where the field is located
- Optionally, the criteria to use to locate the record

To add the supplier contact, open the Products form in Design view and then add a text box with the label Contact Name. The expression to use for this text box is:

=DLookup("[ContactName]","[Suppliers]","[SupplierID]=" & Forms!Products!SupplierID)

Add the supplier contact text box

1. In the Navigation Pane, right-click the main form that you want to change and click Design View on the shortcut menu.
2. On the Design tab, in the Controls group, click Text Box.
3. Locate the area in the form to which you want to add the control, and then drag the pointer on the form to create the text box.
4. Right-click the text box and click Properties.

   -or-

   On the Design tab, in the Tools group, click Property Sheet.
5. Click the All tab.
6. Set the property values, as shown in the following table.

Property	***Setting***
Label	Contact Name
ControlSource	=DLookup("[ContactName]","[Suppliers]","[SupplierID]=" & Forms!Products!SupplierID)

7. Save your changes and then close the property sheet.

This expression searches in the Suppliers table and returns the contact name of the supplier whose supplier ID matches the value in the SupplierID control on the Products form. Note how the & operator is used to construct the third argument. A common error that you should avoid is placing quotation marks around the entire argument instead of around only the text before the & operator.

As an alternative to using the DLookup function, you can alter the underlying query to include only the information that you need. Using a query is often more efficient.

Add a printed date to a report

Report users often want to know when a report was printed. That small piece of information can tell them whether or not they have current data. To have Access fill in a date for you, use either the Now function or the Date function. The Now function returns the current date and time, as stored in your computer's clock. The Date function returns only the current date. You can use the Format function to format the result of either of these functions in any one of the available date and time formats.

Add the printed date to a report

1. In the Navigation Pane, right-click the report that you want to change and click Design View on the shortcut menu.
2. If you cannot see the footer section of the report, click the Report Footer bar, and then drag the lower edge of the bar downward to expand the report.
3. On the Design tab, in the Controls group, click Text Box.
4. In the report footer section, drag the pointer to create the text box.
5. Right-click the text box and click Properties.

   -or-

   On the Design tab, in the Tools group, click Property Sheet.
6. Click the All tab, and then set the property values as shown in the following table.

Property	***Setting***
Name	DatePrinted
ControlSource	="Printed " & Date()
Format	Medium Date

7. Save your changes and then close the property sheet.

Printing the page number on a report

When you design a report that fills more than one printed page, you should add page numbers. You can add page numbers by using the Page property, which automatically numbers the pages when you preview or print the report. The Page property is available only when you preview or print a report, so it doesn't appear in the report's property sheet. To use the Page property, you place a text box in the header or footer of the report and then type **Page** in the ControlSource property of the text box.

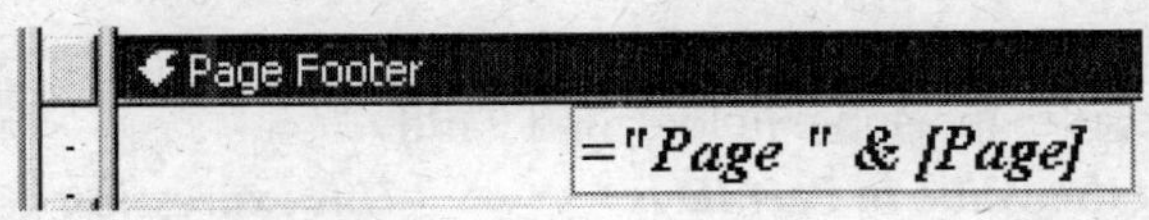

This is the same procedure that you follow when using a function such as Now or Date, except that you don't include parentheses after the Page property.

This figure shows how you can add the Page property directly to a text box control:

In addition, you can also construct an expression that uses the Page and Pages properties. The Pages property returns the total number of pages in the report. For example, the following expression produces page numbering in the format Page 1 of 10.

="Page " & [Page] &" of " & [Pages]

The following steps explain how to add an expression that uses both properties to the footer of a report. The steps explain how to add page numbers in Design view, and by using Layout view.

Use Design view to add page numbering

1. In the Navigation Pane, right-click the report that you want to change and click Design View on the shortcut menu.
2. If you cannot see the footer section of the report, click the Report Footer bar, and then drag the lower edge of the bar downward to expand the report.
3. On the Design tab, in the Controls group, click Text Box.
4. In the report footer section, drag the pointer to create the text box.
5. Right-click the text box and click Properties.

   -or-

   On the Design tab, in the Tools group, click Property Sheet.
6. Click the Data tab, and then change the value in the Control Source property box to: **="Page " & [Page] &" of " & [Pages]**.
7. Save your changes and then close the property sheet.

Use Layout view to add page numbering

1. In the Navigation Pane, right-click the report that you want to change and click Layout View.
2. On the Formatting tab, in the Controls group, click Page Numbers.
3. The Page Numbers dialog box appears.
4. Under Format, click Page N of M.
5. Under Position, select an option.
6. Under Alignment, select an option from the list.
7. Select or clear the Show Number on First Page check box, and then click OK.

Printing a portion of a value on a report

If the first or last few characters in a field have a special meaning, you can organize a report around them. For example, if the first two characters in a product identification code indicate the type of product, you can group the products by the first two characters in the code and then identify each group by printing the characters in a group header.

You use the Left function to extract the first *n* characters of a value in a Text field and the Right function to extract the last *n* characters. In both cases, the first argument is the field name or text expression, and the second argument is the number of characters that you want to extract.

The following table shows expressions that employ these functions. The functions assume that the data resides in a table field called PartID.

If the value in Part ID is	*This expression*	**Returns**
AA105	=Left([PartID],2)	AA
AA105	=Right([PartID],3)	105

Using letter separators in an alphabetical list

For fast identification in a list of products, you can group the products by the first letter of their names and print the letter in a group header, as shown in the following illustration.

To start a new group each time the first letter of the product name changes, and then sort the products within each group alphabetically, you create two groups in the Group, Sort, and Total pane and then set each group as shown in the following tables.

Group on ProductName	with A on top with title click to add keep whole group together on one page	by first character with a header section	with no totals without a footer section
Sort on ProductName	with A on top with title click to add with a header section do not keep whole group together on one page	by entire value with a footer section	with no totals

Display the Group, Sort, and Total pane

1. In the Navigation Pane, right-click the report that you want to change and click Design View on the shortcut menu.
2. On the Design tab, in the Grouping & Totals group, click Group & Sort.

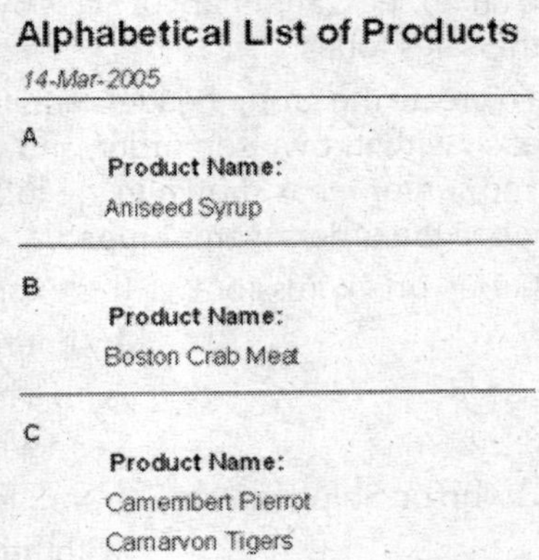
Alphabetical List of Products
14-Mar-2005
A
Product Name:
Aniseed Syrup
B
Product Name:
Boston Crab Meat
C
Product Name:
Camembert Pierrot
Carnarvon Tigers

To print only the first letter of the name at the beginning of a new group, use this expression in the text box in the ProductName header:

= Left([ProductName],1)

Printing the numeric equivalent of a date

You can organize the records in a report by using numeric date values for a period of time — a period such as a year, quarter, month, or week. For example, a year is divided into 53 calendar weeks (The first and last weeks of the year are often partial weeks). Using that numeric value, you can group the orders that were shipped by the week of the year.

To find a portion of a numeric date value, such as just the month or year, you use the DatePart function. The function uses the following syntax:

DatePart (*interval, date*[, *firstdayofweek*] [, *firstweekofyear*])

The *interval* argument is the abbreviation for the part of the date that you want returned. Examples of valid abbreviations are "yyyy" for a four-digit year, "q" for a calendar quarter, and "m" for a month. The *date* argument is a field name or a literal date, such as "1-Jul-07."

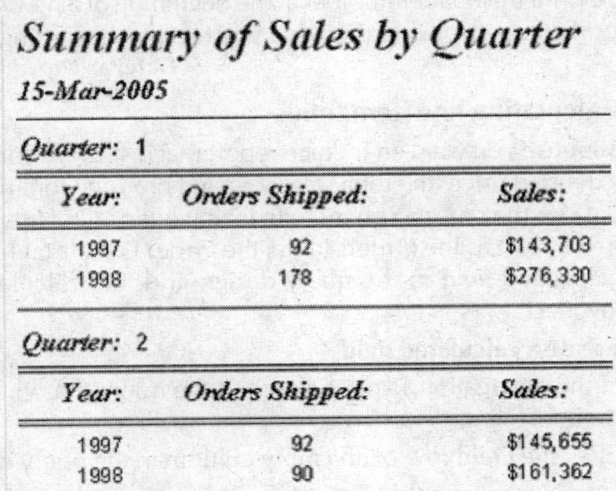
Summary of Sales by Quarter
15-Mar-2005

Quarter: 1

Year:	Orders Shipped:	Sales:
1997	92	$143,703
1998	178	$276,330

Quarter: 2

Year:	Orders Shipped:	Sales:
1997	92	$145,655
1998	90	$161,362

The *firstdayofweek* and *firstweekofyear* arguments are optional. The *firstdayofweek* argument returns Sunday, unless you specify otherwise. To specify a different day, enter a value between 2 and 7 (1 is the default value). The *firstweekofyear* returns the week in which January 1 occurs. To specify a different week, enter 2 or 3. Use 2 to specify the first week that has at least four days in the new year; use 3 to specify the first full week of the year.

The following table lists examples of the results that are returned for a field named "Holiday." The Holiday field can store the holidays that are celebrated in the countries or regions where your company does business.

If the value in Holiday is	*This expression*	*Returns*
1-Jan-07	= DatePart("w",[Holiday])	2 (day of week)
31-Dec-07	= DatePart("ww",[Holiday])	53 (week of year)
31-Dec-07	= DatePart("yyyy",[Holiday])	2010 (four-digit number of year)

Comparing the results of multiple years

When you want to analyze the sales results from more than one year, it's convenient to group the results by a period of time, such as a quarter or month. That way, you can quickly see how the performance for a time period in one year compares with the same time period in another year. For example, suppose you want to see a Summary of Sales by Quarter report that shows the number of orders that were shipped and the sales totals.

To create the group headers and footers and specify the sort order for this report, you create two groups, each with its own sort order, and you set the properties in the Group, Sort, and Total pane for each group and sort order as shown in the following tables. Note that you use an expression to group by the quarter when the orders were shipped.

Group on expressionUse this expression: = DatePart("q",[ShippedDate])			ascending
	by entire value	with no totals	with title Quarter
	with a header section	with a footer section	
	keep whole group together on one page		
Group on ShippedDate	from oldest to newest	by year	with no totals
	with title click to add	without a header section	with a footer section
	do not keep group together on one page		

Display the Group, Sort, and Total pane

1. Open the report in Design view.
2. On the Design tab, in the Grouping & Totals group, click Group & Sort.

To print the quarter number at the beginning of a new group, you place a text box in the group header by using the same expression that you used in the Sorting and Grouping box:

= DatePart("q", [ShippedDate])

Calculating line item totals

Suppose you want an invoice report that displays information about an order. You need to calculate the extended price (the total sales for each product) for line items. You first create a query that provides the data for the report. You include in that query all of the fields that you need from all of the tables that you need, such as the Orders table, the Order Details table, and the Customers table. You can then create a calculated field in the query design grid that calculates the extended price for each product on the invoice.

Create a calculated field

In the Navigation Pane, right-click the query that you want to change and click Design View on the shortcut menu.

Click the Field row of an empty column in the query design grid.

Type a name, a colon (:), and an expression in the Field cell. The name and colon define a user-friendly name for you calculated field. To calculate an extended price, you can use an expression like this:

ExtendedPrice: CCur([Order Details].Unit Price*[Quantity]*(1-[Discount])/100)*100

Note that when you create a calculated field in the query design grid, do not precede your expression with the = operator.

Identifying orders that were shipped late

Under the best of circumstances, orders are shipped on time. Occasionally, some orders may go out after the required date, and you want to identify these on a report. To mark all orders that were shipped late on a report that tracks shipments, you can print a check mark in a check box that is labeled Shipped Late. Because most orders are shipped on time, the check mark is easier to spot than text that spells out On time or Late.

The expression for this report compares the value in the Shipped Date field to the value in the Required Date field. If the value in the Shipped Date field is greater (that is, a later date) than the value in the Required Date field, the expression returns the value True, and the report shows a check mark in the check box. If the value is False, the report leaves the check box empty.

Add the ShippedLate check box to a report

1. In the Navigation Pane, right-click the report that you want to change and click Design View on the shortcut menu.
2. On the Design tab, in the Controls group, click Check Box.
3. Drag the pointer in the detail section of the report to create the check box.
4. Right-click the check box, click Properties on the shortcut menu, and then click the All tab in the property sheet.
5. Set the properties for the check box as shown in the following table.

Property	*Setting*
Name	ShippedLate
ControlSource	=[Shipped Date]>[Required Date]
Visible	Yes

   If you are adapting these steps to work with your own data, remember to change the field names in the identifiers to match your own database.

6. Save your changes and then close the property sheet.

Table of operators

Access supports a variety of operators, including arithmetic operators such as +, -, * (multiply), and / (divide), in addition to comparison operators for comparing values, text operators for concatenating text, logical operators for determining true or false values, and other operators specific to Access. For details about using these operators, see the following tables:

Arithmetic operators

You use the arithmetic operators to calculate a value from two or more numbers or to change the sign of a number from positive to negative.

Operator	*Purpose*	*Example*
+	Sum two numbers.	[Subtotal]+[SalesTax]
-	Find the difference between two numbers or indicate the negative value of a number.	[Price]-[Discount]
*	Multiply two numbers.	[Quantity]*[Price]
/	Divide the first number by the second number.	[Total]/[ItemCount]
\	Round both numbers to integers, then divide the first number by the second number. Then, truncate the result to an integer.	[Registered]\[Rooms]

Mod	Divide the first number by the second number and return only the remainder.	[Registered] Mod [Rooms]
^	Raise a number to the power of an exponent.	Number ^ Exponent

Comparison operators

You use the comparison operators to compare values and return a result that is true, false, or null.

Operator	*Purpose*
<	Determine if the first value is less than the second value.
< =	Determine if the first value is less than or equal to the second value.
>	Determine if the first value is greater than the second value.
> =	Determine if the first value is greater than or equal to the second value.
=	Determine if the first value is equal to the second value.
< >	Determine if the first value is not equal to the second value.

In all cases, if either the first value or the second value is null, the result is then also null. Because null represents an unknown value, the result of any comparison with null is also unknown.

Logical operators

You use the logical operators to combine two values and return a true, false, or null result. You might also see the logical operators referred to as *Boolean* operators.

Operator	Usage	Description
And	Expr1 And Expr2	True when Expr1 and Expr2 are true.
Or	Expr1 Or Expr2	True when either Expr1 or Expr2 is true.
Eqv	Expr1 Eqv Expr2	True when both Expr1 and Expr2 are true or both Expr1 and Expr2 are false.
Not	Not Expr	True when Expr is not true.
Xor	Expr1 Xor Expr2	True when either Expr1 is true, or Expr2 is true, but not both.

Concatenation operators

You use the concatenation operators to combine two text values into one.

Operator	*Usage*	*Description*
&	string1 & string2	Combines two strings to form one string.
+	string1 + string2	Combines two strings to form one string and propagates null values.

Special operators

You use the special operators as described in the following table.

Operator	*Description*
Is Null or Is Not Null	Determines whether a value is Null or Not Null.
Like "pattern"	Matches string values by using wildcard operators ? and *.
Between val1 And val2	Determines whether a numeric or date value falls within a range.
In(string1,string2...)	Determines whether a string value is found within a set of string values.

CHAPTER 10

Microsoft Access 2010 Specifications

Introduction

An expression consists of a number of elements that you use, alone or in combination, to produce a result.

Databases

Attribute	*Maximum*
ACCDB or MDB file size, including all database objects and data.	2GB, minus space needed for system objects (Because your database can include attached tables in multiple files, its total size is limited only by available storage capacity.)
Total number of objects in a database (tables, queries, forms, reports, and so on)	32,768
Number of modules, including modules attached to forms and reports	1,000
Number of characters in object names	64
Number of characters in a database password	14
Number of characters in a username or group name	20
Number of concurrent users	255

Tables

Attribute	*Maximum*
Number of characters in a table name	64
Number of characters in a field name	64
Number of fields in a record or table	255
Number of open tables	2,048, including system tables opened by Microsoft Access internally
Table size	2GB (minus space needed for system objects)
Number of characters in a Text field	255
Number of characters in a Memo field	65,535 when entering data through the user interface; 1GB when entering data programmaticaily
Size of OLE object field	1GB
Number of indexes in a record or table (including composite indexes, primary key indexes, and other indexes)	32
Number of fields in an index	10
Number of characters in a validation message	255
Number of characters in a validation rule (including punctuation and operators)	2,048
Number of characters in a table or field description	255
Number of characters in a record	4,000 (excludes Memo and OLE Object fields)
Number of characters in a field property setting	255

Queries

Attribute	*Maximum*
Number of tables in a query	32

Number of enforced relationships	32 per table, minus indexes that are on the table for the fields or combinations of fields that are not involved in the relationship
Number of fields in a record set	255
Dynaset size	1 GB
Sort limit	255 characters in one or more fields
Number of levels of nested queries	50
Number of characters in a cell of the design grid	1,024
Number of characters in a parameter name for a parameterized query	255
Number of ANDs in a WHERE or HAVING clause	99
Number of characters in a SQL statement	64,000 (approximately)

Forms and Reports

Maximum	***Attribute***
Number of characters in a label	2,048
Number of characters in a text box	65,535
Form or report width	22 inches (55.87 cm)
Section height	22 inches (55.87 cm)
Height of all sections plus section headers in design view	200 inches (508 cm)
Number of levels of nested forms or reports	7 (form-subform-subform)
Number of fields/expressions you can sort or group on (reports only)	10
Number of headers and footers in a report	1 report header/footer, 1 page header/footer, 10 group headers/footers
Number of printed pages in a report	65,536
Number of characters in a SQL statement that is the Recordsource or Rowsource property of a form, report, or control (both .mdband .adp)	32,750
Number of controls or sections you can add over the lifetime of the form or report	754
Number of characters in a SQL statement that serves the RowSource property of a form or report, or the ControlSource property of a control	32,750

Macros

Maximum	***Attribute***
Number of actions in a macro	999
Number of characters in a condition	255
Number of characters in a comment	255
Number of characters in an action argument	255
Number of modules (including all forms and reports with HasModule property set to True)	1,0000

Access Data Projects (ADP) Specifications

Access Project

Attribute	*Maximum*
Number of objects in a Microsoft Access project (. adp)	32,768
Modules (including forms and report modules)	1,000
Number of characters in an object name	64
Number of columns in a table	1,024 (MS SQL Server 2000 and 2005)

Forms and Reports

Maximum	*Attribute*
Number of characters in a label	2,048
Number of characters in a text box	65,535
Form or report width	22 inches (56 cm)
Section height	22 inches (56 cm)
Height of all sections plus section headers in design view	200 inches (508 cm)
Number of levels of nested forms or reports	7 (form-subform-subform)
Number of fields/expressions you can sort or group on	10 (reports only)
Number of headers and footers in a report	1 report header/footer, 1 page header/footer, 10 group headers/footer
Number of printed pages in a report	65,536
Number of characters in a SQL statement that is the Recordsource or Rowsource property of a form, report, or control (both .mdb and .adp)	32,750
Number of controls or sections you can add over the lifetime of the form or report	754

Macros

Attributes	*Maximum*
Number of actions in a macro	999
Number of characters in a condition	255
Number of characters in a comment	255
Number of characters in an action argument	255

Microsoft SQL Server 2008 Database Specifications

The capacities of SQL Server 2008 databases are the same as SQL Server 2008. With the exception of database size, the values in this table apply equally to Microsoft SQL Server 2008 Express Edition. The maximum size of a SQL Server 2008 Express database is 4GB.

The maximum size of data managed by SQL Server 2008 is practically unlimited because of SQL Server's ability to be configured as clustered database servers.

Microsoft SQL Sever 2008 Capacities

SQL Server 2008 Database Engine Object	*Maximum Sizes/Numbers for SQL Server 2008 (32-bit)*	*Maximum Sizes/Numbers forSQl Server 2008 (64-bit)*
Batch size	65,536 x Network Racket Size	65,536 x Network Packet Size
Bytes per short string column	8,000	8,000
Btes per GROUPBY, ORDER BY	8,060	8,060
Bytes per index key	900	900
Bytes per foreign key	900	900
Bytes per primary key	900	900
Bytes per row	8,060	8,060
Bytes in source text of a stored procedure	Lesser of batch size or 250MB	Lesser of batch size or 250MB
Bytes per varchar (max), varbinary (max), xml, text, or image column	1,073,741,823	1,073,741,823
Characters per ntext or nvarchar (max) column	536,870,910	536,870,910
Clustered indexes per table	1	1
Columns in CROUP BY, ORDER BY	Limited only by number of bytes	Limited only by number of bytes
Columns or expressions in a GROUP BY WITH CUBE or WITH ROLLUP statement	10	10
Columns per index key	16	16
Columns per foreign key	16	16
Columns per primary key	16	16
Columns per base table	1,024	1,024
Columns per SELECT statement	4,096	4,096
Columns per INSERT statement	1,024	1,024
Connections per client	Maximum value of configured connections	Maximum value of configured connections
Database size	1,048,516TB	1, 048,51 6TB
Databases per instance of SQL Server	32,767	32,767
File groups per database	32,767	32,767
Files per database	32,767	32,767
File size (data)	16TB	16TB
File size (log)	2TB	2TB
Foreign key table references per table	253	253
Identifier length (in characters)	128	128

Instances per computer	16	16
Length of a string containing SQL statements (batch size)	65,536 x Network packet Size	65,536 x Network packet size
Locks per connection	Maximum locks per server	Maximum locks per server
Locks per instance of SQL Server	Up to 2,147,483,647	Limited only by memory
Nested stored procedure levels	32	32
Nested subqueries	32	32
Nested trigger levels	32	32
Nonclustered indexes per table	249	249
Parameters per stored procedure	2,100	2,100
Parameters per user-defined function	2,100	2,100
REFERENCES_pertable	253	253
Rows per table	Limited by available storage	Limited by available storage
Tables per database	Limited by number of objects in a database	Limited by number of objects in a database
Partitions per partitioned table or index	1,000	1,000
Statistics on nonindexed columns	2,000	2,000
Tables per SELECT statement	256	256
Triggers per table	Limited by number of objects in a database	Limited by number of objects in a database
UNIQUE indexes or constraints per table	249 nonclustered and 1 clustered	249 nonclustered and 1 clustered
User connections	32,767	32,767
XML indexes	249	249

CHAPTER 11

Keyboard Shortcuts of Microsoft Access 2010

Introduction

Shortcut keys are key combinations that start commands. For example, you can press CTRL + O to open a file and CTRL + S to save a file, which is the same result as choosing Open and Save from the File menu. .

General shortcut keys

Opening Databases

To do this	*Press*
Open a new database	Ctrl + N
Open an existing database	Ctrl + O
Exit Office Access 2007Access	Alt + F4

Printing and Saving

To do this	*Press*
Print the current or selected object	Ctrl + P
Open the Print dialog box from Print Preview	P or Ctrl + P
Open the Page Setup dialog box from Print Preview	S
Cancel Print Preview or Layout Preview	C or Esc
Save a database object	Ctrl + S or Shift + F12
Open the Save As dialog box	F12

Using a combo box or list box

To do this	*Press*
Open a combo box	F4 or Alt + Down Arrow
Refresh the contents of a Lookup field (Lookup field: A field, used on a form or report in an Access database, that either displays a list of values retrieved from a table or query, or stores a static set of values.) list box or combo box	F9
Move down one line	Down Arrow
Move down one page	Page Down
Move up one line	Up Arrow
Move up one page	Page Up
Exit the combo box or list box	Tab

Finding and replacing text or data

To do this	*Press*
Open the Find tab in the Find and Replace dialog box (Datasheet view and Form view only)	Ctrl + F
Open the Replace tab in the Find and Replace dialog box (Datasheet view and Form view only)	Ctrl + H
Find the next occurrence of the text specified in the Find and Replace dialog box when the dialog box is closed (Datasheet view and Form view only)	Shift + F4

Working in Design view

To do this	*Press*
Switch between Edit mode (with insertion point displayed) and Navigation	

mode (Navigation mode: The mode in Microsoft Access in which an entire field is selected and the insertion point is not visible. In Navigation mode, you can move between fields by using the arrow keys.) in a datasheet. When working in a form or report, press Esc to leave Navigation mode.	F2
Switch to the property sheet (Design view in forms and reports in both Access databases and Access projects)	F4
Switch to Form view from form Design view	F5
Switch between the upper and lower portions of a window (Design view of queries, and the Advanced Filter/Sort window)	F6
Cycle through the field grid, field properties, Navigation Pane, access keys in the Keyboard Access System, Zoom controls, and the security bar (Design view of tables)	F6
Open the Choose Builder dialog box (Design view window of forms and reports)	F7
Open the Visual Basic Editor from a selected property in the property sheet for a form or report	F7
Switch from the Visual Basic Editor back to form or report Design view	Shift+F7 or Alt+F11

Editing controls in form and report Design view

To do this	***Press***
Copy the selected control to the Clipboard	Ctrl+C
Cut the selected control and copy it to the Clipboard	Ctrl+X
Paste the contents of the Clipboard in the upper-left corner of the selected section	Ctrl+V
Move the selected control to the right (except controls that are part of a layout)	Right Arrow or Ctrl+Right Arrow
Move the selected control to the left (except controls that are part of a layout)	Left Arrow or Ctrl+Left Arrow
Move the selected control up	Up Arrow or Ctrl+Up Arrow
Move the selected control down	Down Arrow or Ctrl+Down Arrow
Increase the height of the selected control	Shift+Down Arrow
Increase the width of the selected control Note If used with controls that are in a layout, the entire layout is resized	Shift+Right Arrow
Reduce the height of the selected control	Shift+Up Arrow
Reduce the width of the selected control Note If used with controls that are in a layout, the entire layout is resized	

Window Operations

By default, Microsoft Office Access 2007 databases display as tabbed documents. To use windowed documents, click the Microsoft Office Button , and then click Access Options. In the Access Options dialog box, click Current Database and, under Document Window Options, click Overlapping Windows.

To do this	***Press***
Toggle the Navigation Pane	F11

Cycle between open windows	Ctrl + F6
Restore the selected minimized window when all windows are minimized	Enter
Turn on Resize mode for the active window when it is not maximized; press the arrow keys to resize the window	Ctrl + F8
Display the Control menu	Alt + Spacebar
Display the shortcut menu	Shift + F10
Close the active window	Ctrl + W or Ctrl + F4
Switch between the Visual Basic Editor and the previous active window	Alt + F11

Working with Wizards

To do this	*Press*
Toggle the focus forward between controls in the wizard	Tab
Move to the next page of the wizard	Alt + N
Move to the previous page of the wizard	Alt + B
Complete the wizard	Alt + F

Miscellaneous

To do this	*Press*
Display the complete hyperlink address for a selected hyperlink	F2
Check spelling	F7
Open the Zoom box to conveniently enter expressions and other text in small input areas	Shift + F2
Display a property sheet in Design view	Alt + Enter
Exit Access or close a dialog box	Alt + F4
Invoke a Builder	Ctrl + F2
Toggle forward between views when in a table, query, form, report, page, PivotTable list, PivotChart report, stored procedure, or Access project (.adp) function. If there are additional views available, successive keystrokes will move to the next available view.	Ctrl + Right Arrow or CRTL + COMMA (,)
Toggle back between views when in a table, query, form, report, page, PivotTable list, PivotChart report, stored procedure, or .adp function. If there are additional views available, successive keystrokes will move to the previous view. Note Ctrl + PERIOD (.) does not work under all conditions with all objects.	

Navigation Pane shortcut keys

Editing and navigating the Object list

To do this	*Press*
Rename a selected object	F2
Move down one line	Down Arrow
Move down one window	Page Down

Move to the last object	End
Move up one line	Up Arrow
Move up one window	Page Up
Move to the first object	Home

Navigating and opening objects

To do this	*Press*
Open the selected table or query in Datasheet view	Enter
Open the selected form or report	Enter
Run the selected macro	Enter
Open the selected table, query, form, report, data access page, macro, or module in Design view	Ctrl + Enter
Display the Immediate window in the Visual Basic Editor	Ctrl + G

Work with menus

To do this	*Press*
Show the shortcut menu	Shift + F10
Show the access keys	Alt or F10
Show the program icon menu (on the program title bar)	Alt + Spacebar
With the menu or submenu visible, select the next or previous command	Down Arrow or Up Arrow
Select the menu to the left or right; or, when a submenu is visible, to switch between the main menu and the submenu	Left Arrow or Right Arrow
Select the first or last command on the menu or submenu	Home or End
Close the visible menu and submenu at the same time	Alt
Close the visible menu; or, with a submenu visible, to close the submenu only	Esc

Work in windows and dialog boxes

Using a program window

To do this	*Press*
Switch to the next program	Alt + Tab
Switch to the previous program	Alt + Shift + Tab
Show the Windows Start menu	Ctrl + Esc
Close the active database window	Ctrl + W
Switch to the next database window	Ctrl + F6
Switch to the previous database window	Ctrl + Shift + F6
Restore the selected minimized window when all windows are minimized	Enter

Using a dialog box

To do this	*Press*
Switch to the next tab in a dialog box	Ctrl + Tab

Switch to the previous tab in a dialog box	Ctrl + Shift + Tab
Move to the next option or option group	Tab
Move to the previous option or option group	Shift + Tab
Move between options in the selected drop-down list box, or to move between some options in a group of options	Arrow keys
Perform the action assigned to the selected button; select or clear the check box	Spacebar
Move to the option by the first letter in the option name in a drop-down list box	Letter key for the first letter in the option name you want (when a drop-down list box is selected)
Select the option, or to select or clear the check box by the letter underlined in the option name	Alt + letter key
Open the selected drop-down list box	Alt + Down Arrow
Close the selected drop-down list box	Esc
Perform the action assigned to the default button in the dialog box	Enter
Cancel the command and close the dialog box	Esc
Close a dialog box	Alt + F4

Editing in a text box

To do this	*Press*
Move to the beginning of the entry	Home
Move to the end of the entry	End
Move one character to the left or right	Left Arrow or Right Arrow
Move one word to the left or right	Ctrl + Left Arrow or Ctrl + Right Arrow
Select from the insertion point to the beginning of the entry	Shift + Home
Select from the insertion point to the end of the entry	Shift + End
Change the size of the selection by one character to the left	Shift + Left Arrow
Change the size of the selection by one character to the right	Shift + Right Arrow
Change the size of the selection by one word to the left	Ctrl + Shift + Left Arrow
Change the size of the selection by one word to the right	Ctrl + Shift + Right Arrow

Work with the Open, File New Database, and Save As dialog boxes

To do this	*Press*
Go to the previous folder ( )	Alt + 1
Open the folder up one level from the open folder (Up One Level button)	Alt + 2
Delete the selected folder or file (Delete button)	DEL
Create a new subfolder in the open folder (Create New Folder button)	Alt + 4
Switch between Thumbnails, Tiles, Icons, List, Details, Properties, and Preview views	Alt + 5
Show the Tools menu (Tools button)	Alt + L

Work with property sheets

Using a property sheet with a form or report

To do this	*Press*
Toggle the property sheet tab	F4
Move among choices in the control drop-down list one item at a time	Down Arrow or Up Arrow
Move among choices in the control drop-down list five items at a time	Page Down or Page Up
Move to the property sheet tabs from the control drop-down list	Tab
Move among the property sheet tabs with a tab selected, but no property selected	Left Arrow or Right Arrow
With a property already selected, move down one property on a tab	Tab
With a property selected, move up one property on a tab; or if already at the top, move to the control drop-down list	Shift+Tab
Toggle forward between tabs when a property is selected	Ctrl+Tab
Toggle backward between tabs when a property is selected	Ctrl+Shift+Tab

Using a property sheet with a table or query

To do this	*Press*
Toggle the property sheet tab	F4
With a tab selected, but no property selected, move among the property sheet tabs	Left Arrow or Right Arrow
Move to the property sheet tabs when a property is selected	Ctrl+Tab
Move to the first property of a tab when no property is selected	Tab
Move down one property on a tab	Tab
Move up one property on a tab; or if already at the top, select the tab itself	Shift+Tab
Toggle forward between tabs when a property is selected	Ctrl+Tab
Toggle backward between tabs when a property is selected	Ctrl+Shift+Tab

Work with the Field List pane

To do this	*Press*
Toggle the Field List pane	Alt+F8
Add the selected field to the form or report detail section	Enter
Move up or down the Field List pane	Up Arrow or Down Arrow
Move to the upper Field List pane from the lower pane	Shift+Tab
Move to the lower Field List pane from the upper pane	Tab

Keyboard shortcuts for using the Help window

To do this	*Press*
Select the next hidden text or hyperlink, or Show All or Hide All at the top of a topic	Tab
Select the previous hidden text or hyperlink, or the Browser View button at the top of a Microsoft Office Web site article	Shift+Tab

Perform the action for the selected Show All, Hide All, hidden text, or hyperlink	Enter
Move back to the previous Help topic	Alt + Left Arrow
Move forward to the next Help topic	Alt + Right Arrow
Open the Print dialog box	Ctrl + P
Scroll small amounts up and down, respectively, within the currently-displayed Help topic.	Up Arrow and Down Arrow
Scroll larger amounts up and down, respectively, within the currently-displayed Help topic.	Page Up and Page Down
Display a menu of commands for the Help window; requires that the Help window have active focus (click an item in the Help window).	Shift + F10

Send e-mail messages

To do this	*Press*
Send the active database object (the object selected in the Navigation Pane) as an e-mail message	Alt + F + E
Open the Address Book from within Outlook	Ctrl + Shift + B
Check the names in the To, Cc, and Bcc boxes against the Address Book	Alt + K or Ctrl + K
Select the next box in the e-mail header or the body of the message when the last box in the e-mail header is active	Tab
Select the previous field or button in the e-mail header	Shift + Tab

Keys for working with text and data

Select text and data

To do this	*Press*
Change the size of the selection by one character to the right	Shift + Right Arrow
Change the size of the selection by one word to the right	Ctrl + Shift + Right Arrow
Change the size of the selection by one character to the left	Shift + Left Arrow
Change the size of the selection by one word to the left	Ctrl + Shift + Left Arrow

Selecting a field or record

To do this	*Press*
Select the next field	Tab
Switch between Edit mode (with insertion point displayed) and Navigation mode (Navigation mode: The mode in Microsoft Access in which an entire field is selected and the insertion point is not visible. In Navigation mode, you can move between fields by using the arrow keys.) in a datasheet. When using a form or report, press Esc to leave Navigation mode.	F2
Switch between selecting the current record and the first field of the current record, in Navigation mode	Shift + Spacebar
Extend selection to the previous record, if the current record is selected	Shift + Up Arrow

Extend selection to the next record, if the current record is selected	Shift + Down Arrow
Select all records	Ctrl + A or Ctrl + Shift + Spacebar

Extending a selection

To do this	*Press*
Turn on Extend mode (in Datasheet view, Extended Selection appears in the lower-right corner of the window); pressing F8 repeatedly extends the selection to the word, the field, the record, and all records	F8
Extend a selection to adjacent fields in the same row in Datasheet view	Left Arrow or Right Arrow
Extend a selection to adjacent rows in Datasheet view	Up Arrow or Down Arrow
Undo the previous extension	Shift + F8
Cancel Extend mode	Esc

Selecting and moving a column in Datasheet view

To do this	*Press*
Select the current column or cancel the column selection, in Navigation mode (Navigation mode: The mode in Microsoft Access in which an entire field is selected and the insertion point is not visible. In Navigation mode, you can move between fields by using the arrow keys.) only	Ctrl + Spacebar
Select the column to the right, if the current column is selected	Shift + Right Arrow
Select the column to the left, if the current column is selected	Shift + Left Arrow
Turn on Move mode (Move mode: The mode in which you can move column(s) in Datasheet view by using the left and right arrow keys.); then press the Right Arrow or Left Arrow key to move selected column(s) to the right or left	Ctrl + Shift + F8

Edit text and data

Moving the insertion point in a field

To do this	*Press*
Move the insertion point one character to the right	Right Arrow
Move the insertion point one word to the right	Ctrl + Right Arrow
Move the insertion point one character to the left	Left Arrow
Move the insertion point one word to the left	Ctrl + Left Arrow
Move the insertion point to the end of the field, in single-line fields; or to move it to the end of the line in multi-line fields	End
Move the insertion point to the end of the field, in multiple-line fields	Ctrl + End
Move the insertion point to the beginning of the field, in single-line fields; or to move it to the beginning of the line in multi-line fields	Home
Move the insertion point to the beginning of the field, in multiple-line fields	Ctrl + Home

Copying, moving, or deleting text

To do this	*Press*
Copy the selection to the Clipboard	Ctrl + C
Cut the selection and copy it to the Clipboard	Ctrl + X
Paste the contents of the Clipboard at the insertion point	Ctrl + V
Delete the selection or the character to the left of the insertion point	Backspace
Delete the selection or the character to the right of the insertion point	Delete
Delete all characters to the right of the insertion point	Ctrl + Delete

Undoing changes

To do this	*Press*
Undo typing	Ctrl + Z or Alt + Backspace
Undo changes in the current field or current record; if both have been changed, press Esc twice to undo changes, first in the current field and then in the current record	Esc

Entering data in Datasheet or Form view

To do this	*Press*
Insert the current date	Ctrl + Semicolon (;)
Insert the current time	Ctrl + Shift + Colon (:)
Insert the default value for a field	Ctrl + Alt + Spacebar
Insert the value from the same field in the previous record	Ctrl + Apostrophe (')
Add a new record	Ctrl + Plus Sign (+)
In a datasheet, delete the current record	Ctrl + Minus Sign (-)
Save changes to the current record	Shift + Enter
Switch between the values in a check box or option button	Spacebar
Insert a new line	Ctrl + Enter

Refreshing fields with current data

To do this	*Press*
Recalculate the fields in the window	F9
Requery the underlying tables; in a subform, this requeries the underlying table for the subform only	Shift + F9
Refresh the contents of a Lookup field (Lookup field: A field, used on a form or report in an Access database, that either displays a list of values retrieved from a table or query, or stores a static set of values.) list box or combo box	

Keys for navigating records

Navigate in Design view

To do this	*Press*
Switch between Edit mode (with insertion point displayed) and Navigation mode	F2

Toggle the property sheet	F4
Switch to Form view from form Design view	F5
Switch between the upper and lower portions of a window (Design view of macros, queries, and the Advanced Filter/Sort window) Use F6 when the Tab key does not take you to the section of the screen you want.	F6
Toggle forward between the design pane, properties, Navigation Pane, access keys, and Zoom controls (Design view of tables, forms, and reports)	F6
Open the Visual Basic Editor from a selected property in the property sheet for a form or report	F7
Invokes the Field List pane in a form, report, or data access page. If the Field List pane is already open, focus moves to the Field List pane.	Alt + F8
When you have a code module open, switch from the Visual Basic Editor to form or report Design view	Shift + F7
Switch from a control's property sheet in form or report Design view to the design surface without changing the control focus	Shift + F7
Display a property sheet	Alt + Enter
Copy the selected control to the Clipboard	Ctrl + C
Cut the selected control and copy it to the Clipboard	Ctrl + X
Paste the contents of the Clipboard in the upper-left corner of the selected section	Ctrl + V
Move the selected control to the right by a pixel along the page's grid	Right Arrow
Move the selected control to the left by a pixel along the page's grid	Left Arrow
Move the selected control up by a pixel along the page's grid Note For controls in a stacked layout, this switches the position of the selected control with the control directly above it, unless it is already the uppermost control in the layout.	Up Arrow
Move the selected control down by a pixel along the page's grid Note For controls in a stacked layout, this switches the position of the selected control with the control directly below it, unless it is already the lowermost control in the layout.	Down Arrow
Move the selected control to the right by a pixel (irrespective of the page's grid)	Ctrl + Right Arrow
Move the selected control to the left by a pixel (irrespective of the page's grid)	Ctrl + Left Arrow
Move the selected control up by a pixel (irrespective of the page's grid) Note For controls in a stacked layout, this switches the position of the selected control with the control directly above it, unless it is already the uppermost control in the layout.	Ctrl + Up Arrow
Move the selected control down by a pixel (irrespective of the page's grid) Note For controls in a stacked layout, this switches the position of the selected control with the control directly below it, unless it is already the lowermost control in the layout.	Ctrl + Down Arrow
Increase the width of the selected control (to the right) by a pixel Note For controls in a stacked layout, this increases the width of the whole layout.	Shift + Right Arrow

Decrease the width of the selected control (to the left) by a pixel Note For controls in a stacked layout, this decreases the width of the whole layout.	Shift + Left Arrow
Decrease the height of the selected control (from the bottom) by a pixel	Shift + Up Arrow
Increase the height of the selected control (from the bottom) by a pixel	Shift + Down Arrow

Navigate in Datasheet view

Going to a specific record

To do this	***Press***
Move to the record number box (record number box: A small box that displays the current record number in the lower-left corner in Datasheet view and Form view. To move to a specific record, you can type the record number in the box, and press Enter.); then type the record number and press Enter	F5

Navigating between fields and records

To do this	***Press***
Move to the next field	Tab or Right Arrow
Move to the last field in the current record, in Navigation mode	End
Move to the previous field	Shift + Tab, or Left Arrow
Move to the first field in the current record, in Navigation mode	Home
Move to the current field in the next record	Down Arrow
Move to the current field in the last record, in Navigation mode	Ctrl + Down Arrow
Move to the last field in the last record, in Navigation mode	Ctrl + End
Move to the current field in the previous record	Up Arrow
Move to the current field in the first record, in Navigation mode	Ctrl + Up Arrow
Move to the first field in the first record, in Navigation mode	Ctrl + Home

Navigating to another screen of data

To do this	***Press***
Move down one screen	Page Down
Move up one screen	Page Up
Move right one screen	Ctrl + Page Down
Move left one screen	Ctrl + Page Up

Navigate in subdatasheets

Going to a specific record

To do this	***Press***
Move from the subdatasheet to move to the record number box; then type the record number and press Enter	Alt + F5

Expanding and collapsing subdatasheet

To do this	***Press***
Move from the datasheet to expand the record's subdatasheet	Ctrl + Shift + Down Arrow
Collapse the subdatasheet	Ctrl + Shift + Up Arrow

Navigating between the datasheet and subdatasheet

To do this	***Press***
Enter the subdatasheet from the last field of the previous record in the datasheet	Tab
Enter the subdatasheet from the first field of the following record in the datasheet	Shift + Tab
Exit the subdatasheet and move to the first field of the next record in the datasheet	Ctrl + Tab
Exit the subdatasheet and move to the last field of the previous record in the datasheet	Ctrl + Shift + Tab
From the last field in the subdatasheet to enter the next field in the datasheet	Tab
From the datasheet to bypass the subdatasheet and move to the next record in the datasheet	Down Arrow
From the datasheet to bypass the subdatasheet and move to the previous record in the datasheet	Up Arrow

Note You can navigate between fields and records in a subdatasheet with the same shortcut keys used in Datasheet view.

Navigate in Form view

Going to a specific record

To do this	***Press***
Move to the record number box; then type the record number and press Enter	F5

Navigating between fields and records

To do this	***Press***
Move to the next field	Tab
Move to the previous field	Shift + Tab
Move to the last control on the form and remain in the current record, in Navigation mode	End
Move to the last control on the form and set focus in the last record, in Navigation mode	Ctrl + End
Move to the first control on the form and remain in the current record, in Navigation mode	Home
Move to the first control on the form and set focus in the first record, in Navigation mode	Ctrl + Home
Move to the current field in the next record	Ctrl + Page Down
Move to the current field in the previous record	Ctrl + Page Up

Navigating in forms with more than one page

To do this	*Press*
Move down one page; at the end of the record, moves to the equivalent page on the next record	Page Down
Move up one page; at the end of the record, moves to the equivalent page on the previous record	Page Up

Navigating between the main form and subform

To do this	*Press*
Enter the subform from the preceding field in the main form	Tab
Enter the subform from the following field in the main form	Shift + Tab
Exit the subform and move to the next field in the master form or next record	Ctrl + Tab
Exit the subform and move to the previous field in the main form or previous record	Ctrl + Shift + Tab

Navigate in Print Preview and Layout Preview

Dialog box and window operations

To do this	*Press*
Open the Print dialog box	P (for forms and reports) or Ctrl + P (for datasheets, forms, and reports)
Open the Page Setup dialog box (forms and reports only)	S
Zoom in or out on a part of the page	Z
Cancel Print Preview or Layout Preview	C or Esc

Viewing different pages

To do this	*Press*
Move to the page number box; then type the page number and press Enter	Alt + F5
View the next page (when Fit To Window is selected)	Page Down or Down Arrow
View the previous page (when Fit To Window is selected)	Page Up or Up Arrow

Navigating in Print and Layout Preview

To do this	*Press*
Scroll down in small increments	Down Arrow
Scroll down one full screen	Page Down
Move to the bottom of the page	Ctrl + Down Arrow
Scroll up in small increments	Up Arrow
Scroll up one full screen	Page Up
Move to the top of the page	Ctrl + Up Arrow
Scroll to the right in small increments	Right Arrow
Move to the right edge of the page	End
Move to the lower-right corner of the page	Ctrl + End

Scroll to the left in small increments	Left Arrow
Move to the left edge of the page	Home
Move to the upper-left corner of the page	Ctrl + Home

Navigate in the Database Diagram window in an Access project

To do this	*Press*
Move from a table cell to the table's title bar	Esc
Move from a table's title bar to the last cell you edited	Enter
Move from table title bar to table title bar, orfrom cell to cell inside a table	Tab
Expand a list inside a table	Alt + Down Arrow
Scroll through the items in a drop-down list from top to bottom	Down Arrow
Move to the previous item in a list	Up Arrow
Select an item in a list and move to the next cell	Enter
Change the setting in a check box	Spacebar
Go to the first cell in the row, orto the beginning of the current cell	Home
Go to the last cell in the row, orto the end of the current cell	End
Scroll to the next "page" inside a table, orto the next "page" of the diagram	Page Down
Scroll to the previous "page" inside a table, orto the previous "page" of the diagram	Page Up

Navigate in the Query Designer in an Access project

Any Pane

To do this	*Press*
Move among the Query Designer panes	F6, Shift + F6

Diagram Pane

To do this	*Press*
Move among tables, views, and functions, (and to join lines, if available)	Tab, or Shift + Tab
Move between columns in a table, view, or function	Arrow keys
Choose the selected data column for output	Spacebar or PLUS key
Remove the selected data column from the query output	Spacebar or MINUS key
Remove the selected table, view, or function, or join line from the query	Delete

Note If multiple items are selected, pressing Spacebar affects all selected items. Select multiple items by holding down the Shift key while clicking them. Toggle the selected state of a single item by holding down Ctrl while clicking it.

Grid Pane

To do this	*Press*
Move among cells	Arrow keys or Tab or Shift + Tab
Move to the last row in the current column	Ctrl + Down Arrow
Move to the first row in the current column	Ctrl + Up Arrow
Move to the top left cell in the visible portion of grid	Ctrl + Home

Move to the bottom right cell	Ctrl + End
Move in a drop-down list	Up Arrow or Down Arrow
Select an entire grid column	Ctrl + Spacebar
Toggle between edit mode and cell selection mode	F2
Copy selected text in cell to the Clipboard (in edit mode)	Ctrl + C
Cut selected text in cell and place it on the Clipboard (in edit mode)	Ctrl + X
Paste text from the Clipboard (in edit mode)	Ctrl + V
Toggle between insert and overstrike mode while editing in a cell	INS
Toggle the check box in the Output columnNote If multiple items are selected, pressing this key affects all seiected items.	Spacebar
Clear the selected contents of a cell	Delete
Remove row containing selected data column from the query Note If multiple items are selected, pressing this key affects all selected items.	Delete
Clear all values for a selected grid column	Delete
Insert row between existing rows	INS (after you select grid row)
Add an Or ... column	INS (after you select any Or ... column)

SQL Pane

You can use the standard Windows editing keys when working in the SQL pane, such as Ctrl + arrow keys to move between words, and the Cut, Copy, and Paste commands on the Edit menu.

Note You can only insert text; there is no overstrike mode.

Work with PivotTable views

PivotTable view

Keys for selecting elements in PivotTable view

To do this	***Press***
Move the selection from left to right, and then down	The Tab key
Move the selection from top to bottom, and then to the right	Enter
Select the cell to the left. If the current cell is the leftmost cell, Shift + Tab selects the last cell in the previous row.	Shift + Tab
Select the cell above the current cell. If the current cell is the topmost cell, Shift + Enter selects the last cell in the previous column.	Shift + Enter
Select the detail cells for the next item in the row area	Ctrl + Enter
Select the detail cells for the previous item in the row area	Shift + Ctrl + Enter
Move the selection in the direction of the arrow key. If a row or column field is selected, press Down Arrow to move to the first item of data in the field, and then press an arrow key to move to the next or previous item or back to the field. If a detail field is selected, press Down Arrow or Right Arrow to move to the first cell in the detail area.	Arrow keys
Extend or reduce the selection in the direction of the arrow key	Shift + arrow keys

Move the selection to the last cell in the direction of the arrow key	Ctrl + arrow keys
Move the selected item in the direction of the arrow key	Shift + Alt + arrow keys
Select the leftmost cell of the current row	Home
Select the rightmost cell of the current row	End
Select the leftmost cell of the first row	Ctrl + Home
Select the last cell of the last row	Ctrl + End
Extend selection to the leftmost cell of the first row	Shift + Ctrl + Home
Extend selection to the last cell of the last row	Shift + Ctrl + End
Select the field for the currently selected item of data, total, or detail	Ctrl + Spacebar
Select the entire row containing the currently selected cell	Shift + Spacebar
Select the entire PivotTable view	Ctrl + A
Display the next screen	Page Down
Display the previous screen	Page Up
Extend the selection down one screen	Shift + Page Down
Reduce the selection by one screen	Shift + Page Up
Display the next screen to the right	Alt + Page Down
Display the previous screen to the left	Alt + Page Up
Extend the selection to the page on the right	Shift + Alt + Page Down
Extend the selection to the page on the left	Shift + Alt + Page Up

Keys for carrying out commands

To do this	*Press*
Display Help topics	F1
Display the shortcut menu for the selected element of the PivotTable view. Use the shortcut menus to carry out commands in the PivotTable view.	Shift + F10
Carry out a command on the shortcut menu	Underlined letter
Close the shortcut menu without carrying out a command	Esc
Display the Properties dialog box	Alt + Enter
Close the Properties dialog box	Alt + F4
Cancel a refresh operation in progress	Esc
Copy the selected data from the PivotTable view to the Clipboard	Ctrl + C
Export the contents of the PivotTable view to Microsoft Office Excel 2007 Office Excel 2007	Ctrl + E

Keys for displaying, hiding, filtering, or sorting data

To do this	*Press*
Show or hide the expand indicators (and boxes) beside items	Ctrl + 8
Expand the currently selected item	Ctrl + Plus Sign (on the numeric keypad)
Hide the currently selected item	Ctrl + Minus Sign (on the numeric keypad)
Open the list for the currently selected field	Alt + Down Arrow
Alternately move to the most recently selected item, the OK button, and the Cancel button in the drop-down list for a field	The Tab key

Move to the next item in the drop-down list for a field	Arrow keys
Select or clear the check box for the current item in the drop-down list for a field	Spacebar
Close the drop-down list for a field and apply any changes you made	Enter
Close the drop-down list for a field without applying your changes	Esc
Turn AutoFilter on or off	Ctrl + T
Sort data in the selected field or total in ascending order (A – Z 0 – 9)	Ctrl + Shift + A
Sort data in the selected field or total in descending order (Z – A 9 – 0)	Ctrl + Shift + Z
Move the selected member up or left	Alt + Shift + Up Arrow or Alt + Shift + Left Arrow
Move the selected member down or right	Alt + Shift + Down Arrow or Alt + Shift + Right Arrow

Keys for adding fields and totals and changing the layout of a PivotTable view

Keys for working with the Field List pane

To do this	*Press*
Display the Field List pane, or activate it if it is already displayed	Ctrl + L
Move to the next item in the Field List pane	Arrow keys
Move to the previous item and include it in the selection	Shift + Up Arrow
Move to the next item and include it in the selection	Shift + Down Arrow
Move to the previous item, but don't include the item in the selection	Ctrl + Up Arrow
Move to the next item, but don't include the item in the selection	Ctrl + Down Arrow
Remove the item from the selection, if the item that has focus is included in the selection, and vice versa	Ctrl + Spacebar
Expand the current item in the Field List pane to display its contents. Or expand Totals to display the available total fields.	Plus Sign (numeric keypad)
Collapse the current item in the Field List pane to hide its contents. Or collapse Totals to hide the available total fields.	Minus Sign (numeric keypad)
Alternately move to the most recently selected item, the Add to button, and the list next to the Add to button in the Field List pane	The Tab key
Open the drop-down list next to the Add to button in the Field List pane. Use the arrow keys to move to the next item in the list, and then press Enter to select an item.	Alt + Down Arrow
Add the highlighted field in the Field List pane to the area in the PivotTable view that is displayed in the Add to list	Enter
Close the Field List pane	Alt + F4

Keys for adding fields and totals

To do this	*Press*
Add a new total field for the selected field in the PivotTable view by using the Sum summary function	Ctrl + Shift + S

Add a new total field for the selected field in the PivotTable view by using the Count summary function	Ctrl + Shift + C
Add a new total field for the selected field in the PivotTable view by using the Min summary function	Ctrl + Shift + M
Add a new total field for the selected field in the PivotTable view by using the Max summary function	Ctrl + Shift + X
Add a new total field for the selected field in the PivotTable view by using the Average summary function	Ctrl + Shift + E
Add a new total field for the selected field in the PivotTable view by using the Standard Deviation summary function	Ctrl + Shift + D
Add a new total field for the selected field in the PivotTable view by using the Standard Deviation Population summary function	Ctrl + Shift + T
Add a new total field for the selected field in the PivotTable view by using the Variance summary function	Ctrl + Shift + V
Add a new total field for the selected field in the PivotTable view by using the Variance Population summary function	Ctrl + Shift + R
Turn subtotals and grand totals on or off for the selected field in the PivotTable view	Ctrl + Shift + B
Add a calculated detail field	Ctrl + F

Keys for changing the layout

Note The following four shortcuts do not work if you press the keys 1, 2, 3, or 4 from the numeric pad of your keyboard.

To do this	***Press***
Move the selected field in the PivotTable view to the row area	Ctrl + 1
Move the selected field in the PivotTable view to the column area	Ctrl + 2
Move the selected field in the PivotTable view to the filter area	Ctrl + 3
Move the selected field in the PivotTable view to the detail area	Ctrl + 4
Move the selected row or column field in the PivotTable view to a higher level	Ctrl + Left Arrow
Move the selected row or column field in the PivotTable view to a lower level	Ctrl + Right Arrow

Keys for formatting elements in PivotTable view

To use the following shortcuts, first select a detail field or a data cell for a total field.

The first seven keyboard shortcuts change the number format of the selected field.

To do this	***Press***
Apply the general number format to values in the selected total or detail field	Ctrl + Shift + ~ (tilde)
Apply the currency format, with two decimal places and negative numbers in parentheses, to values in the selected total or detail field	Ctrl + Shift + $
Apply the percentage format, with no decimal places, to values in the selected total or detail field	Ctrl + Shift + %
Apply the exponential number format, with two decimal places, to values in the selected total or detail field	Ctrl + Shift + ^

To do this	Press
Apply the date format, with the day, month, and year, to values in the selected total or detail field	Ctrl + Shift + #
Apply the time format, with the hour, minute, and AM or PM, to values in the selected total or detail field	Ctrl + Shift + @
Apply the numeric format, with two decimal places, thousands separator, and a minus sign for negative values, to values in the selected total or detail field	Ctrl + Shift + !
Make text bold in the selected field of the PivotTable view	Ctrl + B
Make text underlined in the selected field of the PivotTable view	Ctrl + U
Make text italic in the selected field of the PivotTable view	Ctrl + I

PivotChart view

Keys for selecting items in a chart

To do this	*Press*
Select the next item in the chart	Right Arrow
Select the previous item in the chart	Left Arrow
Select the next group of items	Down Arrow
Select the previous group of items	Up Arrow

Keys for working with properties and options

To do this	*Press*
Display the Properties dialog box	Alt + Enter
Close the Properties dialog box	Alt + F4
When the Properties dialog box is active, select the next item on the active tab	The Tab key
When a tab in the Properties dialog box is active, select the next tab	Right Arrow
When a tab in the Properties dialog box is active, select the previous tab	Left Arrow
Display a list or palette when a button that contains a list or palette is selected	Down Arrow
Display the shortcut menu	Shift + F10
Carry out a command on the shortcut menu	Underlined letter
Close the shortcut menu without carrying out a command	Esc

Keys for working with fields

To do this	*Press*
Open the list for the currently selected field	Alt + Down Arrow
In the drop-down list for a field, alternately move to the most recently selected item, the OK button, and the Cancel button	The Tab key
In the drop-down list for a field, move to the next item	Arrow keys
In the drop-down list for a field, select or clear the check box for the current item	Spacebar
Close the drop-down list for a field and apply any changes you made	Enter
Close the drop-down list for a field without applying your changes	Esc

Keys for working with the Field List pane

To do this	*Press*
Display the Field List pane, or activate it if it is already displayed	Ctrl + L
Move to the next item in the Field List pane	Arrow keys
Move to the previous item and include it in the selection	Shift + Up Arrow
Move to the next item and include it in the selection	Shift + Down Arrow
Move to the previous item, but don't include the item in the selection	Ctrl + Up Arrow
Move to the next item, but don't include the item in the selection	Ctrl + Down Arrow
Remove the item from the selection if the item that has focus is included in the selection, and vice versa	Ctrl + Spacebar
Expand the current item in the Field List pane to display its contents, or expand Totals to display the available total fields	Plus Sign (numeric keypad)
Collapse the current item in the Field List pane to hide its contents, or collapse Totals to hide the available total fields.	Minus Sign (numeric keypad)
In the Field List pane, alternately move to the most recently selected item, the Add to button, and the list next to the Add to button	The Tab key
Open the drop-down list next to the Add to button in the Field List pane. Use the arrow keys to move to the next item in the list, and then press Enter to select an item.	Alt + Down Arrow
Add the highlighted field in the Field List pane to the drop area that is displayed in the Add to list	Enter
Close the Field List pane	Alt + F4

Ribbon

Ribbon	Press Alt.

The KeyTips are displayed over each feature that is available in the current view. The following example is from Office Word 2007.

Press the letter shown in the KeyTip over the feature that you want to use.

Depending on which letter you press, you might be shown additional KeyTips. For example, if the Home tab is active and you press I, the Insert tab is displayed, along with the KeyTips for the groups on that tab.

Continue pressing letters until you press the letter of the command or control that you want to use. In some cases, you must first press the letter of the group that contains the command.

Note To cancel the action that you are taking and hide the KeyTips, press Alt.

Online Help

Keyboard shortcuts for using the Help window

The Help window provides access to all Office Help content. The Help window displays topics and other Help content.

In the Help window

To do this	*Press*
Open the Help window.	F1
Close the Help window	Alt+F4
Switch between the Help window and the active program.	Alt+Tab
Go back to Program Name Home.	Alt+Home
Select the next item in the Help window.	Tab
Select the previous item in the Help window.	Shift+Tab
Perform the action for the selected item.	Enter
In the Browse Program Name Help section of the Help window, select the next or previous item, respectively.	Tab or Shift+Tab
In the Browse Program Name Help section of the Help window, expand or collapse the selected item, respectively.	Enter
Select the next hidden text or hyperlink, including Show All or Hide All at the top of a topic.	Tab
Select the previous hidden text or hyperlink.	Shift+Tab
Perform the action for the selected Show All, Hide All, hidden text, or hyperlink.	Enter
Move back to the previous Help topic (Back button).	Alt+Left Arrow or Backspace
Move forward to the next Help topic (Forward button).	Alt+Right Arrow
Scroll small amounts up or down, respectively, within the currently displayed Help topic.	Up Arrow, Down Arrow
Scroll larger amounts up or down, respectively, within the currently displayed Help topic.	Page Up, Page Down
Display a menu of commands for the Help window. This requires that the Help window have the active focus (click in the Help window).	Shift+F10
Stop the last action (Stop button).	Esc
Refresh the window (Refresh button).	F5
Print the current Help topic. Note If the cursor is not in the current Help topic, press F6 and then press Ctrl+P.	Ctrl+P
Change the connection state.	F6, and then press Enter to open the list of choices
Switch among areas in the Help window; for example, switch between the toolbar and the Search list.	F6
In a Table of Contents in tree view, select the next or previous item, respectively.	Up Arrow, Down Arrow
In a Table of Contents in tree view, expand or collapse the selected item, respectively.	Left Arrow, Right Arrow

Microsoft Office basics

Display and use windows

To do this	*Press*
Switch to the next window.	Alt + Tab
Switch to the previous window.	Alt + Shift + Tab
Close the active window.	Ctrl + W or Ctrl + F4
Move to a task pane from another pane in the program window (clockwise direction). You might need to press F6 more than once. Note If pressing F6 doesn't display the task pane you want, try pressing Alt to place focus on the menu bar or Ribbon and then pressing Ctrl + Tab to move to the task pane.	F6
When more than one window is open, switch to the next window.	Ctrl + F6
Switch to the previous window.	Ctrl + Shift + F6
When a document window is not maximized, perform the Size command (on the Control menu for the window). Press the arrow keys to resize the window, and, when finished, press Enter.	Ctrl + F8
Minimize a window to an icon (works for only some Microsoft Office programs).	Ctrl + F9
Maximize or restore a selected window.	Ctrl + F10
Copy a picture of the screen to the Clipboard.	PRINT SCREEN
Copy a picture of the selected window to the Clipboard.	Alt + PRINT SCREEN

Move around in text or cells

To do this	*Press*
Move one character to the left.	Left Arrow
Move one character to the right.	Right Arrow
Move one line up.	Up Arrow
Move one line down.	Down Arrow
Move one word to the left.	Ctrl + Left Arrow
Move one word to the right.	Ctrl + Right Arrow
Move to the end of a line.	End
Move to the beginning of a line.	Home
Move up one paragraph.	Ctrl + Up Arrow
Move down one paragraph.	Ctrl + Down Arrow
Move to the end of a text box.	Ctrl + End
Move to the beginning of a text box.	Ctrl + Home
In Microsoft Office PowerPoint 2007, move to the next title or body text placeholder. If it is the last placeholder on a slide, this will insert a new slide with the same slide layout as the original slide.	Ctrl + Enter

Repeat the last Find action.	Shift+F4

Move around in and work in tables

To do this	*Press*
Move to the next cell.	Tab
Move to the preceding cell.	Shift+Tab
Move to the next row.	Down Arrow
Move to the preceding row.	Up Arrow
Insert a tab in a cell.	Ctrl+Tab
Start a new paragraph.	Enter
Add a new row at the bottom of the table.	Tab at the end of the last row

Access and use task panes

To do this	*Press*
Move to a task pane from another pane in the program window. (You might need to press F6 more than once.) Note If pressing F6 doesn't display the task pane you want, try pressing Alt to place focus on the menu bar and then pressing Ctrl+Tab to move to the task pane.	F6
When a menu or toolbar is active, move to a task pane. (You might need to press Ctrl+Tab more than once.)	Ctrl+Tab
When a task pane is active, select the next or previous option in the task pane.	Tab or Shift+Tab
Display the full set of commands on the task pane menu.	Ctrl+Down Arrow
Move among choices on a selected submenu; move among certain options in a group of options in a dialog box.	Down Arrow or Up Arrow
Open the selected menu, or perform the action assigned to the selected button.	Spacebar or Enter
Open a shortcut menu; open a drop-down menu for the selected gallery item.	Shift+F10
When a menu or submenu is visible, select the first or last command on the menu or submenu.	Home or End
Scroll up or down in the selected gallery list.	Page Up or Page Down
Move to the top or bottom of the selected gallery list.	Ctrl+Home or Ctrl+End

Access and use smart tags

To do this	*Press*
Display the menu or message for a smart tag. If more than one smart tag is present, switch to the next smart tag and display its menu or message.	Alt+Shift+F10
Select the next item on a smart tag menu.	Down Arrow
Select the previous item on a smart tag menu.	Up Arrow
Perform the action for the selected item on a smart tag menu.	Enter
Close the smart tag menu or message.	Esc

Tips

- You can ask to be notified by a sound whenever a smart tag appears. To hear audio cues, you must have a sound card. You must also have Microsoft Office Sounds installed on your computer.
- If you have access to the World Wide Web, you can download Microsoft Office Sounds from the Microsoft Office Online Web site. After you install the sound files, do the following in Access, Office Excel 2007, and Office Word 2007:

Click the Microsoft Office Button, and then click Program Options.

Click Advanced.

Under General, select the Provide feedback with sound check box, and then click OK.

When you select or clear this check box, the setting affects all Office programs that support sound.

Resize and move toolbars, menus, and task panes

Press Alt to select the menu bar.

Press Ctrl + Tab repeatedly to select the toolbar or task pane that you want.

Do one of the following:

- Resize a toolbar
- On the toolbar, press Ctrl + Spacebar to display the Toolbar Options menu.
- Click the Size command, and then press Enter.
- Use the arrow keys to resize the toolbar. Press Ctrl + the arrow keys to resize one pixel at a time.

Move a toolbar

- On the toolbar, press Ctrl + Spacebar to display the Toolbar Options menu.
- Click the Move command, and then press Enter.
- Use the arrow keys to position the toolbar. Press Ctrl + the arrow keys to move one pixel at a time. To undock the toolbar, press the Down Arrow repeatedly. To dock the toolbar vertically on the left or right side, press the Left Arrow or the Right Arrow, respectively, when the toolbar is positioned all the way to the left or the right side.

Resize a task pane

- In the task pane, press Ctrl + Spacebar to display a menu of additional commands.
- Use the Down Arrow key to select the Size command, and then press Enter.
- Use the arrow keys to resize the task pane. Use Ctrl + the arrow keys to resize one pixel at a time.

Move a task pane

- In the task pane, press Ctrl + Spacebar to display a menu of additional commands.
- Use the Down Arrow key to select the Move command, and then press Enter.
- Use the arrow keys to position the task pane. Use Ctrl + the arrow keys to move one pixel at a time.

When you finish moving or resizing, press Esc.

Use dialog boxes

To do this	*Press*
Move to the next option or option group.	Tab
Move to the previous option or option group.	Shift + Tab
Switch to the next tab in a dialog box.	Ctrl + Tab

Switch to the previous tab in a dialog box.	Ctrl + Shift + Tab
Move between options in an open drop-down list, or between options in a group of options.	Arrow keys
Perform the action assigned to the selected button; select or clear the selected check box.	Spacebar
Open the list if it is closed and move to that option in the list.	First letter of an option in a drop-down list
Select an option; select or clear a check box.	Alt + the letter underlined in an option
Open a selected drop-down list.	Alt + Down Arrow
Close a selected drop-down list; cancel a command and close a dialog box.	Esc
Perform the action assigned to a default button in a dialog box.	Enter

Use edit boxes within dialog boxes

An edit box is a blank in which you type or paste an entry, such as your user name or the path to a folder.

To do this	***Press***
Move to the beginning of the entry.	Home
Move to the end of the entry.	End
Move one character to the left or right.	Left Arrow or Right Arrow
Move one word to the left.	Ctrl + Left Arrow
Move one word to the right.	Ctrl + Right Arrow
Select or cancel selection one character to the left.	Shift + Left Arrow
Select or cancel selection one character to the right.	Shift + Right Arrow
Select or cancel selection one word to the left.	Ctrl + Shift + Left Arrow
Select or cancel selection one word to the right.	Ctrl + Shift + Right Arrow
Select from the insertion point to the beginning of the entry.	Shift + Home
Select from the insertion point to the end of the entry.	Shift + End

Use the Open and Save As dialog boxes

To do this	***Press***
Go to the previous folder.	Alt + 1
Up One Level button: open the folder up one level above the open folder.	Alt + 2
Search the Web button: close the dialog box and open your Web search page	Alt + 3
Delete button: delete the selected folder or file.	Alt + 3
Create New Folder button: create a new folder.	Alt + 4
Views button: switch among available folder views.	Alt + 5
Tools button: show the Tools menu.	Alt + L
Display a shortcut menu for a selected item such as a folder or file.	Shift + F10
Move between options or areas in the dialog box.	Tab
Open the Look in list.	F4 or Alt + I
Refresh the file list.	F5

CHAPTER 12

Questions

Introduction

Questions help you in revising the matter read in the various chapters.

ANSWER THE FOLLOWING QUESTIONS

OBJECTIVE TYPE QUESTIONS

1. For getting information from the database we use :
   (a) Table (b) Query
   (c) Report
2. It consists of various records having data:
   (a) Table (b) Query
   (c) Report
3. For printing the information from the Table we use:
   (a) Table (b) Query
   (c) Report
4. You can create a database using :
   (a) Home panel (b) Wizard
   (c) Programs
5. Main controlling point in Access is:
   (a) Switchboard (b) Home panel
   (c) Edit panel
6. Easy way of creating a Table is by using:
   (a) Wizard (b) Design View
   (c) New
7. A Table is a collection of :
   (a) Queries (b) Data
   (c) Reports
8. Forms are filled with :
   (a) Data (b) Database
   (c) Information
9. The number of forms which you can create from a Table:
   (a) One (b) Many
   (c) None
10. You can modify your report using :
    (a) Wizard (b) AutoFormat
    (c) Printer
11. Report can be created using :
    (a) Wizard (b) AutoFormat
    (c) Printer
12. For clearning the data from the screen, we use ________ key.
    (a) Delete (b) Ctrl + C
    (c) Ctrl + W (d) Enter.
13. For closing the open file, we use:
    (a) Delete (b) Ctrl + C
    (c) Ctrl + W (d) Enter.

14. For copying the data, we use:
    (a) Delete (b) Ctrl + C
    (c) Ctrl + W (d) Enter.
15. To create a new paragraph, we use:
    (a) Delete (b) Ctrl + C
    (c) Ctrl + W (d) Enter.
16. For cutting the selected data or object, we use:
    (a) Cut (b) Ctrl + Q
    (c) Ctrl + F (d) Ctrl + B
17. To exit or quit, we use:
    (a) Cut (b) Ctrl + Q
    (c) Ctrl + F (d) Ctrl + B
18. To find the next word, we use:
    (a) Cut (b) Ctrl + Q
    (c) Ctrl + F (d) Ctrl + B
19. To make the selected text Bold, we use:
    (a) Cut (b) Ctrl + Q
    (c) Ctrl + F (d) Ctrl + B
20. To make the text italics, we use:
    (a) Ctrl + I (b) Shift + F4
    (c) End (d) Page Down
21. To minimize all windows, use the key-combination of:
    (a) Ctrl + I (b) Shift + F4
    (c) End (d) Page Down
22. To move to the end of the line, use the key-combination of:
    (a) Ctrl + I (b) Shift + F4
    (c) End (d) Page Down
23. To move the page down, use the key-combination of:
    (a) Ctrl + I (b) Shift + F4
    (c) End (d) Page Down
24. To move to page up. use ________ key.
    (a) Page Up (b) Home
    (c) Tab (d) Ctrl + N.
25. To move to start of a line, use the ________ key.
    (a) Page Up (b) Home
    (c) Tab (d) Ctrl + N.
26. To move the next cell, we use the _______ key.
    (a) Page Up (b) Home
    (c) Tab (d) Ctrl + N.
27. To create a new document, we use:
    (a) Page Up (b) Home
    (c) Tab (d) Ctrl + N.

28. For opening an existing document file, we use:
    (a) Ctrl + O (b) Ctrl + Shift + S
    (c) Ctrl + S (d) Double Click
29. To Save As a file, we use:
    (a) Ctrl + O (b) Ctrl + Shift + S
    (c) Ctrl + S (d) Double Click
30. To Save a file, we use:
    (a) Ctrl + O (b) Ctrl + Shift + S
    (c) Ctrl + S (d) Double Click
31. To select a word, we use:
    (a) Ctrl + O (b) Ctrl + Shift + S
    (c) Ctrl + S (d) Double Click
32. To Select All items on the screen, we use:
    (a) Ctrl + A (b) Ctrl + Shift + Left Arrow
    (c) Ctrl + Shift + Right Arrow (d) Ctrl + +(Plus)
33. To Select word on the left, we use::
    (a) Ctrl + A (b) Ctrl + Shift + Left Arrow
    (c) Ctrl + Shift + Right Arrow (d) Ctrl + +(Plus)
34. To Select word on the right, use the key-combination of:
    (a) Ctrl + A (b) Ctrl + Shift + Left Arrow
    (c) Ctrl + Shift + Right Arrow (d) Ctrl + +(Plus)
35. To Zoom in site map, use the key-combination of:
    (a) Ctrl + A (b) Ctrl + Shift + Left Arrow
    (c) Ctrl + Shift + Right Arrow (d) Ctrl + +(Plus)

ANSWERS TO OBJECTIVE TYPE QUESTIONS

1. b	2. a	3. c	4. b
5. a	6. a	7. b	8. a
9. b	10. b	11. a	12. a
13. c	14. b	15. d	16. a
17. b	18. c	19. d	20. a
21. b	22. c	23. d	24. a
25. b	26. c	27. d	28. a
29. b	30. c	31. d	32. a
33. b	34. c	35. d	

SUBJECTIVE TYPE QUESTIONS

Chapter 1 — Introduction to Microsoft Office 2010

1. Describe the various constituents of Microsoft Office 2010.
2. What's new in the newer version?
3. Describe how would you use the mouse?

Chapter 2 — What's new in Microsoft Access 2007

1. Describe the various new features of Microsoft Access 2010.

Chapter 3 — Introduction to Relational Database

1. What is a Database?
2. What is Information?
3. Why do we need RDBMS?
4. Describe Relational Data Structure.
5. Describe Data Integrity.

Chapter 4 — Creating a Database in Microsoft Access 2010

1. How would you create a database using Wizard?
2. Describe the method of creating a database using Template.
3. How would you set the Type and Size of a Field?
4. What is Five-Step Design Method?

Chapter 5 — Creating a Table in Microsoft Access 2010

1. How would you create a New Table?
2. How would you change the Table design?
3. Describe the process of setting the Primary Key.
4. How would you index Access Tables

Chapter 6 — Creating a Form in Microsoft Access 2010

1. How would you create a Form?
2. Describe the method of Searching a Database.
3. How would you Manipulate Controls?
4. How would you group controls?
5. What are Properties?

Chapter 7 — Creating a Query in Microsoft Access 2010

1. How would you create a Simple Query?
2. How would you create a Crosstab Query?
3. Describe the working with Table/Query Pane.
4. How would you add fields from more than one table?
5. What is Multi-Table Query Limitations?
6. Describe the process of creating and working with Query Joins.

Chapter 8 — Creating a Report in Microsoft Access 2010

1. How would you create a report?
2. How would you Insert, Add or Create new fields in a table?
3. How would you set a field's data type in Datasheet view?
4. Describe the working with Text boxes.
5. How would you sort and group data?
6. How would you set the data type?

Chapter 9 — Expressions in Microsoft Access 2010

1. What is an expression?
2. Why do we use expression?
3. Where do we use expressions?
4. How would you combine text values?
5. Describe the method of creating the control.
6. What options do you have for printing a report?
7. Describe the various types of operators.
8. How would you sum and group a number of records?
9. How would you look up the value in a table?
10. How would you use expression to do the following:

Form and report controls	Creating calculated fields in a query
Validation Rule property of a table field	Validation Rule property of a control
Setting default values for a table field	Setting default values for controls
Carrying out macro actions	Grouping and sorting data in reports